Essays in Seventeenth-Century Literature, 2

"Bright Shootes of Everlastingnesse"

The Seventeenth-Century
Religious Lyric

Edited by
Claude J. Summers
and
Ted-Larry Pebworth

University of Missouri Press
Columbia, 1987

Library of Congress Cataloging-in-Publication Data
"Bright shootes of everlastingnesse."

Papers presented at the sixth biennial
Renaissance Conference, University of Michigan–
Dearborn, Oct. 18–20, 1984.

Includes index.
1. English poetry—Early modern, 1500–1700—
History and criticism—Congresses. 2. Religious
poetry, English—History and criticism—Congresses.
3. Christian poetry, English—History and
criticism—Congresses. I. Summers, Claude J.
II. Pebworth, Ted-Larry. III. Renaissance Conference
(6th : 1984 : University of Michigan-Dearborn)
PR545.R4B7 1987   821'.04'09382   86-16132

ISBN 0-8262-0618-2 (alk. paper)

For
Judith Scherer Herz
and
Leah Sinanoglou Marcus

Contents

Introduction

Claude J. Summers and
Ted-Larry Pebworth

Much of the greatest lyric poetry in English was written during the seventeenth century, and much of that poetry is religious. As Anthony Low has noted, until fairly recently the irreducibly religious content of this poetry has been something of an embarrassment to modern critics, many of whom have attempted to divorce such major poets as Donne, Herbert, and Milton from the religious dimension of their work and thereby to present them as poets of apparently greater universality and more relevance for twentieth-century readers.[1] In the process, however, the poetry has frequently been lessened and distorted, both removed from its historical context and robbed of its urgent preoccupation with timeless issues of the spirit. Happily, however, this embarrassment has dissipated and there has recently been a new willingness to read the seventeenth-century religious lyric on its own terms and a new appreciation of the complexity of its roots in the various cultural and ecclesiastical traditions and in the turbulent religious and political controversies of the seventeenth century. This new recognition of the spectacular flowering of the religious lyric in the late Renaissance has led to an intensified interest and a truer understanding of the period's literary achievement as a whole.

This volume is a contribution toward the better understanding of the seventeenth-century religious lyric, both as poetry and as historical and cultural artifact. The twelve essays presented here originated as submissions to the sixth biennial Renaissance conference at the University of Michigan-Dearborn, 18–20 October 1984; and the original, abbreviated versions of nearly all of them were presented there.[2] The purpose of the

1. *Love's Architecture: Devotional Modes in Seventeenth-Century English Poetry* (New York: New York University Press, 1978), p. ix.
2. Selected papers from the first five Dearborn conferences have been pub-

conference was to explore the lyric in the seventeenth century from the vantage points of literary criticism and history, while taking seriously the continuing relevance of the spiritual questions insistently posed by the individual works. In "The Retreate," Henry Vaughan speaks of the happiness of his childhood when he "felt through all this fleshly dresse / Bright *shootes* of everlastingnesse" and explains his longing "to travell back / And tread again that ancient track!"[3] The contributors to this volume desire not so much to recapture Vaughan's "Angell-infancy" as to move backwards in time in order to understand both the historical and the timeless dynamics that conspired to create the period's extraordinary explorations of spiritual mysteries in the medium of the lyric. Thus, while the emphasis in these studies is on the religious lyric as a seventeenth-century cultural phenomenon, the historical and critical approaches exemplified here are unself-consciously alert and sympathetic to the difficulties the poets of the time faced in expressing spiritual quests and emotions that are at once personal and universal, rooted in a particular time and place but by no means limited by the temporal and the spatial. In other words, these studies acknowledge the complexities of seventeenth-century religious lyrics as artistic products of individual poets that strive to transcend art and individuality even as they are necessarily (and sometimes triumphantly) mired in both. The contributors recognize that the religious lyric exists in a plane somewhere between the spiritual and the temporal, but recognize also that it finally encapsulates peculiarly human experience, exposing

lished: those from the 1974 conference on Robert Herrick as *"Trust to Good Verses": Herrick Tercentenary Essays*, ed. Roger B. Rollin and J. Max Patrick (Pittsburgh: University of Pittsburgh Press, 1978); those from the 1976 conference on seventeenth-century prose as a special issue of *Studies in the Literary Imagination* 10, no. 2 (1977), ed. William A. Sessions and James S. Tillman; those from the 1978 celebration of Herbert as *"Too Rich to Clothe the Sunne": Essays on George Herbert*, ed. Claude J. Summers and Ted-Larry Pebworth (Pittsburgh: University of Pittsburgh Press, 1980); those from the 1980 conference on Jonson and the Sons of Ben as *Classic and Cavalier: Essays on Jonson and the Sons of Ben*, ed. Claude J. Summers and Ted-Larry Pebworth (Pittsburgh: University of Pittsburgh Press, 1982); and those from the 1982 conference on Donne as *The Eagle and the Dove: Reassessing John Donne*, ed. Claude J. Summers and Ted-Larry Pebworth (Columbia: University of Missouri Press, 1986).

3. *The Works of Henry Vaughan*, ed. L. C. Martin, 2d ed. (Oxford: Clarendon Press, 1957), p. 419.

the poet not only to God but (and perhaps especially) to other men and women as well.

The final versions of almost all the essays included here have profited significantly from the stimulating exchanges and responses afforded by the Dearborn conference, but they were written without consultation among the authors. No topics or approaches were suggested or assigned, and none were proscribed. Most of the essays are both historical and critical in approach, but the authors vary a great deal in their historical and critical presuppositions. They bring to bear on their topics a number of critical and scholarly techniques, from new critical close reading to formalist analysis and source study, and while some are interested in new interpretations of familiar lyrics, others attempt new syntheses of broad categories of works. Some of the essays explore connections between works by several poets, while others examine the achievement of a single author or even a single poem. Some of the studies challenge accepted orthodoxies, while others add to our understanding of seventeenth-century poetry by reading it in the light of fresh contexts. The only criterion for selection has been that each essay contribute to the understanding and informed appreciation of the religious lyric, either in the aggregate or in the particular.

Probably the most wide-ranging and ambitious essay presented here is that by William Sessions. In a rich and suggestive holistic analysis, Sessions discovers within the structures of the greatest religious texts of the period a dialectic of abandonment that leads a reader into the deepest experience of these texts, an experience necessarily involving vulnerability and fear. Touching on important texts by Vaughan, Crashaw, Herbert, Donne, and Milton, Sessions relates the seventeenth-century religious lyric to a mode of abandonment used by classical, medieval, mystical, and dramatic writers from Sappho to Chaucer to Petrarch to Shakespeare. Sessions thus reads the seventeenth-century religious lyric within the broad context of secular and profane literature, explaining its ability to touch our emotions by reference to archetypal human predicaments.

Although limited to the discussion of a single poet, R. V. Young's essay also has wide implications for the study of devotional poetry throughout the period. Challenging the recent designation of a distinctively Protestant poetics as the source of the English tradition of religious poetry, Young compares Donne's Holy Sonnets with the works of a number of Spanish Counter-Reformation poets and argues that the view of the Holy Sonnets as doctrinally and aesthetically Protestant results from a simplistic understanding of the theological issues of Donne's time and from an attempt to force the Holy Sonnets into an inappropriate doctrinal frame. Young concludes his corrective by noting that seventeenth-century religious poets "bring to their poetic encounter with God varied experiences and draw upon a number of Christian resources—Catholic and Protestant, Medieval and Renaissance."

Two other essays—those by Mary Ann Radzinowicz and M. Thomas Hester—also concentrate on Donne. Radzinowicz demonstrates that in several of Donne's Holy Sonnets and occasional poems he uses the poetic device of the address to one's own soul, a device found in eight psalms. This borrowing from the psalter helped Donne create the complex poetic voices of his religious poetry, sanctioning for him "a stance both learned and impassioned, both personal and vicarious, both univocal and congregational." Hester's close reading of "As due by many titles" concentrates not on biographical or theological issues but on that characteristic of Donne's poetry that has most attracted modern readers, its wit. Viewing "As due by many titles" as a poem about the problematic nature of the religious lyric, Hester reveals it to be "an exploration of the kind-ness of the religious lyric, a search for traces of the divine Word in the typology of the self."

Donne also figures in the essay by Claude J. Summers, which discovers in book 1 of *The Faerie Queene* an important analogue (and possible source) for Donne's "Show me deare Christ" and Herbert's "The British Church." Summers's study helps place the two seventeenth-century poems in a tradition of quests for true religion and demonstrates how the image of the Bride of the Apocalypse functions for all three poets as a mirror of their own religio-political assumptions. Summers argues that Donne's skeptical "Show me deare Christ" is an expression of liberal tolerance, while Herbert's affirmative "The British Church" is a statement of conservative reaction.

Herbert is also the focus of two other essays. William Shullenberger examines the art of preaching in Herbert's poetry, pointing out that a preaching poet like Herbert found himself facing a double jeopardy: "a scriptural text which is inherently metaphoric, and the ruin, through the Fall, of the human power of naming." Touching on many poems, but dwelling particularly on "The Windows" and "Prayer (I)," Shullenberger argues that the poet's predicative style helps discover a new language, one that has been renovated by the power of the indwelling Word. In an absorbing essay, Michael C. Schoenfeldt places "Love (III)" in the context of Renaissance courtesy literature and reads the last lyric of "The Church" as a comedy of manners. According to Schoenfeldt, in "Love (III)" Herbert creates a dramatic situation fraught with great social anxiety and political significance in order "to reveal the immense difficulty of responding properly to God's overwhelming beneficence."

Poems by Crashaw and Marvell are the subjects of the essays by Lorraine Roberts and James Andrew Clark. Arguing that the Epiphany Hymn manifests a conscious control of structure and theme not always recognized by critics, Roberts concentrates on the function of the conversion of Dionysius the Areopagite in Crashaw's poem. Roberts explains the presence of Dionysius in the poem as one whose example points the way to epiphany, rather than as an advocate of the *via negativa*. She concludes that what is most striking about the Epiphany Hymn is not its emotionalism or mysticism, but its intellectual depth and consummate control. Clark explores the related acts of quoting, alluding, and echoing in Marvell's "The Coronet." The poem's echoes of and allusions to Herbert, Spenser, and Sidney are critically important, Clark concludes: "Weaving what he cannot disentangle, quoting what he cannot unquote, Marvell uses allusion to express, at once, the despondency and assurance of a poet who attempts to make from other texts an offering acceptable unto God." Almost inevitably, the attempt fails; but "The Coronet"—"a successfully allusive text about that failure"—succeeds.

The essays by Patricia G. Pinka and Stella P. Revard compare the different approaches of various poets to the nativity poem and the religious ode, respectively. Mentioning poems by Jonson, Herrick, and Vaughan, but concentrating on Herbert's

"Christmas" and Milton's "On the Morning of Christ's Nativity," Pinka explores the complexity of time in the nativity poem. She finds in Hooker's remarks on the significance of festival days a parallel to the process by which the speakers of Herbert's and Milton's poems imaginatively experience something of eternity through their celebrations of Christmas. Revard explains why Milton, Crashaw, and Cowley turned to the classical hymns and odes as a model for the religious lyric and compares their adaptations of this model in Milton's "On the Morning of Christ's Nativity," Crashaw's "In the Holy Nativity of Our Lord," and Cowley's "The Resurrection." As adapted by Milton and Crashaw, the religious ode celebrates an important public occasion, but nevertheless keeps its character as a devotion of private faith. In Cowley's adaptation, however, the ode is less a celebration of religious devotion than a vehicle for poetic performance.

In the final essay collected here, Joseph A. Wittreich offers an impressive study of the interactions of the religious lyric and secular literature, of how the latter impinges on the former. Surveying the successive retellings of and allusions to the Samson story in the period preceding *Samson Agonistes*, Wittreich illustrates the limitations of the typological lyric, particularly in its disfigurement of biblical narratives. He acknowledges that lyric poets used typology obliquely and ambiguously, as well as selectively and obviously, and demonstrates that "Typology is both a peril of and a procedure in the seventeenth-century lyric."

In total, the essays in this volume attempt to illuminate the devotional poetry of the seventeenth century by paying careful attention to its texts and contexts. In its entirety, the volume is by no means comprehensive. A number of important religious lyrics and poets are neglected or absent altogether, as, for example, Herrick, Vaughan, Traherne, and Edwards. And many important questions and issues are treated sparingly or not at all, including, for example, many aspects of the relationship between secular and religious poetry and several vexing questions of definition and theory. Nevertheless, the essays included here both individually and collectively shed light on the seventeenth-century religious lyric, fostering an increased understanding of both the genre as a whole and some of its most accomplished practitioners, especially Donne, Herbert,

Crashaw, and Milton. This collection of essays does not pretend to a definitive account of devotional poetry in the late Renaissance, but it furthers substantially our historical and critical appreciation of the seventeenth century's lyric expression of "Bright *shootes* of everlastingnesse."

*   *   *

This book and the conference from which it originated have benefited from the unstinting devotion of time and expertise on the part of the members of the conference steering committee, who helped referee the submissions to the conference and who offered invaluable suggestions for revision: Judith Scherer Herz, Robert B. Hinman, Frank L. Huntley, Leah S. Marcus, John R. Roberts, John T. Shawcross, and Gary A. Stringer. Their contributions have been extensive, and we join the authors of the essays in expressing gratitude to them. It is also our pleasure to acknowledge the support of the Horace H. Rackham Graduate School of the University of Michigan, the University of Michigan-Dearborn Campus Grants Committee, and the University of Michigan-Dearborn Twenty-fifth Anniversary Committee. We are particularly grateful for the support of the following administrators at the University of Michigan-Dearborn: Christopher C. Dahl, Chair, Department of Humanities; Victor K. Wong, former Dean, College of Arts, Sciences, and Letters; and Eugene Arden, Vice Chancellor for Academic Affairs and Provost.

1

ABANDONMENT AND THE ENGLISH RELIGIOUS LYRIC IN THE SEVENTEENTH CENTURY

William A. Sessions

In the twentieth century the English religious lyrics of the early seventeenth century have been easily and even popularly identified within "the whole body of the anthology," to use the contemporary poet A. R. Ammons's phrase.[1] Ironically, however, in the recent theorizing ferment of Renaissance criticism, these texts have been viewed less as a whole body themselves and more as works of individual poets. The reasons for this lack of holistic analysis are not hard to find in our revolutionary new readings of all poetic texts. It is not that such readings are necessarily more secular and less theoretically religious than earlier twentieth-century readings but rather that they challenge all general perspectives of canon, object, and source. Even traditional assumptions of revolution—so vital to secular readings of these texts like Empson's, for example—are no longer adequate, as Lawrence Lipking, commenting on revolutionary feminist thought, has noted.[2] In such ferment a traditional antinomy like that of Catholic-Protestant readings seems even more an endless debate, confusing for many readers the place of text. Indeed the text in this antinomy often becomes a critic's

1. *Sphere: The Form of a Motion* (New York: W. W. Norton and Company, 1974), pp. 15, 10.
2. "Aristotle's Sister: A Poetics of Abandonment," *Critical Inquiry* 10 (September 1983): 63.

weapon, especially in recent "Protestant" readings. As in other such "Protestant" readings elsewhere in Renaissance criticism, an apparently random use of doctrine to support a critical position betrays a general insensitivity not least to actual religious beliefs of all practicing Christians. In short, in such readings we are still repeating the quintessential debate, I believe, of all critical discussions on the whole body of these texts, that between Empson and Tuve over thirty years ago on Herbert's "The Sacrifice." We are repeating, with little change of larger perspective, a pattern that, only with differing positions and names, moves from Empson's eccentric, historically incorrect reading to Tuve's Catholic correction to Empson's apology and final crucial rebuttal: Herbert himself wrote the text, invented "a new style."[3]

Although it is uncertain just how influential this debate has been, Empson's conclusion did offer at the time a practical critical method almost universally followed as a way out of the ideological antinomy. The individual lyric, however intertextually defined, became for many readers and critics a representation and stylistic repository of various aspects of biography, variously interpreted. The style was the man. At least, a reader who concentrated on the lyric text within its own textuality may avoid something so vulgar as an "intentional fallacy" (the man was not necessarily the style) or ideological bias, positions that had in fact started the Empson-Tuve debate. The result of such a method is often deeper understanding of the poem or even of that composite called the poet, but very little understanding of the whole body of these seventeenth-century texts.

Even for a larger interpretation of these lyrics, however, beginning with the experience of a text rather than an elaborate scheme, even in a conceptual analysis of a whole body, is still the best critical method. Indeed Empson's direction of the reader toward the experience of the text itself rather than abstracting beyond that experience is simply an earlier recall to

3. This debate is summarized in Louis L. Martz, *The Poetry of Meditation: A Study in English Religious Literature of the Seventeenth Century* (New Haven and London: Yale University Press, 1954), pp. 91–92. But see also the original arguments in William A. Empson, *Seven Types of Ambiguity* (2d ed.; London: Chatto and Windus, 1947), and Rosemond Tuve, "On Herbert's 'Sacrifice,'" *Kenyon Review* 12 (1950): 51–75, the latter elaborated in her *A Reading of George Herbert* (London: Faber and Faber, 1952).

what recent critical theory, from all voices, has reminded us. As Roland Barthes remarked in his parody, "l'oeuvre propose, l'homme dispose."[4] Further, as most readers now know from hard experience, methods of syntactic ambiguity, deconstructing irony, and shifting perspective demand, in any textual interpretation, a reader's humility as well as cunning. As Lipking notes in the development of his thesis: "Abandoned women know that the world can shift too fast to be imitated, that the harmony of art is made to be broken."[5] Although it may be questionable whether the harmonies of these seventeenth-century "well-wrought urns" were designed to be broken, quite so easily and deliberately, it is nevertheless true that the greatest of these religious texts contain within their structures a dialectic that opens to a "desire" that for Julia Kristeva "organizes its logical structure on what can be called nothingness or the zero in logic."[6] Against one side that opens to structure and logic, action and consummation, this dialectic of desire posits its other firmly not only in an experience of its own deconstructing of its own meaning but also in an experience even greater than its own deconstruction: the absence of meaning of any kind in the dialectic, of being abandoned or being *as* abandonment, the death of dialectic, a lover without a beloved. As I shall argue, it is this mode of abandonment and its representation that leads a reader into the deepest experience of these seventeenth-century texts.

Abandonment as read in this mode of dialectic directs the reader toward an openness defined by "the zero in logic." Experience here is read with an openness not unlike what Heidigger calls *Gelassenheit*,[7] although Heidiggerian openness expresses more of a positive epistemology—the actual usefulness of the accepting subject in the order of *Dingheit*—than the greatest of these religious texts allows. Far more useful as models of such openness for readers of these texts are the literary texts and met-

4. *Critique et Verité* (Paris: Editions du Seuil, 1966), pp. 52–53.

5. "Aristotle's Sister," p. 78.

6. *Revolution in Poetic Language*, trans. Margaret Waller (New York: Columbia University Press, 1984), p. 130.

7. For the most accessible understanding of this term in Heidigger, see the citations in William Richardson, S.J., *Heidigger: Through Phenomenology to Thought*, preface by Martin Heidigger (The Hague: M. Nijhoff, 1963), especially pp. 502–12.

aphors of abandoned women, especially those of Greece and Rome, where, as in these seventeenth-century religious texts, openness as "the zero in logic" defines a structure of human vulnerability neither necessarily without, nor necessarily with, meaning and harmony (at least as expressed in the actual text to be read). Free structural relationships seem to offer possibilities, often as point to counterpoint, within the totality of the text, the concerted "harmony" so beloved by seventeenth-century literary critics. The dialectic of the text thus represents a mode of human existence that, as far as the text and the reading of the text go, begins in openness and a readiness of choice to read and ends in closure and inevitable abandonment. The text itself must end, the free relationships of Eros collapse, if only to go on to another text. The single lyric text simply cannot provide stasis or absolute certainty, only an experience of openness. This is the problematic to be faced by the imposition of antinomies on single texts, whatever kind. The larger critical frame will only suffice, if even that, for these texts that will not be so simply nailed down. Even here the frame can only be as ideological as Paul Valery's caveat about a writer's text: poems are not finished, they are abandoned.[8] Valery's observation remains the qualifying basis for any reader's construction of a grand theory of the English religious lyric.

ii

Yet, even in the act of reading and abandoning these texts, there emerges a dialectic of action for the reader, a dialectic of possibility, if not a moral stance. In their brief epigrammatic statements (often sonnets and never long unless, as in "Lycidas" and Traherne's *Centuries*, the form is virtually discontinuous) the dialectic in these seventeenth-century lyrics is almost self-contradictory, starting from a previous act of abandonment and ending in another. There even appears no action leading from these brief texts outward, no inspiration for overt social action so typical of communal liturgical and ideological language. On the surface, these religious texts appear to lack the assurance or praise typical of religious poetry throughout all cultures—

8. For discussion of this concept in Valery, see Jean Hytier, *The Poetics of Paul Valery*, trans. Richard Howard (Garden City, N.Y.: Doubleday and Co., 1966), especially pp. 240–46.

poetry which can give the reader a special sense of his or her own action in society and even the ideological forms to direct individual experience beyond itself. On the contrary, though written by men, these seventeenth-century texts often sound like the hopeless cries of the abandoned women of classical tradition—a not-surprising possibility since all of these male poets studied such outcries in the texts of Catullus, Virgil, Ovid, and the Greeks in their Humanist grammar schools. Yet these compelling late Renaissance texts express a truth about human existence that amounts to hardly less than a call to action or at least an interpretation for living, a kind of Stoic propaedeutic for survival. The problem is that the call to action, if it is that, implicit in the classical text or the seventeenth-century lyric, is never single but is always qualified and contingent. And this failure to recognize its contingency has been a failure of our reading since the late Renaissance, especially of religious texts, where we discount any action or moral stance unless it is certain and unqualified and preferably ideological.

But it is likely we have been misreading religious poetry in general and the Psalms in particular. The traditionally assumed models for these lyrics, the Psalms themselves, reveal a structure often contrary to frequent institutional interpretations. To be sure, readers of the Psalms, like readers of the Upanishads, will find hymns of praise for the goodness of divine creation and the special place of human beings in this creation. Thus, in Psalm 8, the speaker is careful to unite the majesty of God and the dignity of man in an ordered creation; in Psalm 122 the human creature loves the house of the Lord and the place of devotion, the rituals that are formal social recognition of the majesty of God. At the same time, the Psalms are special among religious documents of the world in their clear questioning of this dignity. In fact, in their expressions of human indignity, they come to grips not only with the self's sense of loss but also with the terror of being abandoned outside the order of love. The dialectic that emerges between these two poles of confidence and abandonment marks the Psalms, even in their affirmations, as a body of texts that dramatize human vulnerability. Indeed, if hope and confidence can exist at all in the whole body of these texts, either personal or collective (as in Psalms 8 and 122), it is only in terms of a recurring possibility of human abandonment, of a person or nation being abandoned and having to abandon. Such a fundamental recognition is particularly expressed in the experience of terror when the self necessarily opens up to loss, as in Psalm 22. The "groaning" speaker of Psalm 38 also echoes the theme of the "broken and contrite heart" of Psalm 51 that runs as a counterpoint throughout the whole of the Psalms, whether calling for the intimate friend who is absent as in Psalm 42, where the soul, like a deer after water, pants for God, or for the absent God in the outcry of Psalm 22.

This last psalm, according to both Mark and Matthew, the earliest Gospels, was sung by Christ himself dying on the cross. In words of vulnerability which Simone Weil praised as the greatest act in Christianity,[9] Christ sings "My God, my God, why hast thou forsaken me?" It is likely, as the Japanese novelist Endo has commented,[10] that the crucified Jesus also sang the rest of this familiar hymn with those other devout Jews below the Cross: "O my God, I cry in the daytime, but thou answerest not; / And in the night season, and am not silent." Through such lyric language, the reader can enter into the intimate desire in each psalm for the ecstatic embrace of what Martin Buber describes as its "I-Thou" encounter.[11] In the same text, at the same time, however, the reader must also confront the singer's own sense of loss, the silence of the beloved, the terror and fear of the self's being abandoned, left open and vulnerable in love.

Such a dialectic at the center of Hebrew experience in many of the Psalms had been so integrated into the whole Christian consciousness of the West by the Renaissance that these seventeenth-century poets, confronted with their own historical and psychological dislocations, must have found especially resourceful the new Protestant translations of the Psalms and the Catholic meditative uses. But by no accident they also found resourceful the new Humanist re-readings of classical texts. Indeed, in Virgil, Ovid, Euripides, and the Greek lyric, abandonment and human vulnerability are often so total that they appear to exist in no dialectic of hope or ecstasy at all.

9. "The Iliad, Or The Poem of Force," in *The Proper Study*, ed. Quentin Anderson and J. A. Mazzeo (New York: St. Martin's Press, 1962), p. 27.

10. Shusaku Endo, *A Life of Jesus*, trans. Richard A. Schuchert, S.J. (New York: Ramsay; Toronto: Paulist Press, 1973), pp. 149–50.

11. *I And Thou*, trans. Ronald Smith (New York: Scribner Book Co., 1958).

These archetypes of terrible abandonment and loss, almost all women, were natural instruments of intertextuality for late Renaissance poets in their new and modern representations. In fact, because of these classical models, these poets likely saw their own versions (and even translations) of the Psalms (and of other Hebrew Wisdom texts) more as simple lyrics than as formal religious expression. In their "translations" as humanist poets, they invented structures of action expressing their own experience, making their own texts or "psalms." Thus, what classical models may help readers understand in the whole body of these religious lyrics, products of Humanist intertextuality as they are, is their emphasis on dramatizations of human vulnerability rather than on formal modes of collective praise and social assurance. The result is that simple religious interpretation, Protestant or Catholic, or any such critical antinomy is no longer possible.

In this secular tradition there was another genre these seventeenth-century poets inherited, which had itself derived from classical models of abandoned women. At the heart of formal imitation in many of these seventeenth-century texts is the literary genre of the love complaint. The most pervasive model of this genre for the English Renaissance was the lament of Chaucer's Troilus. Significantly early in Chaucer's *Troilus and Criseyde* the young Trojan expressed his overwhelming sense of loss in loving: "If no love is, O God, what fele I so? / And if love is, what thing and which is he? / If love be good, from whennes cometh my woo?" (*Troilus* 1.400–402). If this cry appears another form of the Jewish Psalmist's dialectic and questioning in Psalm 22, it is nevertheless in Chaucer a direct translation of Petrarch, in fact the first in English. Moreover, it is Petrarch who links us with that fusion of courtly love and Augustinian psychology, as Greene[12] and Quinones[13] have shown, that dominated the Renaissance heroic mode, directly or inversely. Thus, given Petrarch's crystallizing influence on the rest of the Renaissance, his texts, which Donne, Herbert, and Milton

12. Thomas M. Greene, *The Light in Troy: Imitation and Discovery in Renaissance Poetry* (New Haven and London: Yale University Press, 1982), chapters 5-7.

13. Ricardo J. Quinones, *The Renaissance Discovery of Time* (Cambridge, Mass.: Harvard University Press, 1972), chapter 3.

knew well, and those of the popular *Petrarchismo* set the pattern. These popular texts defined the experience of human love for generations in a legacy not likely to be missed by any poet of the seventeenth century.

Behind Petrarch himself lay Virgil and the figure of Dido. Dido's love story and laments not only profoundly affected the young Saint Augustine, as he tells us in his *Confessions* (1.13), but also pointed Petrarch and his English imitators Chaucer, Wyatt, and Surrey, and the sixteenth-century poets in general, toward their understanding of the nature of love. Given this influence, one might argue that perhaps no line is more focal in later Western literature than the narrator's outburst in book 4 of the *Aeneid:* "Improbe amor, quid non mortalia pectora cogis?" (Fierce love, to what have you not driven mortal hearts?).[14] Behind this line and the figure of "infelix Dido" lie the women of Euripides and, quite likely behind them all, the figure of Sappho. In fact, it is Sappho's very ancient love complaint which I take as the absolute topos for the experience of abandonment that I am arguing is the basis of the seventeenth-century religious lyric. Whatever Sappho's direct influence in the late Renaissance, nowhere is this experience of abandonment and vulnerability in love more graphically revealed than in epigrams attributed to Sappho, the most famous being: "The moon is set, and the Pleiades; midnight, the hour hurries along; I lie alone."[15]

But in fact Sappho is not unknown in the texts of the seventeenth century, and one of the more spectacular translations of the century, what Robert Lowell would have called an "imitation," was made of a fragment of hers by John Donne. The poem "Sapho to Philaenis" was denied authenticity by Helen Gardner in her edition of Donne's Elegies and Songs and Sonnets. Earlier, Grierson had rescued what he denominated "an heroical epistle" from its place in the editions of Donne's poetry 1635–1669 "among the sober *Letters to Severall Personages*" and had related it to the Ovidian epistolary mode popular in the late

14. *Aeneid* 4.412, in P. Vergili Maronis, *Opera*, ed. A. Sidgwick (Cambridge: Cambridge University Press, 1934). The translation is my own.
15. *Greek Lyric*, ed. David A. Campbell, Loeb Classical Library (Cambridge: Harvard University Press, 1982), 1:173. The translation is my own.

1590s, especially through Drayton's imitations.[16] Gardner found "it difficult to imagine" Donne "wishing to assume the love-sickness of Lesbian Sappho" and objected to repetition of language and style and lack of argumentation, both characteristics, however, of the Ovidian monologue.[17] Furthermore, as John Carey noted, such repetition was the clue to the development of this "first female homosexual love poem in English: a limpid pool of sensuousness, swimming with twinned words and images like a deep mirror." Carey in fact marks the dramatic stance in the poem that releases the monologue: Donne's Sappho is standing before a mirror, touching herself as she speaks to her absent lover, who is nevertheless there, "for Sappho feels her when she feels herself."[18] The merging of duality, a persistent theme in all of Donne's work, is the issue here, as in Donne's other dramatized love poems: "My two lips, eyes, thighs, differ from thy two, / But so, as thine from one another doe"; and so "Hand to strange hand, lippe to lippe none denies; / Why should thy brest to brest, or thighs to thighs?" As Carey concludes, "Sappho's homosexuality recommended itself as the answer to another imaginative problem."[19]

But whatever Donne's poem solves, it is first and foremost the poem of an abandoned woman, or at the least one lying or standing alone, literally reflecting on herself and her desire and its center in absence. This is precisely the effect Donne must have intended, for his source of imitation is rather certainly Ovid's *Heroides*, the series of epistolary monologues from abandoned women such as Ariadne, Penelope, and Dido. Out of Propertius, Ovid invented a new genre, more monologue than epistle, and clearly a stage for elaborate, even theatrical *ethopoeia*. English imitations of Ovid's epistles of abandoned women can be found in the Renaissance as early as Surrey's "O happy dames, that may embrace" and "Good ladies, you that have your pleasure in exyle" in *Tottel's Miscellany*, but the

16. Herbert J. C. Grierson, ed., *The Poems of John Donne* (London: Oxford University Press, 1912), 1:124, 2:91.
17. *John Donne: The Elegies and the Songs and Sonnets* (Oxford: Clarendon Press, 1965), p. xlvi.
18. *John Donne: Life, Mind and Art* (New York: Oxford University Press, 1981), pp. 270–71.
19. Ibid., p. 271.

vogue of imitation of the *Heroides* reached a kind of zenith in France and Italy in the sixteenth century and provided English poets with ongoing Continental models. Most remarkable about Donne's generally neglected poem, at least for the purposes of this thesis, is its textual history. Gardner had reluctantly denied the poem for her canon because it had appeared in all the best manuscripts and, most authentically, in the first edition of Donne's poems. Grierson notes the placement of the poem in this 1633 edition but does not elaborate: "follows Basse's *Epitaph upon Shakespeare* and precedes *The Annunciation and Passion*."[20] Donne's reenactment of an abandoned Sappho thus lay between a death-poem for the greatest man of theater in Donne's time, a poem that ends in an image of Shakespeare's sleeping in death all alone, and a religious poem that begins: "Tamely fraile body'abstain to day; to day / My soule eates twice, Christ hither and away."[21] Furthermore, the poem is in the midst of religious poems in the 1633 edition, followed two poems later by "Good Friday, 1613," then "The Litanie," and then "A Nocturnal," and, before the Shakespeare epitaph, preceded by a psalm translation, "Resurrection, Imperfect," and "An Hymn to the Saints." Thus for the reader of 1633 the dialectic and duality of desire of abandoned Sappho merely continues a dialectic in the progression of the book. Whether deliberately ordered or not, the dialectic progresses, through a pagan mode, of course, but marking desire nonetheless—and carrying the momentum of the greater religious texts.

Yet, even if Donne's Sappho is only an exercise of the 1590s and its placement and composition meaningless, the most enduring representation in a classical text of an abandoned woman, Dido, had in fact never left the Western world and had become more important (if that is possible) in the Renaissance. It is even likely that Virgil and possibly Petrarch were read as frequently as the Psalms in the formative years of the authors of these seventeenth-century texts, and, more important, given the synthesizing minds of the period, all read in terms of each other. Such primary levels of reading inspired passions that in their certitude probably did not see the differences we see. Cer-

20. *The Poems of John Donne*, 1:124.
21. Helen Gardner, ed., *John Donne: The Divine Poems*, 2d ed. (Oxford: Clarendon Press, 1978), p. 29.

tainly, among the contemporary religious traditions surrounding these poets, the Spanish mystics reflect the popular courtly *Petrarchismo* and, almost a century before these English poets, make their own parody of erotic love, with the same dialectic of abandonment. The Eros of God, for Saint John of the Cross, visits in the night, the moment of greatest natural and human abandonment. This is the moment Vaughan, reflecting this tradition in his poem "The Night," calls "this worlds defeat" (l. 25). Saint John says that God visits the soul "in total darkness and concealment from the enemy" so that no other being can "know the intimate and secret communications which take place there between the soul and God."[22] John's Dark Night of the Soul is thus more than Dionysius the Areopagite's "superessential Darkness," the traditional Greek theological definition for such a mystic experience; rather, Vaughan's "deep, but dazzling darkness" (l. 50) expresses John's intimate experience wherein God's "touches" are like those entreated by the Bride in the Song of Solomon. With this Bride John identifies, crying out, "Let him kiss me with the kisses of his mouth!"[23] For Vaughan also, ending his poem, there is the outcry: "O for that night! where I in him / Might live invisible and dim."

For Teresa of Avila, abandonment implied no sense of personal vulnerability (a quality apparently lacking in all her texts, including that of her life). Rather, open and free surrender to the repeated "attacks" of God, the repeated plunges of God's arrow of love, define her loss and its inevitable pain. This is the ecstatic union most graphically represented by Bernini and depicted by Crashaw in his "Hymn to the Name and Honor of the Admirable Sainte Teresa." Teresa is, says Crashaw, "love's victim" (l. 75) with "a sweet & subtle Pain" (l. 98) and "a Death, in which who dyes / Loues his death, and dyes again, / and would for euer so be slain" (ll. 100–103). For Crashaw, Teresa's logic is paradoxical and inexorable: "How kindly will thy gentle Heart / Kisse the sweetly-killing Dart" (ll. 105–6). Thus, following Bernini's representation, Crashaw emphasizes in his love-dialectic not so much the terror of abandonment, although Teresa's surrender to the physical nothingness of

22. *Dark Night of the Soul*, trans. and ed. E. Allison Peers (Garden City, N.Y.: Doubleday and Co., 1959), 2:23, 11.

23. Ibid., p. 16.

death is clearly there for him and Bernini. Rather, as in "The Flaming Heart," abandonment reveals "thy brim-fill'd bowls of feirce desire" (l. 99). This is Teresa's ecstatic love that rises up from such openness and abandonment of self: "the full king-dome of that finall kisse / That . . . seal'd thee his" (ll. 101–2).

iii

With different emphasis, the same dialectic in the Spanish mystics appears in the structure of the seventeenth-century English religious lyric. The difference arises from another trans-formation, that of the English tradition of the love complaint, beginning with Chaucer's version of Petrarch, and transmitted into the English Renaissance setting through early collections like the 1557 *Tottel's Miscellany*. In this English dialectic, strengthened by the medieval lyric tradition and its themes of mutability and the early personal influence of Wyatt and, to some degree, Surrey,[24] loss and its melancholy are generally more dominant, as in *Troilus* itself, than the erotic life-giving ecstasy of the Spanish dialectic. Therefore, whether following the Psalmist or the lamenting Troilus, Dido, and Sappho, all of whom in their abandonment long for the ecstasy they have known, these English religious texts give us lyrics of human experience that define both sides of a dialectical contradiction, constantly qualifying ecstasy in terms of abandonment.

For this dialectical representation, the abandoned women of the classical world (and their inverted transfiguration in Troilus and the Petrarchan hero) set the mode. In fact, these lyr-ics express, more often than not, this same classical sense of loss, abandonment, and vulnerability in erotic love just when they are most authentically religious, most open to the love of God. This kind of intense, seemingly contradictory dialectic can be traced and exemplified throughout the whole body of

24. For the influence of *Troilus* in the early Renaissance, see Raymond Southall, *The Courtly Maker: An Essay on the Poetry of Wyatt and His Contemporaries* (Oxford: Basil Blackwell, 1964). For the background of the medieval lyric, see Patricia Thomson, *Sir Thomas Wyatt and His Background* (Stanford: Stanford University Press, 1964), and also Douglas L. Peterson, *The English Lyric from Wyatt to Donne* (Princeton: Princeton University Press, 1967). For a general discussion of Dido, Troilus, and their place in the inception of the Renaissance love lyric, see my book *Henry Howard, The Poet-Earl of Surrey* (Boston: G. K. Hall and Co., 1986).

these religious lyrics of the seventeenth century, but in three of its greatest lyric statements, poems by Herbert, Milton, and Donne, literary representations of abandonment and vulnerability are as profound as any "in the whole body of the anthology."

Thus in Herbert, texts of abandonment, especially those not in the Williams manuscript, make any definition of religious experience in *The Temple* nothing simple at all. These texts are certainly not the simple assertion and assurance so reductively assigned by numerous Herbert commentators to his lyrics. Language of religious encounter is always difficult and ambiguous in Herbert, even though sometimes reduced to a deceptive simplicity like "something understood" ("Prayer [1]," l. 14). Even the ultimate sign of God can become a "strange and uncouth thing" ("The Crosse," l. 1). In "The Crosse," appearing with "The Flower" at a crucial juncture in Herbert's book, the effect of abandonment is almost total. After "much wrestling" and "so much desired to take away," this lover lies "bleeding on the ground." In his complaint, the lover-speaker feels the "ague" of what might have been, "groans" for "harmony." The lover is, in all, "a weak disabled thing." In an image with Petrarchan overtones (probably originating in a love lyric of Surrey's), certainly one echoing Donne's ending for his "Hymne to God my God, in my sicknesse"—"that he may raise the Lord throws down"—Herbert's lover suffers in this text the agony of being at the mercy of a lover who casts away according to his desire: "taking me up to throw me down." The lover, "a weed in paradise," knows what the Eros of completion might mean but he is simply abandoned, lonely in what one might call his night-desire. These contraries, paradoxes that dominate late medieval and early Renaissance love complaints, are, in Herbert's text, transformed cross-actions that crush the lover-speaker.

At the other end of the dialectic, in "Love (III)" the lover is welcomed, coaxed, even wooed by the taking of his hand, and told that the eyes, the focus of all sexual play in *Petrarchismo*, were the gift of the wooer. Although the lover has marred them and now wants his "shame" to go "where it doth deserve" (ll. 13–14), the lover of this lover has borne their blame. This service is the service of courtly love, in which lover accepts lover in submission and as model. But Herbert is truer than the poets of courtly love to the dialectic within his text, truer, that is, to the subtext of the erotic lyric. He takes the acceptance a step further. The divine lover has a meal and specific directions for its consummation: "You must sit down, sayes Love, and taste my meat" (l. 17). The once-abandoned lover immediately acts at the call of Eros, fully entering into his desire and its completion: "So I did sit and eat" (l. 18).

Erotic imagery may seem quite distant from Milton's "Lycidas," but the dialectic I have been describing certainly is not. In this pastoral elegy, where the lyric persona assumes a virtually anonymous ritual mask, Milton builds a constant antithesis between the poles of abandonment and fulfillment. These forces of absolute sudden death and of subtle, if also absolute, Eros dominate the experience of the young shepherd singing his text of the elegy. There are three key moments of abandonment, at least as I have been developing the term, for the anonymous singer in "Lycidas." Each is followed rather quickly by its antithesis in which a holy figure offers an answer or an expanding hope. The most terrible moment of loss, at least as the structure of the text reveals it, is the first. Hoping "to burst into sudden blaze," the speaker finds instead "the blind Fury with the abhorr'd shears" who "slits the thin-spun life" (ll. 74–76). Milton's deliberate concatenation of mismatched myths, blindness and madness that have the power to determine life and death, is a dislocation that in itself could give Humanist culture utter abandonment. Even Apollo's loving admonition and answer is but a leap to another world, however, that cannot dissipate the moment in the text defining a young male's final nothingness. Similarly Peter's "dread voice" with its male fatherly security merely confirms the mad catachresis of universal "blind mouths," and his prophecy, intended to show ultimate love, only reveals, at least on one level, just how truly lost and drowned Lycidas now is. Not even the confident "dear might" of the young Christ walking on this deadly water that kills bright young men can finally overcome that moment in the text, however comforting to have the clear implication that the Eros-figure of the walking Christ can, in fact, overcome nothingness. In Milton's finale, the erotic young male Christ who saves and gives life marries, in effect, the drowned young shepherd. His muddy locks have just been bathed with "nectar pure," and in that general group-marriage, marked by singing, the young man restored in Eros has overcome the utter abandonment of death. In the structure of the poem and its total text, however, the question of survival still remains open for the reader, in a dialectic of vulnerability.

iv

What is remarkable about this sense of vulnerability as a center of lyric experience is precisely its openness. The innate meditative structure of the seventeenth-century text, circling the event of the poem, opens up toward the reader's "text," the reader's own sense of experience. Thus, when this openness of the voice is most clear in these English texts, the speaking voice hardly ends in its own freedom, like a sentimental gesture. It opens toward the reader, carrying, at best, its own honesty. Yet the written text can never become the reader's "text"; it can lead or point the reader only. Even its honesty here is a sword that cuts both ways. The text carries its own dangers that the reader must accept or not read. If a reader refuses these dangers, the dialectic and its tension that describes the life and common act of reading no longer exist. The reader qua reader no longer exists. This is the price and danger of all acts of reading; their freedom exists only in terms of received texts and the choices therein.

In this sense the act of reading, like the act of life, is only choice, and as act, exists only as choice among contingencies. As the voice in these English religious lyrics demonstrably faces the potential dangers in its own language and action—in its own text, the lies that always threaten—so must the reader, now open to that voice. Each must confront lies with the possibility of the terrible consequences that Simone Weil, speaking of Homer's *Iliad*,[25] has suggested may be in store for any such confrontation. The human being, she notes, "who does not wear the armor of the lie" will be "touched by it to the very soul. Grace can prevent this touch from corrupting" such a human being "but it cannot spare" the person "the wound." This vulnerability, she suggests, this openness to being wounded—the absolute condition of readership—may teach us to "recover that

25. "The Iliad, Or The Poem of Force," p. 28.

simplicity that renders so poignant every sentence in the story of the Passion"—which story, one may add, is the central religious mystery most frequently enacted as the formal and psychological root of these seventeenth-century texts.

Therefore, where these religious lyrics offer such openness, without lies, they dramatize, it seems to me, dangerous voices conscious of abandonment, even of suicide if the dialectic breaks down, as with Dido. In this they offer texts as profound as those texts written only a few years earlier and essentially contemporary: the final lessons of the surviving Hamlet to Horatio or of Edgar to Gloucester, calls to "readiness" and "ripeness" in human existence. These lyrics suggest that such "readiness" for the reader may also lead to confrontation. Readers of these lyrics may thus encounter, at its deepest and simplest, a text whose dialectic represents the embrace of Eros but not at the price of truth. The text includes the look into the abyss of Thanatos opening at every moment of human existence.

Few religious texts express such reader-confrontation or the lover's moment of vulnerability, the lover-reader's edge of abandonment and openness, in more discursive terms than Donne's sonnet "Oh, to vex me."[26] This remarkable text is a lyric whose overt contradictory linguistic structure concentrates the drama inevitable in any dialectic of abandonment at the same time that it emphasizes, in a positive sense, its triviality. As such, it becomes a model text about the nature of love, whatever kind. As model text, it begins with the agony of division of self—"Oh, to vex me contraryes meete in one"—and ends in a moral stance and resolution, a unity of action that springs from honest self-recognition: "Those are my best dayes, when I shake with feare." In its text the "wound" of human existence is never denied. At all times, in its threatening dialectic of existence, "Inconstancy unnaturally" becomes "constant," even with the highest ideals of "vowes" and "devotione." These ideals of Eros may be abandoned in this poem of contingency. They may be reduced to the humiliating level of sheer sexual lust—Donne's speaker's "my prophane love"—a reduction to absurdity for a reflective, self-conscious being like Donne's speaker. More dreadfully "and as soone forgott," however, these

26. Gardner, ed., *Divine Poems*, pp. 14–15.

ideals are reduced to the nothingness and concatenation of changing moments (a motion dramatized in the text by sharp metronomic rhymes and self-reflecting figures like asyndeton, anaphora, and polyptoton). This flux allows neither permanent meaning to individual being and action nor secure meaning or direction for any existence, no matter how collective a "people of God." Contingency is everywhere. To "court God" or "quake with true feare of his rod," this lover seeking that "God/rod" is always on an edge, a dialectical tension for which sexual tension is both part and analogue. Always threatened with abandonment, the lover is equally stretched out, like the arms and bodies of Sappho, Dido, or their male descendant, Troilus, toward fulfillment. The irony is that "Devout fitts" containing promise of such fulfillment are themselves stretched out in time, will themselves "come and go away." Donne's lover-speaker thus learns the basic potential deadliness of time: to turn all love and devotion, even the passage of life itself, into hallucination, the fever of illusion, "a fantastique Ague."

In such a frank confrontation with Donne's abyss—dramatized in a text whose sputtering convolutions are "As ridlingly distemperd" as Hopkins's texts of abandonment—Donne's speaker does nevertheless achieve closure and moral statement, but at a price. He can never be secure. Donne's closure is latent with the possibility of further action in time, the next "text," literary or otherwise, but only because the lover shakes "with feare." In fact, Donne's dialectic of fear and trembling as condition for Eros (long before Kierkegaard's redefinition for the modern world) reduces time to nothing less than the motions of desire. Time as Eros had long been the terrible recognition of the lovers, most of them abandoned or threatened by abandonment, in certain key texts of the Western world. Dido, Sappho, Saint John of the Cross, Teresa, all are, in this perspective, the true workers in time and of time. This is because only Eros can encounter the abyss of Thanatos and possibly cross it, although never without being permanently wounded or, at the least, as crippled as the biblical Jacob, who even had to change his name (like a woman being married) to mark his wound.

Thus, what makes for work or action or "best dayes" in Donne's dialectic is the self-recognition of one's "wound." To "shake with feare" before the beloved, the motion of Donne's sonnet, is such recognition. It is an act of love and, for a lover threatened by abandonment, it is his act of faith—but faith only in the life-giving existence of the ongoing dialectic between lover and beloved, nothing more. Such faith as closure for the text can never subsume the rest of the text or even leap beyond it. It can only exist within it and therefore, like everything else, "shake with feare" in the presence of the Beloved and do nothing more, or less. Although the nature of his love is different, this lover is as limited in choices as Dido. He only knows at the end of the poem when are his "best dayes."

Donne's Holy Sonnet may lack the transcendent imagery of the Spanish mystics or Sappho's absolute moment of desire for the Other, but it is nevertheless discourse for an everyday encounter. The encounter is with a dialectic always as sharp as a razor's edge, and language for such an encounter must be comprehending but simple. It must by its nature be difficult to read and write. On the one hand, this dialectical language works toward the moment of ecstasy but at the same time recognizes that the moment of the "I-Thou" is daily contingent on the threat of lies and the fear of abandonment. In Donne's world, like those of abandoned women, the days of the lover-speaker's own nature "can shift too fast to be imitated" and the "harmony of art" can "be broken." Fragmentation, rough prosody, or antithetical order in the concentration of the sonnet are natural forms for such a world. If there can be any harmony or "best dayes," it too must be in a dialectic where the lover shaking with fear is open to that flow of contradictory experience he or she cannot necessarily call one's own.

Thus, finally to enter the embraces of love, as in Herbert's last poem or in "Lycidas," is to have survived in an action whose openness to experience Hamlet understood: "Readiness is all." Such a "ready" text lies open to the embraces of Eros, but by the very definition of Donne's sonnet, these embraces cannot exist, at least in time and human language, without vulnerability and even abandonment, at all times the threat of division of self and the fear of dissolution of being in death. Such recognition is "readiness" in a dialectic of love, a dialectic of action, to be found in the best seventeenth-century religious lyrics. Beyond that dialectic no text will take us or can take us. In fact, whether Sappho's text or Saint John of the Cross's or Donne's, being open to the text, with all its own openness, what Donne's voice shaking with fear is asking, is about as far as any reader in "readiness" can go.

2

DONNE'S HOLY SONNETS AND THE THEOLOGY OF GRACE

R. V. Young

The flowering of the English devotional lyric, long treated as an Anglican phenomenon with Catholic overtones distinct from Puritanism,[1] is now widely regarded as unambiguously Protestant, with negligible debts to Continental Catholicism. With increasing frequency in recent years, a distinctively Protestant poetics has been designated the source of the English tradition of devotional poetry.[2] The Holy Sonnets of John Donne have furnished especially fertile ground for theological speculation. Once seen as examples of the influence of Ignatian meditation on Anglican poetry, the Holy Sonnets are now more often interpreted as an expression of the final crisis in the poet's conversion from Catholic recusancy to a Calvinist orientation consistent with Anglican orthodoxy. Despite the broad acceptance

1. See especially Helen C. White, *The Metaphysical Poets* (1936; rpt. New York: Collier, 1962); Helen Gardner, ed., *John Donne: The Divine Poems*, 2d ed. (Oxford: Clarendon, 1978); Louis L. Martz, *The Poetry of Meditation*, 2d ed. (New Haven: Yale University Press, 1962); and Anthony Low, *Love's Architecture: Devotional Modes in Seventeenth-Century English Poetry* (New York: New York University Press, 1978).

2. See especially William Halewood, *The Poetry of Grace: Reformation Themes and Structures in English Seventeenth-Century Poetry* (New Haven: Yale University Press, 1970); Barbara K. Lewalski, *Donne's Anniversaries and the Poetry of Praise* (Princeton: Princeton University Press, 1973); Andrew Weiner, *Sir Philip Sidney and the Poetics of Protestantism: A Study of Contexts* (Minneapolis: University of Minnesota Press, 1978); and Lewalski, *Protestant Poetics and the Seventeenth-Century Religious Lyric* (Princeton: Princeton University Press, 1979). "Protestant Poetics" was the topic of a special session at the 1983 MLA convention in New York.

it now enjoys, this view of the Holy Sonnets is flawed in several ways. First, it is based on a simplistic and inaccurate view of the theological issues of Donne's era. Second, it attempts to establish the existence of an exclusively Protestant mode of poetry without determining whether the same features of theme and style are available in contemporaneous Catholic poetry. Finally, it forces the Holy Sonnets into a doctrinal frame that often overlooks the equivocal resonance and play of wit in Donne's poetry.

Scholars who espouse the notion of Protestant poetics are fond of observing that the Reformation maintained that man's justification begins with what is called *prevenient grace.* William Halewood quotes one of Donne's sermons on this point: "He is as precise as Taylor in his use of the nomenclature of Reformation theology," Halewood writes. "The grace which provokes the faith which leads to justification is *preventing* or *prevenient:* 'no man can prepare that worke, no man can begin it, no man can proceed in it of himselfe. The desire and the actual beginning is from the preventing grace of God' (*Sermons,* 2:305)."[3] Barbara Lewalski is even more emphatic:

> Because man's natural state is so desperate, there can be no question (as in some Roman Catholic formulations) of man's preparing himself through moral virtue for the reception of grace, or of performing works good and meritorious in themselves; everything that he does himself is necessarily evil and corrupt. As the tenth of the Thirty-nine Articles of the established church put it, "The condition of man, after the fall of Adam is such that he cannot turne, and prepare himselfe by his owne naturall strength, and good workes, to faith, and calling upon God, wherefore we have no power to doe good workes pleasant, and acceptable to God, without the grace of God preventing us, that we may have a good will, and working with us when we have that good will."[4]

Now this is all very puzzling. "Prevenient grace" hardly seems to qualify as a decisive example of "the nomenclature of Reformation theology" since the term is used in the Council of Trent's *Decree on Justification* (1547), which states quite explicitly that the work of salvation begins not with man's efforts, but with the unmerited grace of God:

3. *The Poetry of Grace,* pp. 62–63.
4. *Protestant Poetics,* pp. 15–16.

[The Council] declares further that the beginning of this same justification in adults must be received from the prevenient grace of God through Christ Jesus; that is, from his call, by which they are called for no existing merit of their own, in order that those who have by sins turned away from God, might be disposed through his awakening and help to turn to their own justification, by freely assenting to and cooperating with that grace. Thus as God touches the human heart with the light of the Holy Spirit, the man himself is not wholly inactive, inasmuch as he might cast it aside. Nonetheless, without God's grace he cannot move himself toward justice in God's sight by his own free will. Hence when it is said in Sacred Scripture, "Turn toward me and I shall turn toward you" (Zach. 1:3), we are reminded of our freedom; and when we respond, "Convert us, Lord, to you and we shall be converted" (Lam. 5:21), we confess that we are anticipated by God's grace.[5]

This is not a Tridentine novelty. St. Thomas Aquinas makes it clear that the "preparation for grace" attributed by Lewalski to "some Roman Catholic formulations" can only come after and as a result of God's prior gift of grace: "But if we speak of grace as it signifies a help from God moving us to good, no preparation is required on man's part anticipating, as it were, the divine help, but rather, every preparation in man must be by the help of God moving the soul to good."[6] Or as the mystic, St. John of the

5. Quoted from *Enchiridion Symbolorum, Definitionum et Declarationum de rebus fidei et Morum*, ed. Henr. Denzinger and Clem. Bannwart, S.J., 17th ed. (Fribourg: Herder, 1927), 797: "Declarat praeterea, ipsius iustificationis exordium in adultis a Dei per Christum Iesum praeveniente gratia sumendum esse, hoc est, ab eius vocatione, qua nullis eorum exsistentibus meritis vocantur, ut qui per peccata a Deo aversi erant, per eius excitantem atque adiuvantem gratiam ad convertendum se ad suam ipsorum iustificationem, eidem gratiae libere assentiendo et cooperando, disponantur, ita ut tangente Deo cor hominis per Spiritus Sancti illuminationem neque homo ipse nihil omnino agat, inspirationem illam recipiens, quippe qui illam et abicere potest, neque tamen sine gratia Dei movere se ad iustitiam coram illo libera sua voluntate possit. Unde in sacris litteris cum dicitur: '*Convertimini ad me, et ego convertar ad vos*' (Zach 1, 3), libertatis nostrae admonemur; cum respondemus: '*Converte nos, Domine, ad te, et convertemur*' (Thr 5, 21), Dei nos gratia praeveniri confitemur."

6. *Summa Theologica*, 1-2.112.2: "Sed si loquamur de gratia secundum quod significat auxilium Dei moventis ad bonum, sic nulla praeparatio requiritur ex parte hominis quasi praeveniens divinum auxilium; sed potius quaecumque praeparatio in homine esse potest, est ex auxilio Dei moventis animam ad bonum." The Latin text is from the Blackfriars edition of St. Thomas Aquinas, *Summa Theologica*, vol. 30, *The Gospel of Grace*, ed. and trans. Cornelius Ernst, O.P. (London: Eyre & Spottiswoode, 1972), p. 148.

Cross, succinctly puts it, "without his grace one is unable to merit his grace."[7]

There are, to be sure, significant differences between Protestant and Catholic versions of justification; the insistence of the Council of Trent on the cooperation of man's free will with God's grace is an example, and will presently receive further consideration. But there is no basis for suggesting that the concept of prevenient grace was a discovery, even a rediscovery, of the Reformation. At times it appears that the proponents of Protestant poetics have derived their concept of Catholic theology wholly from Reformation polemics. In any case, many commentators of recent years have read Donne's devotional poems, along with those of his English contemporaries, as expositions of an exclusively Protestant, indeed a Calvinist, view of election and grace. According to one critic, Donne's Holy Sonnets "yield more fully to an analysis of their biblical motifs, their anguished Pauline speaker, their presentation of states of soul attendant upon the Protestant drama of regeneration, than they do to any other meditative scheme," and the first of these sonnets, "As due by many titles," has been called a treatment of "the problem of election."[8]

Here and there in the Holy Sonnets there are explicitly Calvinist terms, as well as passages that suggest a Calvinist theology of grace—the phrase "Impute me righteous" in Sonnet 3, for instance, or the famous paradox that closes "Batter my heart," Sonnet 10. But neither the first sonnet, "As due by many titles," nor the Holy Sonnets generally can be read as a specifically Calvinist, nor even Protestant, exposition of grace. In fact, the persona of the Holy Sonnets seems almost to be "trying out" different versions of grace in order to arrive at a theologically moderate position. We know from his letters that Donne inclined this way. Writing to Henry Goodyere within a year of

7. *Cántico espiritual*, 32.5: "sin su gracia no se puede merecer su gracia." *Vida y obras completas de San Juan de la Cruz*, ed. Crisógono de Jesús, O.C.D., Matías del Niño Jesús, O.C.D., and Lucinio del SS. Sacramento, O.C.D., 5th ed. (Madrid: BAC, 1964), p. 718.

8. Lewalski, *Protestant Poetics*, pp. 265–66. Unlike Lewalski, I follow the order of the first twelve sonnets in the Gardner edition of the *Divine Poems*, which seems to have been vindicated by Patrick F. O'Connell, "The Successive Arrangements of Donne's 'Holy Sonnets,'" *Philological Quarterly* 60 (1981): 323–42, esp. p. 334.

the time he is believed to have composed most of the Holy Sonnets, he praises his own verse litany, "That neither the Roman Church need call it defective, because it abhors not the particular mention of the blessed Triumphers in heaven; nor the Reformed can discreetly accuse it, of attributing more then a rectified devotion ought to doe"; and in another letter to Goodyere, written about the same time, he says of Catholic and Protestant churches, "The channels of Gods mercies run through both fields; and they are sister teats of his graces, yet both diseased and infected, but not both alike."[9] This is hardly the attitude of militant Calvinism.

Donne's "ecumenical" inclination is further developed in his *Essays in Divinity*, probably composed during the three or four years before his ordination. As Evelyn Simpson observes, this work would hardly have commended Donne to Anglican orthodoxy, as represented by the Calvinist archbishop of Canterbury, George Abbot, since "Abbot was a narrow-minded man, bitterly hostile to the Church of Rome."[10] In the *Essays* Donne maintains, however, that despite sharp differences between the Anglican and Roman communions, they share the same foundation: "yet though we branch out *East* and *West*, that Church concurs with us in the root, and sucks her vegetation from one and the same ground, *Christ Jesus.*" Donne continues, "so Synagogue and Church is the same thing, and of the Church, *Roman* and *Reformed*, and all other distinctions of place, Discipline, or Person, but one Church, journying to one *Hierusalem*, and directed by one guide, Christ Jesus." Most remarkably, Donne even goes so far as to prefer a unity based on the form of *any* of the principal churches—Roman, Genevan, or Anglican—to the disunity prevailing in his day:

> And though to all my thanksgivings to God, I ever humbly acknowledg, as one of his greatest Mercies to me, that he gave me my Pasture in this Park, and my milk from the brests of this Church, yet out of a fervent, and (I hope) not inordinate affection, even to such an Unity, I do zealously wish, that the whole catho-

9. *Letters to Severall Persons of Honour* (1651), introd. M. Thomas Hester (fac. rpt.; New York: Delmar, 1977), pp. 34, 102. Hester gives as the dates of these letters 1608 and 1609 respectively, in the Schedule, pp. xviii-xxii.

10. See the Introduction to her edition of Donne's *Essays in Divinity* (Oxford: Clarendon, 1952), p. xi.

lick Church, were reduced to such Unity and agreement, in the form and profession Established, in any one of these Churches (though ours were principally to be wished) which have not by any additions destroyed the foundation and possibility of salvation in Christ Jesus; That then the Church, discharged of disputations, and misapprehensions, and this defensive warr, might contemplate Christ clearly and uniformely.[11]

Again, this is not the tone of Calvinist rigor, and the emphasis on the corporate unity of the Church seems incompatible with the stress on individual election urged by Calvin and his more vociferous English followers.

Hence when Donne plainly repudiates Calvin on the specific matter of grace in a subsequent passage of the *Essays in Divinity*, his theology is perfectly consistent. Although in his reply to Cardinal Sadoleto, Calvin names "justification by faith, the first and keenest subject of controversy between us,"[12] his own *Antidote to the Council of Trent* clearly establishes that the central theological issue of the Protestant Reformation was freedom of the will. Calvin says "amen" to the Council's first three canons on justification, which stipulate, respectively, that man cannot be justified by his own human works or the law without the grace of Christ; that this grace does not merely make salvation easier, but is absolutely necessary; and that prevenient grace is requisite to dispose man even to desire salvation. Calvin only begins to take exception with the fourth canon, which says, "If anyone say that the free will of man, moved and excited by God, in no way cooperates by assenting to God's stimulus and call, by which it disposes and prepares itself for receiving the grace of justification, and that it is unable to resist, if it would, but that as a thing inanimate it is able to do nothing and is held merely passive, let him be anathema."[13] Calvin's rejoinder: "the efficacy of divine grace is such, that all opposi-

---

11. *Essays in Divinity*, pp. 50, 51, 51–52.

12. *John Calvin: Selections from His Writings*, ed. John Dillenberger (New York: Doubleday, 1971), p. 95.

13. *Enchiridion Symbolorum*, ed. Denzinger and Bannwart, 814: "Si quis dixerit, liberum hominis arbitrium a Deo motum et excitatum nihil cooperari assentiendo Deo excitanti atque vocanti, quo ad obtinendam iustificationis gratiam se disponat ac praeparet, neque posse dissentire, si velit, sed velut inanime quoddam nihil omnino agere mereque passive se habere: anathema sit."

tion is beaten down, and we who were unwilling are made obedient, it is not we who assent, but the Lord by the Prophet, when he promises that he will make us to walk in his precepts."[14] Calvin raises similar objections to canons 5 through 7, which assert that Adam's sin did not obliterate free will; that man does evil only on his own with God's permissive will and not his proper consenting; and that man is not utterly incapable of doing good before justification.

When Donne meditates on God's mercy in the *Essays in Divinity*, his discussion of grace and nature is Thomistic, his view of the human will far more Tridentine than Calvinist:

> in our repentances and reconciliations, though the first grace proceed only from God, yet we concurr so, as there is an union of two Hypostases, *Grace* and *Nature*. Which, (as the incarnation of our Blessed Saviour himself was) is conceived in us of the Holy Ghost, without father; but fed and produced by us; that is, by our will first enabled and illumined. For neither God nor man determine mans will; (for that must either imply a necessiting therof from God, or else *Pelagianisme*) but they condetermine it.

Above all Donne denies Calvin's notion of irresistible grace by which "all opposition is beaten down": "And yet we may not say, but that God begins many things which we frustrate; and calls when we come not."[15] The issue would not go away for Donne, even after his ordination. Of course, in his very public sermons far more discretion was required than in his letters or *Essays*, which remained unpublished during his lifetime. Still, Donne clung consistently to an un-Calvinist belief in freedom of the will. In a sermon of 1626, for example, he affirms what seems to be predestination: "Christ doth not now begin to make that man his, but now declares to us, that he hath been his from all eternity. . . ." But a few pages further, immediately after referring to "the Eternal Decree of my Election," he attacks what—for Calvin—seems the necessary corollary, the doctrine of irresistible grace (which Donne attributes to "the later School"): "He came not to force and compel them, who would not be brought

14. *Calvin: Selections*, ed. Dillenberger, p. 194.
15. *Essays in Divinity*, pp. 80, 81.

into the way: Christ saves no man against his will."[16] Like the fathers of the Council of Trent, Donne seeks to formulate the delicate balance between grace and nature, predestination and free will. If his conclusions differ from theirs, they likewise differ from Calvin's.

It is not surprising, therefore, to find many of the theological features of the Holy Sonnets paralleled in the devotional poems of Donne's Catholic contemporaries, who exhibit an equal concern over the problem of election and grace. A good example is furnished by the *Heráclito cristiano* (*Christian Heraclitus*, 1613) by Francisco de Quevedo (1580–1645). Like Donne's Holy Sonnets, it is a collection of penitential lyrics that focus on the spiritual condition of the poetic persona. The parallels begin to emerge with the first poem of each set. The octave of Donne's "As due by many titles" establishes the misery of man's natural condition by seeing his situation as that of an unreliable debtor who tries to cancel his debts by inviting God to foreclose on his hopelessly overmortgaged self:

> As due by many titles I resigne
> My selfe to thee, O God, first I was made
> By thee, and for thee, and when I was decay'd
> Thy blood bought that, the which before was thine,
> I am thy sonne, made with thy selfe to shine,
> Thy servant, whose paines thou hast still repaid,
> Thy sheepe, thine Image, and till I betray'd
> My selfe, a temple of thy Spirit divine . . . .[17]

The proliferation of metaphors, suggesting various relationships with God, is an indication of the speaker's uncertainty and the feebleness of his position. Hence it is not surprising that the sestet dwells queasily on the prospect that the proffered self may not be worth the cost of refurbishing, that only the devil is still interested:

> Why doth the devill then usurpe in mee?

---

16. "A Sermon Preached to the Household at White-hall, April 30, 1626," in *The Sermons of John Donne*, ed. George R. Potter and Evelyn M. Simpson, 10 vols. (Berkeley: University of California Press, 1953–1962), 7:153, 156.

17. The Holy Sonnets are quoted from Gardner's second edition of the *Divine Poems*.

Why doth he steale, nay ravish that's thy right?
Except thou rise and for thine owne worke fight,
Oh I shall soone despaire, when I doe see
That thou lov'st mankind well, yet wilt'not chuse mee,
And Satan hates mee, yet is loth to lose mee.

Like this first of the Holy Sonnets, the first poem of Quevedo's *Heráclito* is an intense reflection of the poet's fearful sense of his utter dependence on divine grace:

A new heart, a new man, Lord,
Are what my soul has need of;
Strip me of myself, for it could be
That in your pity you might pay what I owe.
    I take doubtful steps in the blind night,
For already I have come to hate the day,
And I fear that I shall find cold death
Wrapped in a deadly bait (although sweet).
    I am of your making; your image, Father, I have been,
And, if you have no concern for me, I believe
That nothing else will take my part.[18]

Donne describes himself as "due by many titles" to God; Quevedo mentions the debt that he "owes" to God, and describes himself as of God's "making" and formerly His "image" until corrupted by sin. Donne says that he is God's "owne worke" and his "image." Both emphasize that God must take their part and "fight for" or "defend" the sinner, who is helpless without such assistance. Indeed, the fundamental theme of both poems is the utter hopelessness of the sinner's situation without divine intervention. Donne closes on the brink of despair, awaiting some sign that God will "chuse" him; Quevedo calls upon God to take decisive action on behalf of a sinner who turns away from spiritual health: "Do what is

18. Quevedo is quoted from Francisco de Quevedo, *Obras completas*, ed. José Manuel Blecua (Barcelona: Editorial Planeta, 1963), 1:20: "Un nuevo corazón, un hombre nuevo / ha menester, Señor, la ánima mía; / desnúdame de mí, que ser podría / que tu piedad pagase lo que debo. // Dudosos pies por ciego noche llevo, / que ya he llegado a aborrecer el día, / y temo que hallaré la muerte fría / envuelta en (bien que dulce) mortal cebo. // Tu haciendo soy; tu imagen, Padre, he sido, / y, si no es tu interés en mí, no creo / que otra cosa defiende mi partido. // Haz lo que pide verme cual me veo, / no lo que pido yo: pues, de perdido, / recato mi salud de mi deseo."

demanded by the way I seem, / Not what I demand; for, like a profligate, / I hide my salvation from my desire."

There are Catholic poets of grace besides Quevedo, and not all are confined to Spain. The Frenchman Jean de la Ceppède (1550–1622), for example, closes one of his *Théorèmes Spirituels* (1613–1621) with the plea of a hapless sinner for divine help: "But it is for you, Lord, to make me capable / Of sharing in your riches: for my guilty soul / Does not know how, without your aid, to return to you."[19] The close of another of La Ceppède's sonnets recalls a figure frequently associated with Luther's view of justification: "Oh Christ, oh holy Lamb, deign to hide / All my scarlet sins, the kindling twigs of the abyss, / Within the bloody folds of the cloak of your flesh."[20] These lines suggest that a Catholic poet can use the metaphor of having his sins covered by the righteous blood of Christ without invoking the Reformation doctrine of imputed, rather than infused, grace. Hence there is little reason to find anything specifically Protestant in the closing lines of Donne's "Hymne to God my God, in my sicknesse":[21]

> Looke Lord, and finde both *Adams* met in me;
>> As the first *Adams* sweat surrounds my face,
>> May the last *Adams* blood my soule embrace.
> So, in his purple wrapp'd receive mee Lord,
>> By these his thornes give me his other Crowne. (ll. 23–27)

19. Quoted from *European Metaphysical Poetry*, ed. Frank Warnke (New Haven: Yale University Press, 1961), p. 104: "Mais c'est à vous, Seigneur, de me rendre capable / D'avoir part en vos biens: car mon ame coulpable / Ne scauroit sans votre aide, à vous s'en revoler."

20. Quoted from *The Baroque Poem*, ed. Harold B. Segel (New York: Dutton, 1974), p. 172: "O Christ, ô saint Agneau, daigne-toi de cacher / Tous mes rouges péchés, brindelles des abîmes, / Dans les sanglants replis du manteau de ta chair." See Luther's *Commentary on Galatians*, in *Martin Luther: Selections from His Writings*, ed. John Dillenberger (New York: Doubleday, 1961), p. 129: "So we shroud ourselves under the covering of Christ's flesh, . . . lest God should see our sin."

21. Cf. Lewalski, *Protestant Poetics*, pp. 16–17; and Richard Strier, *Love Known: Theology and Experience in George Herbert's Poetry* (Chicago: University of Chicago Press, 1983), p. 130. On La Ceppède's relation to the Counter-Reformation, see P. A. Chilton, *The Poetry of Jean de la Ceppède: A Study in Text and Context* (Oxford: Oxford University Press, 1977), pp. 24, 50–52. Terence Cave, *Devotional Poetry in France, c. 1570–1613* (Cambridge: Cambridge University Press, 1969), pp. 22–23, observes that the differences between Catholic and Protestant poetry in France are largely negative; i.e., some subjects available to Catholics are not available to Protestants.

Obviously here, as in the Holy Sonnets, Donne is concerned with the problem of grace, conceived in terms of Pauline typology; however, this is hardly a theme unique to the Protestant Reformation. As the examples of Quevedo and La Ceppède indicate, Continental Catholic poets were equally sensitive to man's hopeless sinfulness before God and radical dependence on his grace. In all of these poems the expression of Christian experience seems more important than the articulation of theological distinctions.

Even in those Holy Sonnets that seem to display most explicitly the severities of Calvinism, it is difficult to find in Donne an uncritical propounder of Reformation theology. At first glance the famous conclusion to Sonnet 10, "Batter my heart," suggests nothing so much as the effects of Calvinist "irresistible" grace: "Take mee to you, imprison mee, for I / Except you'enthrall mee, never shall be free, / Nor ever chast, except you ravish mee." But even the critic who has recently been most resolute in turning up Calvinism in the Holy Sonnets finds it hedged in by important reservations. John Stachniewski writes that "the essential subject matter" of Sonnet 10 is "the conflict between [Donne's] personal integrity and the demands of a theology which brutalized self-esteem." Stachniewski concludes that Donne's Calvinism in the Holy Sonnets is a temporary phase in his transition from Catholic to High Anglican, arising from his sense of worldly disappointment at the time of the poems' composition: "Donne felt his dependence on God to resemble his dependence on secular patronage with its attendant frustration, humiliation, and despair."[22]

It is not necessary, however, to turn the Holy Sonnets into a sublimated manifestation of the poet's socioeconomic frustration to question whether a few scattered suggestions of Calvinism make the poems a Calvinist work. "Batter my heart" is precisely a prayer to God for grace, which, if the Calvinist notion of the irresistibility of grace be true, is essentially point-

22. "John Donne: The Despair of the 'Holy Sonnets,'" *ELH* 48 (1981): 690, 702-3. See also Wilbur Sanders, *John Donne's Poetry* (Cambridge: Cambridge University Press, 1971), pp. 120-31; Lewalski, *Protestant Poetics*, pp. 120-31; John Carey, *John Donne: Life, Mind, and Art* (New York: Oxford University Press, 1981), pp. 51-59. There is a similar politicizing of Donne's *Songs and Sonets* and his *Devotions* in Jonathan Goldberg, *James I and the Politics of Literature* (Baltimore: Johns Hopkins University Press, 1983), pp. 66-67, 80-83, 107-12, 211-19.

less. However inappropriate the use of quasi-mystical imagery at the end of Donne's sonnet may be, Hugh Richmond has pointed out a striking parallel in a similar sonnet by the French Catholic poet Ronsard.[23] In any case, Donne pleads that God stop tinkering with him ("for, you / As yet but knocke, breathe, shine, and seeke to mend") and instead reforge him altogether: "That I may rise, and stand, o'erthrow mee,'and bend / Your force, to breake, blowe, burn and make me new" (ll. 1–4). Now this may quite plausibly be read as a plea for infused sanctifying grace (*gratia gratum faciens*) which, as Barbara Lewalski insists, is an idea contrary to the Protestant Reformation: "The Reformers were adamant in their insistence that this justification is only imputed to the sinner, not infused into him as the Roman Catholics held, so as actually to restore God's image in him; however, the imputed righteousness is really his because he is joined to Christ as body to head."[24] Of course, there is no denying that Donne's sonnet expresses a sense of profound depravity and fear of damnation—not without Calvinist reverberations—for the very reason that the poet has abandoned Catholic sources of consolation without yet discovering or devising acceptable alternatives. This is a matter of rather delicate discriminations, however, and it is questionable whether the close of "Batter my heart" yields a clear theological resolution.

The trouble with theological categorizing of the Holy Sonnets is that it is likely to flatten out the wit and daring that are characteristic of Donne's poetry. The equivocal implication of the third of these sonnets, "This is my playes last scene," with its explicit reference to imputed righteousness, furnishes a good example. The octave presents a traditional meditative theme, the deathbed:

> This is my playes last scene, here heavens appoint
> My pilgrimages last mile; and my race
> Idly, yet quickly runne, hath this last pace,
> My spans last inch, my minutes last point,
> And gluttonous death will instantly unjoynt
> My body,'and soule, and I shall sleepe a space,
> But my'ever-waking part shal see that face,
> Whose fear already shakes my every joynt.

23. *Divine Poems*, ed. Gardner, pp. 152–53.
24. *Protestant Poetics*, p. 17.

Clearly this poem is based on the standard Ignatian meditative topos of the Four Last Things.[25] Even as the octave evokes death and judgment, so the sestet adds heaven and hell:

> Then, as my soule, to'heaven her first seate, takes flight,
> And earth-borne body, in the earth shall dwell,
> So, fall my sinnes, that all may have their right,
> To where they'are bred, and would presse me, to hell.
> Impute me righteous, thus purg'd of evill,
> For thus I leave the world, the flesh, and devill.

This closing couplet could be seen as turning the Ignatian meditation into something emphatically Calvinist. Yet this almost magical invocation of the Calvinist dogma has troubled more than one critic. Wilbur Sanders calls these lines "blatant theological sophistry" and adds that "the spiritual malady so obviously won't give way to the patent medicine applied to it, that it seems almost to be a part of the poetic strategy to make us aware of this fact."[26] There is perhaps more to what Sanders says than he realizes: it is quite as likely that Donne is playing with a theological concept in a dramatic and witty fashion as it is that he is writing bad verse theology.

With this approach in mind, it is instructive to consider two other references to "imputation" in the Donne canon. The first comes from Satyre III, "Of Religion":

> and shall thy fathers spirit
> Meete blinde philosophers in heaven, whose merit
> Of strict life may be imputed faith, and heare
> Thee, whom hee taught so easie wayes and neare
> To follow, damn'd? (ll. 11–15)[27]

In raising the theme of the virtuous heathen—a lively topic in

---

25. *The Spiritual Exercises*, 1st week, 5th exercise, in *Obras completas de San Ignacio de Loyola*, ed. Ignacio Iparraguirre, S.J. (Madrid: BAC, 1963), pp. 214–16. Lewalski, *Protestant Poetics*, p. 268, argues that the use of the pilgrimage and race tropes in the opening lines of this sonnet make it Protestant in mood. But the notion of life as a pilgrimage is too familiar an idea in the Middle Ages to require illustration. St. Thomas More combines the theme of life as a pilgrimage with the contemplation of death in a Latin epigram, *Vita Ipsa cursus ad mortem est*, in Fred Nichols, ed., *An Anthology of Neo-Latin Poetry* (New Haven: Yale University Press, 1979), p. 462.

26. *John Donne's Poetry*, p. 128.

27. Quoted from *The Complete Poetry of John Donne*, ed. John T. Shawcross (Garden City, N.Y.: Doubleday/Anchor, 1967), p. 23.

the Middle Ages and among Renaissance humanists—Donne simply stands Calvinism on its head: instead of Christ's righteousness imputed to a man on the basis of his faith, Donne speculates that virtuous pagans might have faith imputed to them on the basis of righteousness. This passage comes in a poem that questions Catholicism, Calvinism, Anglicanism, and indifferentism alike on behalf of the sincere individual believer, who is exhorted to "doubt wisely" (l. 77). Thus the severe Calvinist version of grace is subverted by a witty turn growing out of a moderate Erasmian attitude amidst the horrors of sixteenth-century religious strife.[28]

The Calvinist concept of imputed righteousness is subjected to an especially extravagant outburst of Donne's wit in Elegy 19, the notorious "Going to Bed," in which the poetic persona is occupied with getting his mistress undressed and into bed as quickly as possible:

> Like pictures, or like bookes gay coverings made
> For laymen, are all women thus arraid;
> Themselves are mystique bookes, which only wee
> Whom their imputed grace will dignify
> Must see reveal'd. (ll. 39–43)[29]

Like his principal classical model, Ovid, Donne uses the erotic elegy as a vehicle for ridiculing the most revered ideals and institutions of respectable society. Amatory figures become quick thrusts in a perilous antiestablishment poetic game. Here, beneath the surface of outrageous wit and blasphemous sensuality, Donne indulges in a momentary gesture of theological satire. In a context of "imputed grace" and the removal of clothing, it is difficult not to recall how Luther explains God's imputation of righteousness to the sinner, in his *Commentary on Galatians*, by comparing it to *covering* his sin by grace and not *seeing* it.[30] For Donne's speaker the woman's "imputed grace" permits him to *uncover* (or *discover*) and *see*. The

28. Donne could well have absorbed a pre-Tridentine Erasmian Catholicity from his Jesuit uncle, Jasper Heywood. See Dennis Flynn, "The '*Annales* School' and the Catholicism of Donne's Family," *John Donne Journal* 2 (1983): 1–9.

29. Quoted from *John Donne: The Elegies and the Songs and Sonnets*, ed. Helen Gardner (Oxford: Clarendon, 1965), p. 16.

30. *Luther: Selections*, ed. Dillenberger, p. 129.

implication of the conceit emerges when it is reversed: the justi-
fication of the elect, an inscrutable act of divine power accord-
ing to the Calvinist formulation, makes God's work of salvation
as arbitrary and fickle as a woman's choice of the lover admitted
to her bed. Hence this risqué poem by a young law student and
flamboyant dandy is also a sly send-up of the dominant theology
of the Reformation.

To be sure, the Satyres and Elegies, if Dame Helen
Gardner's dating is reliable, were written more than ten years
before the Holy Sonnets; and when the latter were composed
Donne had already undertaken the labor of an Anglican pol-
emicist, and the idea of entering Anglican orders had at least
been broached to him. But the Holy Sonnets, like almost all
Donne's poetry, are private exercises, circulated for the most
part among his friends. There are undeniable marks of the poet's
Catholic upbringing in their themes and structures, and the spe-
cifically Calvinist elements are handled tentatively, even with
an air of provisionality. Sonnet 3, "This is my playes last scene,"
with its reference to imputed righteousness, a doctrine
ridiculed by Donne in other poems, seems to ask, "Does this
work? Will my sins simply drop away into hell as I am 'purg'd of
evill' by imputation?" There is an air of nervousness here—a
result, perhaps, of Donne's embarrassed or even guilty recollec-
tion of earlier flippant treatments of matters of eternal life and
death. Still, a negative answer is implied in the nine remaining
sonnets of the set, which keep seeking different approaches to
the problem of justification and grace.

This is not to say that the doctrines of the Reformation,
especially Calvin's view of justification, had no bearing on the
Holy Sonnets, but that the impact of Calvinism was oblique
rather than direct. In fact, there is often a Calvinist subtext, like
a magnetic field, exerting a subtle but continuous force over the
most unlikely of the Holy Sonnets. For instance, the ninth son-
net, "What if this present were the worlds last night?," discloses
under scrutiny the spiritual strains generated by the terrifying
yet fascinating concept of irresistible grace.

At first glance the octave of the poem seems an extravagant
sacred parody of a Petrarchan love sonnet, done in Continental
style. Donne's anguished meditator, recalling the counsel of
Astrophil's muse, attempts to convince himself that he need

only "looke in [his] heart and write."[31] What he sees there is a graphic, Spanish baroque crucifix:

> What if this present were the worlds last night?
> Marke in my heart, O Soule, where thou dost dwell,
> The picture of Christ crucified, and tell
> Whether that countenance can thee affright,
> Teares in his eyes quench the amasing light,
> Blood fills his frownes, which from his pierc'd head fell,
> And can that tongue adjudge thee unto hell,
> Which pray'd forgivenesse for his foes fierce spight?

Even as Astrophil assures "sleepe" that no better image of Stella is available than what is in his mind (*Astrophil and Stella*, sonnet 39), so Donne's speaker assures himself by means of the image of Christ in his mind. Yet the octave ends, literally, with a question mark; and, though Christ "pray'd forgivenesse for his foes fierce spight," when he returns as Judge of the world, some at least will indeed be adjudged "unto hell."

The sestet undertakes a strengthening of the persona's assurance of salvation by encouragement of an emotional and aesthetic response to the interior image of Christ that he has evoked. Again the conventions of Petrarchan/Neoplatonic love poetry are parodied:

> No, no; but as in my idolatrie
> I said to all my profane mistresses,
> Beauty, of pitty, foulness onely is
> A signe of rigour: so I say to thee,
> To wicked spirits are horrid shapes assign'd,
> This beauteous forme assures a pitious minde.

The very slyness of these lines is troubling. In a poem resonant with echoes of Sidney, one can hardly forget that "two Negatives affirme" according to the "Grammer rules" of *Astrophil and Stella*, sonnet 63. Can Donne's "No, no," like Stella's, be construed as an implicit *yes*? The speaker of "What if this present" must fear a certain poetic justice, since as a youthful seducer he seems, like Astrophil, to have distorted the conventions. In his Neoplatonic discourse in the *Book of the Courtier*, Pietro

---

31. *Astrophil and Stella*, sonnet 1, cited here and below from *The Poems of Sir Philip Sidney*, ed. William A. Ringler, Jr. (Oxford: Clarendon, 1962).

Bembo tells us that a "beauteous forme" is a "signe" not of "a pitious minde" but of a virtuous soul.[32] Samuel Daniel's Delia, after all, was "faire, and *thus* vnkinde."[33] In view of the evident duplicity of the persona's addresses to his "profane mistresses" in the past, his present analogous address to his own soul—patently intended to be overheard by the divine lover—is at best questionable, and a dubious means of assuring oneself of salvation.

In a Calvinist perspective this is a crucial issue, for the interpretation of the "picture" in the persona's heart—is it a "marke" of election or condemnation?—is contingent upon the speaker's emotional response to Christ's countenance. To find this tearful, bloody visage beautiful is not a natural response; it requires grace, grace that in Calvin's view is irresistible. The picture of the suffering Christ within will be an image of beauty to the man who has faith, when faith means the subjective, unpremeditated realization that one is in fact saved. "A right definition of faith," Calvin says in *The Institutes* (3.2.7), is "a firm and certain knowledge of God's benevolence toward us, founded upon the truth of the freely given promise in Christ, both revealed to our minds and sealed upon our hearts through the Holy Spirit." Seeking a "signe" of "pitty" instead of "rigour," seeking, that is, the "marke" of his faith and election, a man has nothing to consult but his feelings; for as Calvin adds, in the next section of *The Institutes* (3.2.8), "that very assent itself . . . is more of the heart than of the brain, and more of the disposition than of the understanding."[34] Donne's persona seems to be trying to stimulate in himself the appropriate feelings toward the crucified Christ—a passionate attraction at least as intense as what he once felt for his "profane mistresses." The

32. Baldasarre Castiglione, *The Courtier*, book 4, trans. Sir Thomas Hoby, in *Three Renaissance Classics*, ed. Burton A. Milligan (New York: Scribner's, 1953), p. 599: "Whereupon doth very seldom an ill soule dwell in a beautifull bodie. And therefore is the outwards beautie a true signe of the inwarde goodnesse . . . ."

33. *Delia*, sonnet 6, in *Poems and a Defence of Ryme*, ed. Arthur Colby Sprague (1930; rpt. Chicago: University of Chicago Press, 1965): "O had she not been faire, and thus vnkinde, / My Muse had slept, and none had knowne my minde."

34. *Calvin: Selections*, ed. Dillenberger, pp. 380, 381.

manipulative insincerity of the erotic analogy, however, infects his expression of desire for Christ.

The air of tentativeness, if not downright factitiousness, in Donne's sonnet becomes apparent when it is set beside an anonymous Spanish sonnet of the same era, "To Christ Crucified":

> No me mueve, mi Dios, para quererte
> el cielo que me tienes prometido;
> ni me mueve el infierno tan temido
> para dejar por eso ofenderte.
>
> Tú me mueves, Señor; muéveme el verte
> clavado en una cruz y escarnecido;
> muéveme ver tu cuerpo tan herido;
> muévenme tus afrentas y tu muerte.
>
> Muéveme, en fin, tu amor, y en tal manera,
> que aunque no hubiera cielo, yo te amara,
> y aunque no hubiera infierno, te temiera.
>
> No tienes que me dar porque te quiera;
> pues aunque cuanto espero no esperara,
> lo mismo que te quiero te quisiera.[35]

(I am not moved, my God, to love you / by the heaven you have promised me; / nor am I moved by fear of hell / to leave off offending you for this. // You move me, Lord; I am moved to see you / nailed to a cross and ridiculed; / I am moved to see your body so wounded; / I am moved by your mistreatment and your death. // Your love, at last, moves me and in a way / that though there were no heaven, I would love you, / and though there were no hell, I would fear you. // You need give me nothing for me to love you; / for though I might not hope as I do hope, / I would love you the same as I do love you.)

Everything about this poem bespeaks a guileless simplicity, a spontaneous and passionate longing for the crucified Christ. The contrast with Donne's sonnet is striking. Although the Donne poem is in many ways compatible with baroque Catholicism and seems, at first, to be on the same theme, Donne introduces an element of uneasy self-consciousness. The Spanish

35. *An Anthology of Spanish Poetry, 1500–1700*, ed. Arthur Terry (Oxford: Pergamon, 1968), 2:96–97. The poem was first published in 1628, but, as Terry points out, it could have been written any time after the middle of the sixteenth century.

poem addresses Christ on the cross; the speaker of the Donne sonnet addresses his "Soule" with Christ as an inferential over-hearer. The speaker of the Spanish poem simply dismisses any consideration of salvation as irrelevant to his exalted love of Christ, while Donne's persona is obsessed with finding suffici-ent love for Christ in his heart to be assured of salvation. Cal-vinist notions of grace pervade the Holy Sonnets in this fashion: not as principal theological inspiration, but as a lingering fear of faithlessness haunting the background of poems that in most of their features resemble the Catholic devotional poetry of the Continent. It is not surprising that Donne should handle such traditional forms with a certain diffidence and trepidation: he was, as he composed the Holy Sonnets, neither still Catholic nor yet Protestant in a settled way that gave his conscience peace; and, as it is phrased in one of his letters, "to be no part of any body, is to be nothing."[36]

But though Donne's persona is hag-ridden by doubts of his own sincerity, and hence by doubts of the validity of his sense of grace, the Calvinist dynamic does not finally dominate the Holy Sonnets. The last sonnet, "Father, part of thy double inter-est," closes with the law of love—not faith—as the ultimate Christian obligation:

> Yet such are those laws, that men argue yet
> Whether a man those statutes can fulfill;
> None doth, but all-healing grace and Spirit,
> Revive againe what law and letter kill.
> Thy lawes abridgement, and thy last command
> Is all but love; Oh let that last Will stand!

These lines are not notably Catholic or Protestant. Donne is not here taking a position on the theology of justification and grace; he is praying for grace and exhorting himself to love. Herein he is typical of the English devotional poets of the seventeenth cen-tury, who, though generally Protestant, are not, *in their poetry*, so much militant proponents of the Reformation as Christians confronting God.

These poets bring to their poetic encounter with God varied experiences and draw upon a number of Christian resources—Catholic and Protestant, Medieval and Renaissance. What is

36. *Letters to Severall Persons of Honour*, p. 51.

conspicuously missing is a definitely Protestant theology of grace embodied in poems decisively incompatible with Catholic theology. Calvin's presence, like that of other divines of the era, remains marginal when it is not equivocal. Instead of versified theological expositions, marks of the strains exerted by competing versions of grace and salvation ought to be the quarry of the critic. For it is the poets' sensitivity to the theological tensions of the era that generates the urgency peculiar to their poems.

3

"ANIMA MEA" PSALMS AND JOHN DONNE'S RELIGIOUS POETRY

Mary Ann Radzinowicz

The poet in the paired Psalms 42 and 43 writes in exile, longing to go to the Temple to worship once more in the presence of his "living God." His song is a personal lament composed of three stanzas, each followed by a refrain the Book of Common Prayer translates as follows:

> Why art thou so full of heaviness, O my soul? and why
>   art thou so disquieted within me?
> O put thy trust in God; for I will yet thank him, which
>   is the help of my countenance, and my God.

Eight psalms use the poetical device of the dialogue of a man with his soul, each to a different rhetorical end.[1] Among John Donne's religious poems probably composed before his ordination, five holy sonnets—"O might those sighes and teares returne againe," "Oh my blacke Soule! now thou art summoned," "What if this present were the worlds last night?,"

1. Psalms in this essay are quoted from the Book of Common Prayer, which uses the translation made by Bishop Coverdale for the Great Bible, 1539, 1540, the translation likeliest to have had any literary influence on Donne's religious poetry. The word *soul* is used some 755 times in the Old Testament with varying significations, according to A. A. Anderson (*The New Century Bible Commentary* [London: Marshall, Morgan and Scott, 1972], 1:266). In the trope of an inner dialogue, it is used in a psychical sense and is endowed with various emotional states. The value of the trope lies in the dialogic relationship of speaker and soul, the speaker aware of identity and difference.

I am grateful to Carol Kaske for having read this essay and for letting me see her draft entry on "Spenser and the Bible" for the forthcoming *The Spenser Encyclopedia*.

"Wilt thou love God, as he thee! then digest," and "If faithfull soules be alike glorifi'd"—and one occasional poem, "Upon the Annunciation and Passion falling upon one day. 1608," use that psalmic device directly. Among those probably composed after his ordination, one holy sonnet, "Since she whome I lovd, hath payd her last debt," and one occasional poem, "Hymne to God my God, in my sicknesse," imply it.

The device in the psalter helped Donne to create the complex poetic voices of his religious poetry, by distinguishing between a speaker and the agency of his inner feeling. The psalmic address to a man's own soul sanctioned for him a stance both learned and impassioned, both personal and vicarious, both univocal and congregational. The *anima mea* psalms—as we might as well call them—not only foster self-examination, they intertwine personal and public worship that encompasses teaching, penitence, praise, and thanksgiving. By attending carefully to the device in each of its contexts, Donne wove himself into the liturgy and wrote himself into the priesthood before taking Holy Orders. Once ordained, Donne wrote almost no poems. But then he celebrated, in the language of the liturgy before a congregation, the fusion of private and public voices that the Psalms and the liturgy had taught him, and he preached in his sermons the combination of believer and teacher he found in the *anima mea* psalms. The value of those psalms to Donne is not just that they validate a "protestant poetic,"[2] for, of course, that is done by the whole psalter. It is that they in particular exemplify the combination of personal and congregational lyric voice that moves his poetry toward his priestly vocation and at every stage of that journey enriches it.[3]

2. See Barbara Lewalski, *Protestant Poetics and the Seventeenth-Century Religious Lyric* (Princeton: Princeton University Press, 1979), especially part 1, for a full discussion of that poetics and its principal exponents. Professor Lewalski does not discuss the *anima mea* motif.

3. Contemporary transcriptions of inward feelings are discussed helpfully in Anne Ferry, *The "Inward" Language: Sonnets of Wyatt, Sidney, Shakespeare, Donne* (Chicago: University of Chicago Press, 1983); poetical self-representation is discussed helpfully in Richard Helgerson, *Self-Crowned Laureates: Spenser, Jonson, Milton, and the Literary System* (Berkeley: University of California Press, 1983); and heroic self-representation, in John Guillory, *Poetic Authority: Spenser, Milton, and Literary History* (New York: Columbia University Press, 1983). My interest in the problem of the transcription and poetic authorization of religious feelings has been whetted by those works, although none takes up the psalm trope.

Eight psalms of the psalter use the device of a dialogue between a man and his own soul. In each the self-exhortation fits into Temple worship within a congregational liturgy, but each speaker anticipates a particular result from his handling of the device. Not only does the self-address play its part within an elaborate diversity of address; the persona of the soul is conceived in a variety of attitudes by a speaker likewise variously conceived in relation to God. On the one hand, the soul embodies passions that must be given a vent, and the authority for singing the poem is the poet's affective transformation, an authority like the spontaneous overflow of powerful emotion. On the other hand, the soul has experienced something about which a wise psalmist has thought a good deal; his authority is didactic and vocational, the communication of truths by a teacher. When the soul seems to disturb the settled thoughts of a Temple servant appointed to sing the representative speech of a congregation, the psalmist may treat it as a surrogate for his congregation's emotions, asking it to be silent and trust him. More simply, the speaker may be seen as a teacher and the congregation pupils; there the soul is asked to endorse the lesson by taking the moral line recommended by the teacher. In the more "romantic" context the official voice runs into genuine intellectual problems with the inequities of human life; nevertheless he knows that in congregational worship he will somehow be sustained in the Temple to the full satisfaction of his innermost soul. He may then experience his God so strongly that he permits his soul to swell the passions felt, not to contain them or redirect them.

This flexible psalmic device is particularly interesting with respect to Donne. For secular occasions, Donne learned to use all the possible registers of passionate, learned, and witty voice in writing love poetry. He is the accomplished poet who comes late to apply his art to religious themes and has trouble writing spiritual poems on the heels of secular ones. The sanction he seems most inclined to use, the "romantic" authority of his sincere feelings, is the most compromised authority. He himself has trivialized the language of devotion by applying it exaggeratedly or tactically to human mistresses; he writes like a startled rake moved by an innocent passion, appropriating the too-familiar words of sexual love to divine love. Thus in the *anima mea* sonnet "What if this present were the worlds last night?," he tells his soul in reference to Christ what he used to say in his "idolatrie" about "all [his] profane mistresses."[4] In "Batter my heart, three person'd God," he entreats God to divorce him from Lucifer by ravishing him. In "Oh, to vex me, contraryes meete in one," he likens his "prophane love" to his "contritione," finding both "as humorous . . . and as soon forgott." And in the most arresting of all these transferrals of sexual language to worship,[5] in "Show me deare Christ, thy Spouse," he asks of God, the "kind husband" of the church, permission to "court thy mild Dove": "Who is most trew, and pleasing to thee, then / When she'is embrac'd and open to most men." A help in this perplexity is the device's power to distinguish between the too-knowing self and the sincere anima, or the authorized congregational self and the privately penitent or disturbed anima.

Donne wrote most of his religious poetry as a preparation for taking holy orders. Once priest, he versified only occasionally, preferring instead to transfer to sermons his energies of persuasion and self-expression. While he wrote religious poetry, however, he composed the distinctive group of poems using the *anima mea* device. That group reflects the complexity of address in their Hebrew original. The psalmist in *anima mea* psalms spoke for himself in a context where those who heard him asked that he speak for them and to them. That gave him

4. All quotations from Donne's poetry will be taken from Dame Helen Gardner, *John Donne: The Divine Poems* (Oxford: Clarendon Press, 1952). She notes of "What if this present were the worlds last night?" that Donne "is addressing his soul" (p. 71); of "Upon the Annunciation and Passion falling upon one day. 1608," "But Donne has a habit of speaking of his soul as distinct from himself; cf. 'Holy Sonnets' (1633) 9.2 and 'Holy Sonnets' (1635) 4.14" (p. 96). She makes no other reference to the trope. John Carey, *John Donne: Life, Mind, and Art* (New York: Oxford University Press, 1981), p. 73, writes that Donne "tells God what he used to say," but the address is to the soul throughout this sonnet.

5. The conversion of sexual language into spiritual has been frequently noted of Donne's poetry. Early comments include Joan Bennett, *Four Metaphysical Poets* (Cambridge: Cambridge University Press, 1953), pp. 26–27; Louis Martz, *The Poetry of Meditation* (New Haven: Yale University Press, 1954), pp. 215–16; George Reuben Potter, "John Donne's Discovery of Himself," *University of California Publications in English*, no. 4 (Berkeley: University of California Press, 1934), p. 5; Milton Rugoff, *Donne's Imagery: A Study in Creative Sources* (New York: Corporate Press, 1939), pp. 86–87; and George Williamson, *The Donne Tradition* (Cambridge: Harvard University Press, 1930), pp. 50–51.

the double sanction of his own religious feelings and his Temple duties. Donne, as the protagonist in his religious poetry, gains by the *anima mea* device the authority of the church liturgy incorporating the device. He learns to help his tattered personal voice by congregational penitence; his psalter teaches him to combine the personal and the vicarious. Once he is priest, writing sermons wholeheartedly as vicar, he resorts to no Old Testament source in the sermons more regularly than to Psalms; almost never writing poems then, his adaptations of the device are covert. Although Donne directly uses the trope on six occasions, and implies it on two, and although the psalter likewise makes use of the trope eight times, Donne does not draw attention to the numerical symmetry between his usage and the psalter's. Furthermore, the device is important to him as a trope and not as the source of any strictly verbal echo taken from any particular translation. Quoting Psalms in his sermons, Donne regularly gives the Latin of the Vulgate and sometimes comments on particular expressions from the Hebrew, suggesting that his primary text was either the *Biblia Polyglotta* of 1514–1517 or the *Biblia Sacra Hebraica, Chaldaice, Graece, et Latine* of 1569–1572. He then cites the translation from the Authorized Version (1611) more often than from the Geneva Bible (1560). The Authorized translation is too late to have influenced him as a religious poet, however. Like most of his contemporaries, Donne would have found the translation that seemed most natural to him that made by Bishop Coverdale for the Great Bible (1539, 1540), because it was the translation printed in the Book of Common Prayer. Unlike some of his contemporaries, however, he never to the best of my knowledge cites any metrical version, notwithstanding the fact that the Sternhold and Hopkins was printed together with the Coverdale translation in some contemporary editions of the Book of Common Prayer.[6] The *anima mea* device is for Donne a recognizable and

6. Two other bibles, the Geneva and the Junius-Tremellius, were significant to Donne. He drew attention to his indebtedness to the latter in the title of "The Lamentations of Jeremy, for the most part according to Tremelius" but in that work the translation itself is based on a comparison of the Vulgate, Tremellius, and Great Bibles. The Geneva Bible was the family Bible of most literate Englishmen before the King James replaced it; numerous printings of it bound the Common Prayer and metrical translations of Psalms at the end, however, as well as offering its own in the proper place.

significant figurative analogue to *prosopopoeia* and *apostrophe* in whatever mediating translation or edition he finds it.

Let us begin with those *anima mea* poems written before Donne's ordination that overtly quote the device. In three holy sonnets, Donne uses the penitential and lament psalms to present the self-examination of a man spiritual by nature but reluctant to take holy orders. The passionate laments in those three *anima mea* holy sonnets—"O might those sighes and teares returne againe," "Oh my blacke Soule! now thou art summoned," and "What if this present were the worlds last night?"—are all fully penitential. The penitence in "O might those sighes and teares returne againe" has long been considered peculiarly Donnean, revealing a man so self-absorbedly melancholy that mourning is the name of his sin: "That sufferance was my sinne, now I repent." Unlike drunkards, thieves and lechers, no memory of "past joyes" comforts his despair: "To (poore) me is allow'd / No ease; for, long, yet vehement griefe hath beene / Th'effect and cause, the punishment and sinne."[7] But the point of the sonnet is missed if it is thought that it works to a climax of passionate self-expression. The sonnet opens with its strongest point; it does not close with it. That point is that penitential grief is so valuable, indeed salvatory, that one must sorrow over wasted sorrow. In sermons Donne finds the refrains of Psalms 42 and 43—"Why art thou cast down, O my soul?"— both restorative and dangerous. He would "joyne with David . . . in that holy increpation [self-reproof] of a dangerous sadnesse"; he considers, nevertheless, that the self-address can "reintegrate that broken and scattered heart, by enabling him to expostulate."[8] Donne addresses the entire sonnet to his own soul "in holy increpation of a dangerous sadness" to hallow his grief at grief. His "vehement grief" should be read not only as cause and effect, punishment and sin, but also as dangerous

---

7. See Gardner, *Divine Poems*, p. 76, who disputes George Williamson's reading "That suffering was the sin which I am now repenting of" and offers instead "The contrast in the line is between past and present, his 'unholy' and his 'holy' discontent. '*That* suffering in the past was sin: *now* I am engaged in a good work, repentance—but I still suffer.'" Both readings neglect, however, Donne's effort to hallow his griefs.

8. These two psalms remained important to Donne, and he cited them in sermons on six occasions. See Troy D. Reeves, *An Annotated Index to the Sermons of John Donne* (Salzburg: Institut für Anglistik, 1979).

indulgence and homeopathic medicine. The paired psalms were not wasted on the sonnet.

Psalms 42 and 43 form a lament in which addresses to *anima mea* function as structural and emphatic refrains. A poem of longing is framed as a prayer to God by a poet surrounded by pagans who taunt him with "Where is now thy God?" He feels inside himself a swelling of emotion. When he speaks to his soul, he treats it as the locus of his passion. "Athirst" and longing, "vexed" and "disquieted," it is told to "put thy trust in God." In the Hebrew psychology of the psalter, a man is his rational consciousness, but his soul is the seat of his feelings, continuous with heart and flesh.[9] The psalmist consoles his passionate soul for the loss of its rapturous worship in the assurance of God's nearness, but simply by asking it to endure the tension in which it exists. The refrains are identical in the Hebrew,[10] but are varied a little in the Book of Common Prayer. Coverdale sought by variation to strengthen the assurance the soul receives, whereas the Hebrew stresses the sense of emotional strain the speaker asks his soul to endure, thus emphasizing the moral power of faith rather than the certainty of grace. The soul should not so insist on the grief it now endures in comparison with its past joy, but should wait in trust; self-rebuke fuels the Hebrew self-expression. Donne, in comparing the sinful sufferings of his self-absorbed past with the penitent sufferings of his contrite present, evokes the Hebrew

9. One might compare Psalm 84, another psalm longing for the house of God, which opens: "My soul hath a desire and longing to enter into the courts of the Lord; my heart and my flesh rejoice in the living God." Here the formulaic triads (soul, heart, flesh; desire, longing, rejoice) imply if not perfect synonymity at least natural extension and similarity.

10. Sir Philip Sidney, in the translations of Psalms 1 through 43 admired by Donne, translates the refrain identically in Psalm 42 as:

Why art Thou my soul so sorry
And in me so much dismaid?
Wait on God, for yet his glory
In my song shall be display'd.

But he translates it in Psalm 43 as:

Why art Thou my soul
Cast down in such dole,
    What ayles Thy discomfort?
Wait on God, for still
Thank my God I will,
    Sure aid present comfort.

The Poems of Sir Philip Sidney, ed. William A. Ringler, Jr. (Oxford: Clarendon Press, 1961), pp. 334–37.

sense of strain in order to claim for himself an even worse despair. His feelings are equally implicated in self-accusation but unequally denied the assurance of former experience. Since the Hebrew soul should and can remember God's presence, it is reminded both as reproach and consolation to rely on the past joy so as to sustain the present anguish. Donne's soul must be rebuked for having indulged its grief in the past on objects so idolatrous that it can have no "remembrance of past joyes, for reliefe / Of comming ills"; even worse, it must be rebuked for having wasted a quantum of grief that could have been used to "Mourne with some fruit." The present is the unconsoled but morally significant moment in which the soul must live.

The sonnet "Oh my blacke Soule! now thou art summoned" sustainedly addresses the soul throughout its fourteen lines. Donne's speaker separates himself from his black soul to admonish it. The separation of self from soul permits the protagonist to stoke up in the soul a necessary penitence. The octave does not so much indict as it terrifies the soul by comparing its feelings to those of two doomed types—the traveler who cannot come home where he faces an indictment for crimes abroad, the prisoner who dreads stepping out of jail for his only exit will be to the gallows. Then with no break between octave and sestet, the speaker reminds his soul that grace is available and sets forth the two means—*contrition*, "Oh make thy selfe with holy mourning blacke, / And red with blushing, as thou art with sinne," and *belief*, "wash thee in Christs blood." The speaker is compassionate but impotent, the soul responsive but helpless; grace affords active compassion and enables response. The hero of the poem is neither the speaker nor the soul, but the suffering Saviour.

This sonnet draws on the *anima mea* device concealed in the first of another pair of psalms, 142 and 143. Both are laments, 143 being the last of the penitential psalms. The Prayer Book translates the psalm so as to preserve the distinction the trope makes between speaker and soul, but it does not use the distinction in direct address. Psalm 142:4–5 reads:

> I looked also upon my right hand, and saw there
>   was no man that would know me.
> I had no place to flee unto, and no man cared for
>   my soul.

The verses sustain the distinction between "me" and "my soul." They imply within a prayer to God a concern both for himself and a distinctive psyche. Similarly the Prayer Book translates the lonely lament of Psalm 143:4–6 as follows:

> Therefore is my spirit vexed within me, and my heart within me is desolate.
> Yet do I remember the time past; I muse upon all thy works; yea, I exercise myself in the works of thy hands.
> I stretch forth my hands unto thee; my soul gaspeth unto thee as a thirsty land.

In these psalm translations, the speaker does not actually address his soul, with whom, however, he has a dialogic relationship.[11] The principal address in 142 is to God; the complaint consists of the prayer of an anguished protagonist who implores God to lead his soul out of prison, as once before when his path was hopelessly beset with snares but God was with him on his journey. The psalm expresses the same impotence of the suffering soul to help itself that Donne dramatizes in "Oh my blacke Soule! now thou art summoned." Attempts to interpret the psalm circumstantially read it as a deathbed poem, and clearly so did Donne. The advantage he derives from the distinction of self and spirit is its emphasis on the helplessness of both the sufferer and his helpless soul to do anything more than turn to his God.

The lament of Psalm 142 is made by a speaker in mental distress unable to help himself. He uses two examples to tell God and his soul his sorrow—the traveler along a path laid with snares and the man in prison, Donne's examples. The psalmist then addresses God only. He expresses his faith, "Thou art my hope, and my portion in the land of the living," and entreats aid, "Bring my soul out of prison, that I may give thanks unto thy name." The twinned instruments of grace in Psalm 142 are faith and prayer, corresponding to the contrition and faith of Donne's sonnet. Like that sonnet, it recognizes the complementarity of God's mercy and power. Nor are the similarities between sonnet and psalm limited to motif and metaphor. The strongest is

11. For a running discussion of the device, see Mitchell Dahood, *The Anchor Bible: Psalms* (Garden City, N.Y.: Doubleday and Company, 1979), 1:275; 2:91; 3:25, 30, 33, 41, 147.

voice, presented in both as that of a sufferer completely convinced of his need of God, and expressing the need in a fully consistent and barely controlled form.

In Psalm 143 the psalmist confesses that his suffering is a deserved punishment for his sins and asks for mercy from God since only mercy can save him. The mood and thematic emphasis rather than the scenario of Psalm 143 can be seen in Donne's sonnet "What if this present were the worlds last night," where the speaker, convinced of his guilt, assures his soul that Christ will be compassionate, his physical beauty guaranteeing his mercy. Both psalm and sonnet are extraordinarily intense; both use the device to augment that intensity by insisting that the suffering speaker contains an even more suffering soul.[12]

If Donne's scenario is baroquely Christian in affirming the beauty of the body on the cross, and the psalm is darkly Hebrew in the desolation in which the suffering soul is shown, that difference does not bar influence from the psalm. Donne ascribes the composition of Psalms to the divine Muse in "Upon the translation of the Psalmes by Sir Philip Sydney . . .":

> The songs are these, which heavens high holy Muse
> Whisper'd to *David*, *David* to the Jewes:
> And *Davids* Successors, in holy zeale,
> In formes of joy and art doe re-reveale
> To us . . .

The "re-revelation" or Christian typologizing of the psalter is the necessary precondition for its usefulness to Donne. That effected, what he found in the *anima mea* device was a pattern of spiritual address that permitted further re-revelations. The three sonnets at which we have glanced not only all consistently use the device in order to express both a fear and a desire for judgment on the part of a penitent, but also use it to contrast the idolatrous past with the contrite present, and to place by

12. See Robert S. Jackson, *John Donne's Christian Vocation* (Evanston: Northwestern University Press, 1970), pp. 107–11, for an analysis of "Oh my Blacke Soule!" and "Wilt thou love God, as he thee!" by reference to Jung's concept of the anima. See Michael Smalling, "Donne's Medieval Aesthetics and His Use of Morally Distant *Personae*," in *New Essays on Donne*, ed. Gary A. Stringer (Salzburg: Institut für Anglistik, 1977), pp. 74–109, for a discussion of the influence of Saint Augustine on Donne's biblical poetics and use of personae.

implication a solitary and single worshiper within the traditions of a commonly experienced faith. We need not deny that the disciplines of meditation are at work in the sonnets to see that the poetical adaptation of the device is also at work.

Finally, before taking holy orders, Donne wrote two poems linked to Psalms 103 and 104, the sonnet "Wilt thou love God as he thee" and the occasional poem "Upon the Annunciation and Passion falling upon one day. 1608." The two psalms instruct the soul to praise God, extolling all his sublime powers in the first, praising his creativity in the second. The speaker in Donne's "Wilt thou love God as he thee" prompts his soul to love God by recollecting the Father surrounded by angels in heaven who chooses not only to live in the temple of man's heart but also to beget the incarnate Son to redeem mankind and make him heir to immortality, a magnanimity also found in Psalm 103: "For look how high the heaven is in comparison of the earth; so great is his mercy also toward them that fear him." Donne's speaker specifies God's care in the ransom theory of atonement and moves beyond the psalm into Christian theology. The final couplet takes its witty force precisely from Donne's awareness of the distinctiveness of psalmic and contemporary hymnology. Because the New Testament fulfills the Old, his forms of praise cap those of David: " 'Twas much, that man was made like God before, / But, that God should be made like man, much more."

The speaker in the occasional poem "Upon the Annunciation and the Passion falling upon one day. 1608" elaborates Christian paradoxes for forty-four lines, phrasing his lines as a third-person admiration uttered by his own soul. She, in a series of "She sees" formulations, admires the nearly irreconcilable mysteries brought to mind when birth and death are celebrated at once. Then in two closing lines, he asks his soul in direct address to bundle all the mysteries she has admired into one treasure and to dispense it daily to him: "This treasure then, in grosse, my Soule uplay, / And in my life retaile it everyday." The paradoxes are not psalmic, the use of paradox as a stimulus to faith is not psalmic, and the address to the soul in the poem is subsidiary to the enjoyment of paradox. Here Donne uses the *anima mea* device to recommend an activity not natural to the soul in the psalter. Nonetheless in 1608 the value of liturgy, the strength of personal faith, and the usefulness of the psalm figure are clearly drawing together in the poet's mind.

Psalms 103 and 104 are thought to have been written by the same Hebrew poet as companion pieces. Both are hymns, opening and closing with a call to worship.[13] Psalm 103 calls on the soul to praise God, specifies a variety of divine acts and attributes worthy of praise, asks a variety of beings—God's angels, hosts, servants, and works in all places of his dominion—to praise him and closes with the same command to the soul with which it opened, *Benedic, anima mea.* Psalm 104 also opens and closes with "Praise the Lord, O my soul," but exhorts only the psalmist's soul to praise only one divine attribute. The hymn focuses on God's creativity majestically manifested by all the orders of being. Although the *anima mea* figure frames each psalm individually, its identical appearance suggests a kind of contrast-pairing of the two. The framing self-exhortation implies of the soul not that it is the locus of passion or resolution or volition but that it is a metonymy for the integral human being, a witness among many witnesses in Psalm 103, a beneficiary of creation among many creatures in Psalm 104. This pair of hymns was translated and adapted again and again by Donne's poetical descendants,[14] and Donne himself used them, although the penitential psalms were far more useful and important to his religious poetry.

But ought it not to follow from the points we have been making about the utility of the figure to Donne as religious poet, that rather than virtually ceasing to write after his ordination Donne should have proliferated such addresses? Such questions cannot, of course, be answered with any color of authority. One can, however, look briefly at the final poem in the pre-ordina-

13. In the version in the Book of Common Prayer, the exhortations read 103:1: "Praise the Lord, O my soul; and all that is within me, praise his holy Name"; 103:2: "Praise the Lord, O my soul, and forget not all his benefits"; 103:22: "O speak good of the Lord, all ye works of his, in all places of his dominion: praise thou the Lord, O my soul"; 104:1: "Praise the Lord, O my soul; O Lord my God, thou art become exceedingly glorious; thou art clothed with majesty and honour"; and 104:36: "Praise the Lord, O my soul. Praise the Lord."

14. Barbara Lewalski draws attention to the value of these hymns and the frequency of their adaptations in a number of the metaphysical poets, *Protestant Poetics*, pp. 45–52, 162, 240, 246–47, 333–34, 383–85.

tion *anima mea* group, for such help as it may give. The sonnet, "If faithfull soules be alike glorifi'd," accepts the distinction between man's discursive and angel's intuitive knowledge and applies it beyond the grave. In the octave the speaker wonders how "[his] mindes white truth" will be judged by the redeemed if in heaven they still understand like men "By circumstances, and by signes . . . not immediately," modes of understanding likely to be deceived by appearances. Will the redeemed not doubt his religious sincerity? Donne had similarly played in his secular poetry with a bystander's difficulties in judging the sincerity of a physical lover—alluding to it variously in "The Paradox," "Loves Exchange," "Loves Deitie," and "Twicknam Garden." In the sonnet's sestet he admonishes his "pensive soule" to concern itself only with God's judgment, not man's: "Then turne / O pensive soule, to God, for he knowes best / Thy true griefe, for he put it in my breast."[15] The dialogic relationship between speaker and soul, each to be understood only by God, is here oddly but interdependently reflected in the personal pronouns—thy grief and my breast. In the other *anima mea* poems, Donne uses the device to enable himself to write religious verse and to find the right kind of sanction for using his poetical skills and emotions in the service of religion. In this sonnet, however, the device doubts the propriety of using verse addresses to beg understanding from any audience whatsoever but God. The ordination led in the end both to so appropriate an

15. Although one can find in the psalter the idea that abasement, silence, or humility is a God-given attitude (for example, see Psalms 90, 123, 130, and 131), the psalm with the closest affinity to Donne's sonnet here is perhaps Psalm 139, recommending total withdrawal into God. An even closer affinity in tone can be found in Jeremiah, whose lamentations Donne paraphrased after his ordination for use in penitential seasons. See Gardner, *Divine Poems*, pp. 103–4; and see also David Novarr, *The Disinterred Muse: Donne's Texts and Contexts* (Ithaca: Cornell University Press, 1980), pp. 144–50. The paraphrase retains from Jeremiah the address to his own soul in chapter 3 to read at verse 18 "My strength, my hope (unto my selfe I said)" and at verse 24 "The Lord is, saith my Soule, my portion, / And therefore in him will I hope alone." And it approaches the content of "If faithfull soules alike be glorifi'd" when Donne paraphrases:

37 Who then will say, that ought doth come to passe,
    But that which by the Lord commanded was?
38 Both good and evill from his mouth proceeds;
    39 Why then grieves any man for his misdeeds?
40 Turne wee to God, by trying out our wayes;
    41 To him in heaven, our hands with hearts upraise.

audience for his creativity in sermons and for his spiritually wholesome self-dramatization in the Eucharist that all Donne's creative impulses found there their fullest possible expression. And in facilitating that ordination a poetical and a ritually liturgical device of Hebrew psalmody played a significant role.

Donne wrote "Hymne to God my God, in my sicknesse" as a death-bed meditation on an illness he thought would be fatal, now generally agreed to be that of 1623, which inspired the *Devotions upon Emergent Occasions* and the prebend sermons, and not, as Walton wrote, that of 1631, which inspired the sermon *Deaths Duell* and was fatal.[16] He took holy orders in 1615; in 1621 he secured the deanery of St. Paul's, a post that carried with it the prebendary of Chiswick. The office of prebendary at Saint Paul's is filled by thirty canons, or prebendaries, including the dean, each of whom is required to recite daily a part of the psalter "for the health of the living and the repose of the departed benefactors of Saint Paul's Cathedral." The psalms assigned to Donne were 62 through 66. After his illness he preached the five great prebend sermons on them.[17] The first of his psalms, 62, is an *anima mea* psalm in the form of a wisdom song spoken by a teacher to God, his congregation, and his own soul, about how God's providence inspires confidence. The concurrence of the theme of this assigned psalm with Donne's illness, his converting his illness into worship in *Devotions on Emergent Occasions*, his decision to write the prebend sermons, and his "Hymne to God my God, in my sicknesse" link the psalm to the poem. The poem considers vocation in the face of death; the psalm trusts in God in the face of death.

The poem is unusually confident of grace, calm in mood, and unified under one metaphor. The speaker investigates the wit of one conceit: as east and west meet on a globe, so death and life meet in the resurrection. His purpose is to use his remaining life to adjust his thoughts to afterlife, or—as he puts it—bound to join the choir of saints, "I tune the Instrument here at the dore, / And what I must doe then, thinke now before." But if

16. See Novarr, *The Disinterred Muse*, pp. 170–75, for the dating of "Hymne to God my God, in my sicknesse" and "A Hymne to God the Father." Novarr dates the former in December 1623.

17. See *Donne's Prebend Sermons*, ed. with introduction and commentary by Janel M. Mueller (Cambridge: Harvard University Press, 1971).

metaphor is unified, the poet's self-representation is various. He represents himself as a chorister, his physicians' map, himself a cosmographer, a geographico-theological lecturer on his own condition who uses the lecturers' "we," "We thinke that Paradise and Calvarie . . . stood in one place," and finally a priest at the offertory, "receive mee Lord . . . give me." He ends converting all his insights into a text for his own soul: "And as to others soules I preach'd thy word, / Be this my Text, my Sermon to mine owne, / Therfore that he may raise the Lord throws down." Such simplicity of figure and complexity of address is the rhetorical hallmark of Psalm 62.

In Psalm 62, the poet likewise lives through conflicting feelings and expresses his trust in God. In this psalm, however, the teaching of trust is the real point of the poem, not the expression of conflict borne in patient tension. From the beginning the psalmist trusts God and advises his soul to trust him. The poet is more interested in teaching instruction through a range of listeners than in encouraging worship through a deepening of tensions. He is objective about himself and deploys a sort of ironic exaggeration in outfacing his enemies. When he sees that they plot his ruin, he turns from exhorting his soul to rely on God and addresses the enemies directly. In contrast to God his fortress, they are a tottering wall. Then he returns to the neutral audience and denounces the enemies: "They give good words with their mouth, but they curse with their heart." Within the four verses of that first movement, the poet uses three forms of address—to the soul, enemies, and bystanders. With the second movement, the psalmist turns again to his soul: "Nevertheless my soul, wait thou still upon God."[18] Then he explains to the onlookers: "In God is my health and my glory." And he advises them as "us" to trust Him "our hope." Those verses too abound in shifts of address—"my strength,"

18. The Book of Common Prayer translation does not make clear the full extent of the device in Psalm 62, translating the first two verses: "My soul truly waiteth still upon God; for of him cometh my salvation. He verily is my strength and my salvation; he is my defence, so that I shall not greatly fall." With this one might compare Dahood, *Psalms II*, p. 89: "The God of gods alone is my mighty castle; My soul, from him will my triumph come. He alone is my mountain of triumph, my bulwark: I will not stumble into the dragnet." The Book of Common Prayer does translate the second occurrence clearly, however: "Nevertheless, my soul, wait thou still upon God; for my hope is in him."

"your trust," "our hope." Only in the last four verses does the poet reveal himself to us sufficiently for all the changes in pronoun and voice to come together in a personality. A mandarin donnish voice begins with some good negative advice: "O trust not in wrong and robbery; give not yourselves unto vanity: if riches increase, set not your heart upon them." The voice proclaims its authority by a schoolmaster's enumeration: "God spake once, and twice I have also heard the same." Then, satisfied with his own craft, balance, and good sense, the wisdom psalmist speaks to his God for the first and last time: "thou, Lord . . . rewardest every man according to his work." The psalmist tells his soul not so much about how the Lord pays out enemies as about how his justice works. This psalm is linked to the occasional poem "Hymne to God my God, in my sicknesse."

Both Donne and the psalmist learn through suffering that God's justice initiates his mercy. Donne phrases the insight: "Therefore that He may raise the Lord throws down"; the psalmist of 62: "power belongeth unto God. Also unto thee, O Lord, belongeth mercy." It has been suggested that whereas "A Hymne to God my God, in my sicknesse" is in a general way hymnic and biblical, it is neither public enough to be a proper hymn nor actually biblical enough so that its "text" can be found in Scripture.[19] Nevertheless the habit of addressing truths to one's own soul, while anticipating the value to others of overhearing them, is both specific to the psalter and congregational in force. The value of the device in Donne's occasional poem lies in the distinction it permits between the protagonist as teacher and his soul as pupil, and in the nature of the wisdom lesson it has to teach about how sufferings lead to mercy and how both educate.

The scenario of "Hymne to God my God, in my sicknesse" derives not from Psalm 62, however, but from another of the *anima mea* psalms. The situation of Donne's fulfilling his prebendary duty by composing a sermon for "others soules" on the lesson contained in his own *anima mea* psalm matches some-

19. Novarr, *The Disinterred Muse*, pp. 180–84, addressing points about the poem made by Gardner, *Divine Poems*, p. 109, and by Clay Hunt, *Donne's Poetry: Essays in Literary Analysis* (New Haven: Yale University Press, 1954), pp. 115–17.

thing of the plot of Psalm 116, a public song dedicated to giving thanks for the poet's personal preservation from death. Psalm 116 is a thanksgiving sung within the Hebrew liturgy by one grateful to have escaped death in a serious illness, who speaks not simply for himself but for everyone in the Temple. The first verses consider the circumstances of narrowly escaping death. The next are the psalmist's dialogue with his soul, this time the soul responding with verses of her own. The psalmist reminds her how he invoked God at the hour of his death and how the Lord helped him to escape. His soul replies that she always believed in God during their sufferings, even when pain made her turn against mankind. The psalmist then addresses the congregation and describes his devotions—blessing the wine, pouring it on the altar, praising God's name. As he blesses and pours, he tells the congregation how during his sickness he prayed for help and vowed a thank offering if his prayer were answered. Recalling that prayer, he recites it again. Finally he turns again to the congregation and completes the thanksgiving ritual with his promised words of praise. The Prayer Book translates the dialogue as follows:

> [Psalmist to Soul] Turn again then unto thy rest, O my
>   soul; for the Lord hath rewarded thee.
> [Psalmist to God] And why? thou hast delivered my soul
>   from death, mine eyes from tears, and my feet from falling.
> I will walk before the Lord in the land of the living.
> [Soul to Psalmist] I believed, and therefore will I speak;
>   but I was sore troubled: I said in my haste,
> All men are liars.[20]

The psalmist speaks of a personal experience so essentially religious as to be best said in the Temple. The aspects of the device in this psalm making it useful to "Hymne to God my God, in my sicknesse" are its retrospection, its plot of restoration, and its meditative force.

But the device in Psalm 116 is notable for another quality that relates it equally to Donne's sonnet on the death of his wife. While the psalmist is dependent on God, his soul is dependent on both God and the psalmist. The possibilities of interdependence, weakness, and subordination in the exchange hinge on

20. Compare Dahood, *Psalms III*, pp. 145–51, and Artur Weiser, *The Psalms* (Philadelphia: Westminster Press, 1962), pp. 718–21.

the Hebrew gender of the soul being feminine and the psalmist using the feminine for "thee" and "thy rest," a point easily taken by Donne, who had as good a grasp of Hebrew as he did not have of Greek. Furthermore the psalm is notable for its eschatological hints. During the near-fatal illness, the psalmist called on his God, who heard his prayers and restored him because that is how God is, "Gracious is the Lord, and righteous; Yea, our God is merciful." Addressing his people, he resolves to pay his vowed thank offering in the Temple. There he tells the congregation of the direct exchange that took place between himself, his soul, and God. The psalmist called on God, "O Lord . . . deliver my soul"; feeling God's response, he said to his soul, "Turn again then unto thy rest, O my soul," and prophesied eschatologically, "I will walk before the Lord In the land of the living." The feminine soul in antiphon declared her personal and precedent trust even in the difficult times. About eschatology, the psalmist is convinced that he will be forever in the presence of his God, who has saved him.

Although the psychological and tonal complexity of Donne's sonnet is greater than the psalm's, the psalm may help us to read the poem more clearly. The poet has lost his wife, whose death has turned his mind exclusively to heaven. While she lived, her goodness made him seek God, the source of her admirable qualities; he found God but, he confesses to end the octave, his thirst for him remains unassuaged. That octave has always been read as a conversion of life into art. Critics recall that in the *Essays in Divinity* Donne thanked God for rescuing him "from the Egypt of lust, by confining [his] affections" to his wife. Conceding her good effect on him, they note how the grief of his bereavement in the sonnet is calmed by Donne's certainty of her salvation: "Her Soule early into heaven [has been] ravished." But the poem not only converts life, it also converts a psalm into art; God has loved both Anne Donne and the poet, and has taken Anne's soul into heaven to be with him there in anticipation of the time Donne too may join them. God has performed that act of love because it is his nature.[21] At the end of the octave, God possesses Anne; John longs to be similarly possessed.

21. For a rather different account, see M. E. Grenander in "Holy Sonnets VIII and XVII: John Donne," reprinted in *Essential Articles for the Study of John Donne's Poetry*, ed. John R. Roberts (Hamden, Conn.: Archon Books, 1975), p. 329.

The sestet questions the poet's need to beg more love and then settles the relationship among husband, wife, and Creator according to the protagonist's most passionate desire, by discovering the full sufficiency of God's care.

> But why should I begg more love, when as thou
> Dost wooe my soule, for hers offring all thine:
> And dost not only feare least I allow
> My love to saints and Angels, things divine,
> But in thy tender jealosy dost doubt
> Least the World, fleshe, yea Devill putt thee out.

Donne may rejoice that God has his wife's soul until his own coming to heaven and meanwhile ardently and jealously woos his soul lest it suffer either the enticements and dangers of the world or the idolatrous worship of the instrumental goods of the spirit, including the saintliness of Anne.[22] It would be doctrinally possible for Donne to rest in an eschatological security at which Psalm 116 hints. But he has ascribed to his God so anthropomorphic a love that he darkens the close of the poem. The jealousy of God extends to misdoubt of Donne, and with that darkening Donne ends. Donne might have aimed in the echo of the psalm to reecho its faithful security, but in the end he characteristically moderated its confidence in the addition of his own psychological misgivings.

The two post-ordination adaptations of the device exhaust its use in the religious poetry of John Donne. The history of the device in seventeenth-century English religious poetry after Donne is the history of Donnean influence and allusion as well as of biblical poetics. The honor of the first adaptations of the trope in the seventeenth century, that is, is surely Donne's, for whom it answered such complex religious, personal, poetical, and vocational needs. George Herbert and his followers pluck the device from Donne for their own uses, uses more often implying dialogue between soul and body or implicating addresses to the heart quite as often as to the soul. Those uses are still to be examined.

---

22. Anne Donne died in 1617, two years after Donne's ordination. Dame Helen Gardner finds the sonnet too calm to suggest composition immediately after Anne's death, and she dates it 1619 (*Divine Poems*, p. 78).

4

RE-SIGNING THE TEXT OF THE SELF: DONNE'S "AS DUE BY MANY TITLES"

M. Thomas Hester

During a class in which I was outlining the "literary" conventions of More's *Utopia*, one of my students pointed out the classification given the book by Yale University Press on the back cover; there in bold letters appears the generic prescription HISTORY/PHILOSOPHY. Attempting to appear undaunted by this rebuttal to my generic classification, I explained that the Press's description was quite accurate, that it was merely following the Sidneyan distinction between those two disciplines and "Poetrie." The generic locus of *Utopia*, I explained, is that seam (or seem/seme) between Philosophy and History, that space (or no-place) traced by the bold virgule on the book cover. In the same vein, one wonders how Donne's Holy Sonnets would be classified by the dust-cover genericists. If they followed the directive of much critical commentary, the back cover would designate BIOGRAPHY/THEOLOGY. Certainly, the wide knowledge of theological controversy of the most famous surviving member of a family of Catholic recusants who was to become a clergyman in the Established Church cannot be denied. Nevertheless, Donne continues to merit our attention as a poet; and what is too frequently slighted in much criticism of his religious lyrics is that characteristic of Donne's verse which most attracts us—his wit. This is not meant to deny the significance of these poems as documents that, in the words of

Dennis Flynn, "dramatize the isolation of an individual soul aware of the odds against salvation without institutional support" or that they might be poetic reflections on Donne's "spiritual malaise" during the Mitcham years (if that indeed is when they were composed); nor is it to deny that the Holy Sonnets could well be Donne's poetic essays of differing theological positions, doctrines, and motifs. It is only meant to suggest that our assessments of these poems should not forget that Donne, in John Shawcross's words, "is a marvelous example of the craftsman at work"[1] —and a craftsman especially and often explicitly concerned with unfolding the dynamics and problematics of the norms and forms with which he works.

An outstanding example of Donne's self-reflexive craftsmanship is provided by the first of his Holy Sonnets, "As due by many titles," for it in many ways is a poem about the problematic nature of the religious lyric. It is, in fact, an exploration of the kind-ness of the religious lyric, a search for traces of the divine Word in the typology of the self. Framed by the central comparison between the poet's witty re-creation and the divine Maker's originary and continuous acts of re-creation, "As due by many titles" applies that central topos of Renaissance homiletics and poetics—man as a word striving to communicate with The Word—in order to explicate the limitations and powers of man to re-create himself *in imagine dei*. Like so many of Donne's poems, it is an anatomy of its own wit and of the central concern of the religious lyric—the power of words to signify the self as an image of The Word, or, in the central terms of the poem, the capacity of "titles" to "re-sign" the self in humble resignation to the handwriting of God.

> As due by many titles, I resigne
> My selfe to thee, O God, first I was made
> By thee, and for thee, and when I was decay'd

---

1. Flynn, "Donne's Catholicism," *Recusant History* 13 (1975): 190; Shawcross, "Remarks on Donne's 400th Anniversary," *Bulletin, The Poetry Society of America* (May 1972), p. 14. For a convincing argument that "at least some of the Holy Sonnets [were composed] much earlier than has been supposed," perhaps even as early as the middle and late 1590s, see Flynn, "The Dating of Donne's Holy Sonnets," in *Theology and the Poetry of Seventeenth-Century England: A Symposium in Honor of Joseph H. Summers*, ed. Mary A. Maleski (forthcoming). All citations of Donne are to the edition by John T. Shawcross, *The Complete Poetry of John Donne* (Garden City, N.Y.: Doubleday/Anchor, 1967).

Thy blood bought that, the which before was thine,
I am thy sonne, made with thy selfe to shine,
Thy servant, whose paines thou hast still repaid,
Thy sheepe, thine Image, and till I betray'd
My selfe, a temple of thy Spirit divine;
Why doth the devill then usurpe in mee?
Why doth he steale, nay ravish that's thy right?
Except thou rise and for thine owne worke fight,
Oh I shall soone despaire, when I doe see
That thou lov'st mankind well, yet wilt not chuse me.
And Satan hates mee, yet is loth to lose mee.

As conveyed by the puns on "titles" and "resigne" in the opening line, the sonnet strives to enact in words a testament to God's glory that is legally "due" because of God's eternal *sermo* with His creation. Enumerating examples of God's merciful re-creations to which the poem is a response, in the octave the speaker first recalls the archetypal Creation pattern that has formed and re-formed man, then elaborates the biblical types on which his own understanding of his appeal for re-creation is based, and then recalls the failure of will that defaced the divine imprint on his soul. The central motif of God as an artist thus establishes a paradoxical analogical pattern of divine re-creation which the speaker meditatively strives to imitate. He is unable, however, to enact this pattern, and the sestet calls into question both the argument and imagery of the octave. Contradicting first the conception of God that was affirmed by the images of the octave and then the octave's typological interpretation of the "selfe," the speaker *re-signs* his poem into an image of the fatal debility of the fallen self. The rational recollection of the just motions of divine mercy is overturned by an emotional appeal for legal "exception" to the eternal pattern; typological identifications become individual separations; the syntax becomes confusing; and even the meter of the lines finally loses its integrity. The sestet, quite simply, de-constructs the poem, as it struggles to assume a different genre in order to become a love complaint instead of a legal petition.[2]

2. As Robert S. Shaw phrases it, "If the anxious soul had temerity enough, it would make its petition not in the language of law but of love" (*The Call of God: Vocation in Donne and Herbert* [Cambridge, Mass.: Cowley, 1981], p. 44). See also Ann Ferry, *The "Inward" Language: Sonnets of Wyatt, Sidney, Shakespeare, Donne* (Chicago: University of Chicago Press, 1983), chap. 5, who suggests that the language of Donne's speakers "evokes in many ways the figure of the poet-

The strain of the sestet intimates, in fact, the central dilemma of Donne's religious lyrics. Conventionally, the speaker of a love sonnet aims to express his love for a beloved, to initiate an exchange of vows or to "obtain grace" by the rhetoric of his words. As Donne's sonnet shows, however, the speaker of the religious lyric is not the lover but the beloved who must respond to the "signs" of God's love that have already been expressed in, and given significance to, human history. He is unable, however, to respond in kind to God's love poem, but can submit only an image of that Poem, which he knows is unlike its divine Type because of his fallen condition: it is always an enigmatic re-signing that should signal the necessity of resigning the self. Thus, the implicit premise of this sonnet paradox— that man, as a word whose creation and re-creation is verified by the "titles" of His Word, must resign himself to his inability to glorify Him—is dramatically explored and poetically mirrored in Donne's witty frustration and surprise of meditative and poetic expectations.

By and large, the problematic character of the poem's opening declaration of humility is not explicit in the octave, which fulfills Puente's prescription for an address to the Trinity in which the meditator offers "titles and reasons, that may move them to grant us what we demand."[3] These lines present a smooth and orderly review of man's covenantal relationship to his Maker. But they also survey man's gradual separation from the Word—what might be termed *man's fall into language*, his progressive separation as a word (or *verba*) from the eternal signification (or *res*) of the eternal conversation of Creator and creature. The octave, in other words, not only recounts the history of man; it enacts it verbally.

The first lines, for instance, are significantly sparse and clear in their specificity: "first I was made / By thee, and for thee." Man is explainable only in terms of his relation to God's

lover as it was developed in the sequences of Sidney and Shakespeare" (p. 227); and Terry Sherwood, *Fulfilling the Circle: A Study of Donne's Thought* (Toronto: University of Toronto Press, 1984), chap. 6, who suggests that the Petrarchan sonnet "provided Donne with a form for scrutinizing the varying motions of the penitential soul" (p. 156).

3. Luis de la Puente, *Meditations upon the Mysteries of our Holie Faith* (Omer, 1619), quoted in Louis L. Martz, *The Poetry of Meditation* (New Haven: Yale University Press, 1954), p. 48.

creativity and glory: he is only by and for God. The simplicity of his nature is reiterated (and mirrored) in the description of man's Fall and Redemption: "when I was decay'd / Thy blood bought *that, the which* before was thine." What he was and is, then, is entirely the result of divine creativity and mercy. But, at the same time, the shift from the personalized "I" to the neutral "that" and "the which" does trace his descent into the *this-ness* of the fallen world, which is also reflected in the increasing ambiguity of the poem. The parallelism of "I was made" and "I was decay'd," for example, creates problems because of its intimation that man's decay, like his creation, was the result of God's choice and "making." The gradually changing (or "decaying") texture of the poem, in other words, mirrors the progressive separation of man from The Word.

The possible confusion of "I" and "thou" continues in the second quatrain, which lists man's "titles." The stabilizing effect of the legal motif is retained by "made" and "repaid," but this catalogue of biblical types creates some troublesome questions, for the list presents "titles" that are not in a sense the speaker's but attributes of Christ. As line 5 admits, his "selfe" is "thy sonne" only in the sense that he is "made with thy selfe to shine." He was, through the re-creative gift of Christ, made to shine, but that does not mean that he does: the indefiniteness of the infinitive form traces simultaneously man's potential likeness and fallen unlikeness to the creative clarity of God's Light. And the suffering servant image is even more troublesome. Christ, of course, is the antetype of the Isaiahic servant who in death ("still") "paid" for man's sins, while man is "still" (yet) a creator of "paines" because of his deadly sins. "Repaid," then, suggests the continuation of man's sins and Christ's pains. If the infinitive of line 5 records in suspension man's potential likeness to God's creative mercy, the pun on "still" in line 6 focuses attention more fully on his unlikeness—now man is the creator, but of "paines" that must "still" be "repaid."

That the speaker is, in fact, not "thy sonne" and "Thy servant" is encouraged more forcefully in the last two lines of the octave, the syntax of which conveys man's present condition. The declaration of titles continues with "Thy sheepe, thine Image," but is suddenly interrupted by "and till I betray'd / My selfe." Whether he is aware that betrayal of "My selfe" is actually a betrayal of "thy selfe" is not clear; but "betray'd" is precisely the correct term, for it suggests both the act of turning his self over to the enemy and turning Christ over to His crucifiers while submitting at the same time an unintentional disclosure of his own character (*OED* 2a). That this submission literally disrupts the list of titles mirrors the effect of man's betrayal and reinforces that Christ must "still" *re*pay for man's denials. The eighth line shows the ultimate effect of man's sinfulness—his loss of unity/similarity to the third member of the Trinity, "thy Spirit divine," by which the (lower case) "temple" has become mere body, suggesting the generic means of betrayal of the self. Thus, the movement from memory to understanding of God's gifts/covenants is disrupted by the interference of the speaker's willful selfishness; recitation of titles that prove God's love is momentarily disrupted by his focus on his "selfe"; and his meditative movement through Father/Son/Spirit is disordered by the willful self-pity of his own words. The "titles" listed by the speaker, in other words, all connote man's dependence on God;[4] but the speaker confesses to an independence of self that denies the natural laws of divine grammar.

The speaker's account of divine repetition and re-making ("the which before," "repaid") and its puns (sonne/sun, "still" as *dead* and as *yet*) should verify, that is, the continuing connection of God with His creation. But the past tense of "till I betray'd" (with the past tense sense of "till" denying the eternality of "still," and "betray'd" denying "I am") indicates a willful denial of the divine course of human history—and thus of all the titles the speaker is supposedly resigning to God. It is in this sense that Donne forces us to consider his most provocative pun in the poem—on "resign" as not only "to yield humbly" (*OED* I, 2b) but also as "to deny" and "to re-write" (*OED* II, IV). The speaker's attempt to submit his rational soul in meditation to his Maker, then, is subverted by his own denial of the efficacy of those "titles," by his own claim that he has the power by his own sinfulness to render them meaningless and void. Perhaps this is why Donne chooses the titles of Christic typology—in order to suggest that the gifts of Christ, the titles He earned for man, are man's only if he chooses them. As Dean

4. Shaw, *The Call of God*, p. 44.

Donne phrased it, "God saves no man without or against his will."[5] When the speaker *re-signs* his self, re-writes the titles of God, he separates himself from the divine Image. His words become mere words.

The speaker's descent into the enigmatic text of his self has been traced, in fact, by the shapes of his language. The clarity and simplicity of the first lines, which record a pure and personal relationship with the Creator, were first replaced by the neutral pronouns and difficult syntax of the lines which report the Fall; then the equivocal suspension of the infinitive in line 5 was replaced by the polysemous pun and ambiguity of line 6, and finally by the piteous interruption of the last two lines of the octave. In the same vein, the increasing impersonality and remoteness of the analogies (son-servant-sheep-image-temple)[6] trace his gradual descent from the essential, creative relationship of the opening lines. Thus, the changing shape of his language in the octave subtly traces man's fall from union with the signifying divine Word into the isolated limitations of human signs.

The effects of this fall are illustrated in the desperate assertiveness of the sestet, which attempts an ingenious but willfully abusive reversal of the imagery and argument of the octave. In lines 9–11, the speaker presents a series of parallel contrasts to the figures of the octave. Presumptuously denying his own admission that his "betrayal" was the source of his sinfulness, he now insists that "the devill . . . usurpe[s] in mee." Thus, the creative Father of the octave is replaced by the devil; and accordingly, "By thee, and for thee" is replaced by "in mee." "Made," the act of creating by speech ("God said"), is replaced with "usurpe," the act of using or appropriating wrongfully or, in this case, the appropriation of another's words, titles, or speech (*OED* 4c). The false logic of the speaker's excuse, then, replaces a creative Speaking that "makes" covenants and "titles" (an originary Word that creates meaning) with an illegal and mendacious speaking that derives from a fallen word ("in mee"), an abusive Liar that denies meaning.

5. *The Sermons of John Donne*, ed. George R. Potter and Evelyn M. Simpson, 10 vols. (Los Angeles: University of California Press, 1953–1962), 5:317.

6. Pointed out by J. W. Lever in notes to his edition, *Sonnets of the English Renaissance* (London: Athlone, 1974), p. 179.

This denial of God's power is followed by abusive contrasts
to the attributes of the Son and the Holy Ghost. The speaker
now seems to question that Christ "bought" and "repaid" his
self "still," claiming instead that the devil "steale[s]" and "rav-
ish[es]" him, therein replacing "due" resignation to the cove-
nant of Christ's "blood" and "paines" with supposed subjection
to the devil's illegal and illicit assaults.[7] The speaker begins, in
fact, to move the psychomachia into a kind of Manichaeism,
transferring God's gift of free choice to Satan's controlling
action. This self-serving view of man as spectator to the battle
for his soul continues in the revealing pun on "rise" and the
ignorant misuse of "fight," in which he obviates the resurrec-
tion of Christ as the bridegroom of the Church Militant. Even
the central legal conceit of the octave is denied: "As due by many
titles" has become "except," the legal bases of the Covenants
replaced with a threatening gesture that demands a legal "exclu-
sion to the course of action or proceeding" (*OED* 2a), that orders
suspension of the divine course of history. And, most telling,
the "selfe" which "before was thine" has now become only
God's "worke," the glance at the *good works* that should ema-
nate from faith now seen as the responsibility of God instead of
the speaker. The presumptuous questions of the speaker, then,
implicate him by their reversals of the language, reason, and
strategy of the octave. Here we see the flawed memory that
denies his Creator in an attempt to erase the origins of his own
culpability and the flawed reason as it makes demands that the
"rise[n]" Christ has already fulfilled for man.

In the same vein, the final three lines present the fugacious
motions of the flawed will as the speaker descends into a hell of
his own making while denying the merciful motions of the Holy
Spirit. Beginning with the emotional and pitiful "Oh," these

7. In a 1617 sermon preached at Whitehall, Donne explains that "though it
be some degree of injustice, to impute all our particular sins, to the devil him-
self, after a habit of sin hath made us spontaneous demones, devils to our selves;
yet we do come too near an imputing our sins to God himself, when we place
such an impossibility in his Commandments, as makes us lazie, that because
we cannot do all, therefore, we will do nothing; or such a manifestation and
infallibility in his Decree, as makes us either secure, or desperate; and say, The
Decree hath damned me, therefore I can do no good. . . . but of the shadow of
death, wherein I sit, there is no cause, but mine own corruption. And this is the
cause, why I do sin; but why I should sin, there is none at all" (*Sermons*,
1:226–27).

lines figure forth the act of "despaire" both thematically and poetically. Restricting the power of the Spirit by the prediction that he shall "see" not election but damnation, the speaker's threatening and bold gamble presents his final self-centered act of self-abnegation and privation. Willfully choosing despair (*despeare*)—"I *shall* soone despaire"—and thus suggesting his own control of the course of human history, he literally enacts the process of dis-pairing (*OED* 1) by separating himself from his God and his fellow man. "Thy Spirit divine," he now insists, "wilt not chuse me." Thus, he not only dis-pairs himself from "mankind," sundering his humanity, but also separates God's justice from His mercy. The saucy pun on "well" as "sinless" in "thou lov'st mankind well" intimates the basis of his despair to be his awareness of his own sinfulness; but he therein facetiously adds an "exception" to the divine covenant that is of his own willful "making." And the result of his own choice is graphically conveyed by the placement of "me" in the line. Helen Gardner misses the point of the dangling eleventh syllable in this line when, in her 1952 edition of *The Divine Poems*, she accepts the 1633 contraction "wilt'not" (which "has no manuscript support") in order to create a decasyllabic line. She then ends up with "a masculine rhyme . . . matched with the second syllable of a feminine rhyme," even though "haunted by the true feminine rhyme 'chuse me' and 'lose mee.'"[8] She rejects the contraction in her 1978 edition, but still does not seem to realize that the *me/mee* is not feminine—the point is that the speaker's choice has literally placed him beyond expression, outside the order of the poetic frame, separated from his own "selfe." And this condition is enforced by the repetition of this hypermetric effect in the dark concluding line, which presents the hellish mental condition of the speaker. The ironic internal rhymes of the final two lines ("wilt"/"loth," "chuse"/"lose") aptly depict his condition: it is his will that has chosen his loathsome loss of meaning. It is his desperation that has separated "mee" from "thee," his words that have "lost" the "titles" "due" to them "by" and "from" the divine Word. It is he who has separated his "selfe" from his poem so that "mee" is finally deprived of a metrical place in the final lines. Having

8. *John Donne: The Divine Poems* (Oxford: Clarendon, 1956), p. 66.

alienated his "titles" and their spiritual significances, his history and its providential sentences, in the final tercet he denies his own humanity and becomes only "mee"—a *verba* without a *res*.

The willful "betrayal" of the lucidity and order of the octave is also reflected in the syntax and sentence structure of the last six lines. The organic, harmonious *abba abba* of the first section, for example, is followed by the revealing stasis of the *cddccc* rhymes of the sestet, in which the dominant focus on the self is reflected in the discarding of rhymes with "thy right"/"thine fight" for the total immersion in "mee"/"I doe see"/"me"/"mee." The poem seems to be struggling to become an English instead of a Petrarchan sonnet; but this discursive scheme is denied by the sentence structure of the lines, which divides them into two tercets. But then even the organic structure of the Italian form is not followed, for the main clause of line 11 has subordinate clauses that carry from line 12 over into line 13;[9] and even the logical sequence of this complex sentence is disrupted by the interjection of the piteous "Oh." It is not only difficult to follow the reasoning of these six lines, but also difficult to scan them—as witnessed by the inverted foot that emphasis demands at the start of line 9 and of line 10, the spondee that begins line 12, and the eleventh syllables in the last two lines. Such a view of the sestet affirms, in fact, the soundness of the period at the end of the thirteenth line, which most accurately conveys the tone and character of these last desperate lines: the last line is not part of a compound sentence, but only another attempt by the speaker to place guilt outside himself, another afterthought, another excuse that tries to shift blame—another lie.[10] Instead of the humble colloquy of a meditation, the "act of correlation" of an Italian sonnet, or the dis-

9. Antony F. Bellette, "'Little Worlds Made Cunningly': Significant Form in Donne's *Holy Sonnets* and 'Goodfriday, 1613,'" *Studies in Philology* 72 (1975): 329. Bellette offers an important alternative to the theological preoccupations of modern criticism of the Holy Sonnets. This paragraph is indebted to his observations.

10. The first edition of *Poems* (1633) and several of the manuscripts give a period at the end of line 13, which Shawcross retains. Grierson emended it to a comma, and Gardner followed his emendation. Creating a compound sentence here may accord more fully with "proper" grammar and with the sequential thought of a Petrarchan sonnet, but Donne is violating those conventions in order to enforce the texture of his suggestive presentation.

cursive resolution of an English sonnet, the sestet "consists of essentially isolated elements at war with themselves."[11]

"As due by many titles," then, does not present the initial step in a contritional progression, but a willful denial of the speaker's ability to enact his own determination. If viewed as the first *preparatio* of a meditative scheme, it might be seen as a dramatic presentation or imaginative composition of the flawed will of man, for what distinguishes the psychological and dramatic intensity of the poem is the picture of the speaker's willful refusal to submit. In this sense, the two major sections of the poem present two attempts at resignation or re-signing. The first considers the reasons why he should submit, typologically applying the movements of the rational soul to an examination of the workings of The Word in human history; the second section re-writes or re-signs this covenantal pattern, accommodating it to the presumptuous and demanding obduracy of the fallen will. Thus, the consequences of man's descent into language intimated in the octave—the movement from an unmediated relationship with The Word, to the mediation between Creator and creature by Christ's active "words," to the interjection of the speaker's own words of "betrayal"—are realized in the sestet by the speaker's selfish, emotional, and desperate displacement of God's promises with his own threats. In this sense, therefore, the final ironic paradox of the poem is that it enacts its major concern: it shows or reveals the dependence of the debilitated soul of man on the mercy of God. The need for the "titles" given to man by God that are recalled in the octave is confirmed by the "titles" or words of the isolated speaker in the sestet. Even his presumptuous words of judicious outrage are finally images that justify his status as an image of God: his enigmatic words only confirm the bases of divine typology, illustrating that Christ's titles are due because of his sinfulness, are necessary because of his debility. The pattern of human history typologically traced in the octave is ironically fulfilled by the "betrayal" of the sestet.

"As due by many titles," therefore, alerts us again to one of the central achievements of Donne as a poet: his ability to present the paradoxes of the human condition. The poem may well

11. Bellette, "Little Worlds," p. 329.

confirm some tenets of Aquinas, Calvin, or Hooker; but its achievement lies not in its successful dramatization of any theological doctrine but in its poetic enactment of the paradox of man as a fallen image of The Word. The refusal of the poem to conform to the therapeutic aims of a meditation and to enact the organic and metrical order of a Petrarchan or an English sonnet—its refusal to accept even its initial premises and motifs—bespeaks its central concern with depicting the refusal of the human will to submit to any form of constructed order, to any set of devotional, poetical, or logical frames of law. It is in these senses that the poem as a series of titles or words illustrates ironically its major premise: that man as a fallen word who is capable only of fallen words has significance only through the mediation of divine mercy.

*   *   *

"To know how to liue by the booke," Donne once wrote in a personal letter, "is a pedantery, & to do it is a bondage. for both hearers & players are more delighted with voluntary then with sett musike. And he that will liue by precept shalbe long without the habite of honesty." Later, after having advised, admonished, and invited rebuttal from his friend, he closed the letter with this affectionate and revealing paradox: "I am so far from pswading yea conselling you to beleeue others that I care not that you beleeue not mee when I say that others are not to bee beleeued: only beleeue that I loue you and I haue enough . . . ." In some ways this advice is similar to that witty warning given to Wotton when Donne sent him a copy of his "paradoxes": "if they make you to find better reasons against them they do their office: for they are but swaggerers: quiet enough if you resist them. . . . they are nothings: therefore take heed of allowing any of them least you make another."[12] Both letters provide instructive glosses on the central strategy of "As due by many titles." This swaggering paradox which refuses to "liue by the booke," that demands its "voluntary" right to deny the "sette musike" of biblical and poetic laws, asks only for a response, a response on its own terms. As a legal disputation to God, then,

12. Cited in Evelyn M. Simpson, *A Study of the Prose Works of John Donne* (Oxford: Clarendon, 1924), pp. 294–96, 298. I have expanded the contractions.

it "allows" only two possible responses—damnation or salvation, the first of which would verify the willful claims of the speaker, the second of which would deny his logic. Either would prove "another" paradox—an overturning of the pattern of divine creation or a bestowing of mercy where it is not logically justified. Thus, whether the speaker has outsmarted his auditor or himself in this poem it is not possible to conclude. And whether Donne has only followed what he read in Hooker or Calvin or Aquinas seems beside the point. What "As due by many titles" does illustrate is Donne's awareness that the significance of his words, his titles, and his "selfe" was to be the response of The Word alone. Only the merciful Maker can finally re-sign the text of the self.

In closing, therefore, I would remind the Yale University Press book designers that the religious lyric is not History or Philosophy. Like the "selfe" it presents, it lives in the seam between time and eternity, type and antetype, history and philosophy. Like all religious lyrics, "As due by many titles" is a poem in search of its own genre, a poetic presentation of man's desire for the closure of divine kind-ness. In this sense, Donne himself provides the best gloss on his poem when, in a March 1608 letter to Henry Goodyere, he writes: "But of the diseases of the minde, there is no *Criterium*, no Canon, no rule; for, our own taste and apprehension and interpretation should be the Judge, and that is the disease it self."[13]

13. *Letters to Severall Persons of Honour* (London, 1651), p. 71.

5

THE BRIDE OF THE APOCALYPSE AND THE QUEST FOR TRUE RELIGION: DONNE, HERBERT, AND SPENSER

Claude J. Summers

John Donne's Holy Sonnet "Show me deare Christ" and George Herbert's "The British Church" are both prompted by schism in the Church. They both explore the question of how to recognize true religion at a time when the seamless garment of Christian faith seems to be rent by the competing claims of rival institutions. Both works are audaciously witty and daring in their conceits, and both contrast the image of the Bride of the Apocalypse with distinctly unbridelike women who represent various manifestations of the visible Church. But the poems reach strikingly different conclusions, and these divergent responses reflect a fundamental difference between the two poets' regard for the earthly Church. Whereas Herbert confidently celebrates the form and liturgy of his "dearest Mother" Church—and "none but thee"—as the divinely favored compromise between Roman Catholicism's gaudy trappings and Genevan Calvinism's indecorous nakedness, the more skeptical Donne implores Christ to reveal the true Church, which for Donne cannot finally be equated with any temporal institution.

The conception of the Church as a woman is a traditional conceit grounded in biblical passages from both the Old and New Testaments, and the comparison of Roman Catholicism and Protestantism in terms of rival women is a Reformation commonplace, repeated both in recondite theological studies and in popular polemical works. Neither Herbert nor Donne needed a source beyond his own highly emblematic and allusive imagination to suggest the appropriateness of these traditional tropes. But what has not been recognized is that both poems are probably indebted to the conflict of Protestantism (as represented by Una) and Roman Catholicism (as represented by Duessa) in the first book of Spenser's *The Faerie Queene.* More specifically, both poems are probably influenced by Spenser's revelation of Una as the Church Triumphant in *The Faerie Queene*, 1.12.22. Recognition of the Spenserian material as an important analogue to the two seventeenth-century poems helps clarify more precisely the rich tradition from which they develop and provides a base against which to gauge their innovative transformations of an image rife with significance in the common quest for true religion. The image of the Bride of the Apocalypse functions for all three poets as a mirror of their own religio-political assumptions.

Book 1 of *The Faerie Queene* ends with the betrothal of the Redcrosse Knight to Una. This betrothal, as Michael O'Connell explains, "conflates history and sacred myth, the accession of Elizabeth and the mystic marriage of the Lamb."[1] Una, who at once represents such abstractions as Wisdom, Truth, Faith, and Protestantism, is finally revealed to symbolize also the Church Triumphant. And in her engagement to Redcrosse, Spenser signifies that England has finally achieved the divine mission of discovering true religion and now assumes the role of its defender, especially against the peril of Roman Catholicism. The continuing danger to true religion posed by Roman Catholicism is indicated by Duessa's false claim of betrothal to Redcrosse at the end of book 1. As O'Connell remarks, "Duessa's threat that her cause 'shall find friends, if need required soe' is of course an accurate reflection of the peril in which England and Elizabeth stood from the forces of Catholic Europe at her accession" (p. 63).

In the evolving and contrasting images of Una, Spenser

1. *Mirror and Veil: The Historical Dimension of Spenser's "Faerie Queene"* (Chapel Hill: University of North Carolina Press, 1977), p. 63. The subsequent quotation from O'Connell is cited parenthetically in the text by page number.

visualizes the political condition of Protestant England. When Una is initially presented in the first canto of *The Faerie Queene*, her face is hidden "Under a vele, that wimpled was full low, / And ouer all a blacke stole she did throw / As one that inly mourned" (1.1.4).[2] But at her betrothal she emerges "As bright as doth the morning starre appeare / Out of the East" (1.12.21). She lays her "mournefull stole aside" and throws away her "widow-like sad wimple" and reveals herself in all her beauty:

> And on her now a garment she did weare,
> All lily white, withouten spot, or pride,
> That seemd like silke and siluer wouen neare,
> But neither silke nor siluer therein did appeare.

> The blazing brightnesse of her beauties beame,
> And glorious light of her sunshyny face
> To tell, were as to striue against the streame.
> My ragged rimes are all too rude and bace,
> Her heauenly lineaments for to enchace. (1.12.22–23)

What identifies Una with the Church Triumphant here is the allusion to the account of the bridal raiment in St. John the Divine's vision of the marriage of Christ the Lamb to his cleansed and completed Church: "for the mariage of the Lambe is come, and his wife hathe made herselfe readie. And to her was granted, that she shulde be araied in fyne linen, and shining: for the fine linen is the righteousnes of Saintes" (Rev. 19:7b-8).[3] The identification of Una with the Bride of the Apocalypse is complemented by the repeated associations of her rival Duessa with the Whore of Babylon, described in Revelation 17:4 as "araied in purple and skarlat, and guilded with golde and precious stones, and pearles, and had a cup of gold in her hand, ful of abominations, and filthines of her fornication." Moreover, the description of Una also echoes passages in the Old Testament that were related typologically and allegorically to the marriage

2. *The Faerie Queene: Book One*, ed. Frederick Morgan Padelford, vol. 1 in *The Works of Edmund Spenser: A Variorum Edition*, ed. Edwin Greenlaw et al., 10 vols. (Baltimore: Johns Hopkins Press, 1932-1949). All quotations from *The Faerie Queene* are from this edition and are cited parenthetically in the text by book, canto, and stanza number.
3. All biblical quotations are from *The Geneva Bible: A Facsimile of the 1560 Edition*, intro. by Lloyd E. Berry (Madison: University of Wisconsin Press, 1969), with *i*, *j*, *u*, and *v* regularized and contractions expanded, and are cited parenthetically in the text.

of Christ and the Church envisioned by St. John. The most important of these are found in the Song of Songs, whose erotic celebration of betrothal was commonly interpreted by Christians as a marriage song of Christ and His Church. Just as Una's bridal raiment is "withouten spot," so the Church in the Song of Songs is, according to the Bridegroom, "all faire, my love, and there is no spot in thee" (4:7). Spenser's insistence that the bridal garment "seemd like silke and siluer wouen neare" but actually contained neither silk nor silver is probably intended to distinguish Una both from the Whore of Babylon and from the bride of Yahweh, the harlot of Jerusalem. The latter is described in Ezekiel: "Thus wast thou dect with golde and silver, and thy raiment was of fine linen, and silke and broydered worke: thou didest eat fine floure, and hony, and oyle, and thou wast very beautiful, and thou didest grow up into a kingdome" (16:13). But whereas Una is without pride, Yahweh's bride, in the words of Ezekiel, "didest trust in thine owne beautie, and plaied the harlot, because of thy renome, and hast powred out thy fornicacions on every one that passed by" (16:15). The bride of Yahweh finds her New Testament fulfillment in the Whore of Babylon, who is similarly associated with "ware of golde, and silver, and of precious stone, and of pearles, and of fine linen, and of purple, and of silke, and of skarlet" (Rev. 18:12).

Although the conception of the Church as a woman and the contrast of Protestantism and Roman Catholicism in terms of rival women are so traditional as to make one hesitate to claim *The Faerie Queene* as a source for Donne's similar conceptions in his sonnet, there are nevertheless a number of reasons for thinking that Donne had Spenser particularly in mind as he composed his poem. Not only do the two works share the common image of the Bride of the Apocalypse and the common technique of contrast, but their descriptions of the Bride in terms of brightness and light are also similar. Spenser emphasizes Una's "celestiall sight" and "The blazing brightnesse of her beauties beame, / And glorious light of her sunshyny face" (1.12.23), and Donne opens his sonnet with the plea, "Show me deare Christ, thy spouse, so bright and cleare."[4] Moreover, Donne's concep-

---

4. All quotations from Donne's poetry are from *The Complete Poetry of John Donne*, ed. John T. Shawcross, The Anchor Seventeenth-Century Series (Garden City, N.Y.: Doubleday, 1967), and are cited parenthetically by line numbers in the text.

tion of the Reformed Church as one that "rob'd and tore / Laments and mournes in Germany and here" (ll. 3–4) may glance at Spenser's early characterization of Una as veiled and wimpled, robed in a black stole "As one that inly mourned" (1.1.4). But most suggestive of a connection between Donne's poem and *The Faerie Queene* is the sonnet's questioning whether Christ's spouse dwells "with us, or like adventuring knights / First travaile we to seeke and then make love?" (ll. 9–10). This curious rhetorical question is usually ignored by commentators on the poem or dismissed lamely as an unusual and unflattering reference to the courtly love tradition. It seems to me, however, that this couplet, placed pivotally to begin the sonnet's sestet, is crucial. It is Donne's acknowledgment of Spenser's earlier quest for true religion—a quest that Spenser depicts in terms of courtly romance—and a recognition of the eroticism of that quest, an eroticism that Donne will still more daringly exploit in the conclusion to his poem. But even as Donne in effect pays homage to the earlier poet, he also qualifies the tribute with irony and implies considerable skepticism as to the validity of the epic poet's claim to have discovered true religion in Elizabethan England.

If Spenser could confidently associate the Church Triumphant with Protestantism, Donne emphatically could not. Donne's doubt is the impetus for his sonnet, the very structure of which encapsulates the poet's skepticism. In a series of questions, the implied answers to which are negative, Donne asks which is the true religion. "What, is it she, which on the other shore / Goes richly painted?" (ll. 2–3), he queries, referring to Roman Catholicism. Or, he continues, is it she who "rob'd and tore / Laments and mournes in Germany and here?" (ll. 3–4), referring to Protestantism. The characterization of Roman Catholicism as "richly painted" may hint at the Reformation equation of Rome with the Whore of Babylon, but it primarily functions to distinguish the sumptuousness of Roman ritual from the plainness of most Protestant worship. Similarly, the characterization of Protestantism as mournful and torn may suggest obliquely a resemblance between the Reformed Church and the afflicted daughter of Zion in Lamentations, but more significantly it acknowledges the bitter divisions within Protestantism.[5] In any case, the point of Donne's questions is not to identify either Roman Catholicism or Protestantism with biblical analogues, but rather to express doubt as to whether either Roman Catholicism or Protestantism can genuinely claim to be Christ's spouse. What both the "richly painted" Church of Rome and the mournful and dishevelled Church of "Germany and here" have in common is that they are distinctly unbridelike and very different from Christ's spouse as described in either Song of Songs or Revelation.

Donne's skepticism also dictates the other questions in the octet, questions that go to the heart of the debate between Roman Catholicism and Protestantism in the late sixteenth and early seventeenth century. Indeed, Donne's method here is extraordinarily witty and effective. Echoing in his queries the acrimonious charges each competitor brought against the claims of the other, Donne suffuses the religious debate with an irony born of profound skepticism. "Sleepes she a thousand, then peepes up one yeare?" (l. 5), Donne asks, raising the question that Roman Catholics and anti-Puritans leveled against some Protestant's purported recovery of primitive discipline after a millennium of Roman hegemony. "Is she selfe truth and errs? now new, now'outwore?" (l. 6), he continues, now echoing the Protestant attack against Rome's pretense to infallibility and doctrinal continuity even in the face of the historical record of numerous reversals and revisions of doctrine. The various claims and counterclaims of the opposing Churches are placed

5. Helen Gardner sees a similarity between the lamenting and mournful woman and the Church in Lamentations and uses this perception to buttress her argument about the poem's date: "I would suggest that Donne has seen a parallel between the captivity of Israel and the total collapse of the Protestants after the defeat of the Elector in the battle of the White Mountain, outside Prague, on 29 October 1620" (Gardner, ed., *John Donne: The Divine Poems*, 2d ed. [Oxford: Clarendon Press, 1978], p. 124). A date of late 1620 for "Show me deare Christ" is not unreasonable, but, as David Novarr remarks of Gardner's suggestion, "Her evidence is not compelling" (*The Disinterred Muse: Donne's Texts and Contexts* [Ithaca, N.Y.: Cornell University Press, 1980], p. 135). Cf. Donne's depiction of Protestantism with that in Dekker's *The Whore of Babylon* (1607), a play heavily influenced by *The Faerie Queene*, where Truth, a lovely young woman representing Anglicanism, is discovered "in sad abiliments; vncrowned: her haire disheueld, and sleeping on a Rock" (*The Dramatic Works of Thomas Dekker*, ed. Fredson Bowers, 2 vols. [Cambridge: Cambridge University Press, 1955], 2:500).

in perspective in the culminating question of the octet: "Doth she,'and did she, and shall she evermore / On one, on seaven, or on no hill appeare?" (ll. 7–8). In other words, can Christ's spouse be identified with the Old Testament temple built by Solomon on Mount Moriah? Or with the institution established on Rome's seven hills? Or with the Reformed Church that emerged near Geneva's lake? The implied answer to this rhetorical question, as to the others, is negative. Donne resists equating the Church Triumphant with any of these visible Churches, which are seen in their temporal discontinuity as merely historical and transient.

The octet-sestet division in the poem is obscure because lines 9 and 10 are, like lines 2–8, also in the form of a question, the resolution of the poem seemingly not beginning until line 11. The apparent absence of the conventional structural division results in additional emphasis on the final lines, the most striking in the sonnet. But the question of lines 9 and 10 is fundamentally different from the earlier questions and properly marks the poem's turn toward resolution. The earlier questions asked whether any of the visible Churches could be identified with Christ's spouse. Beginning in line 9, the focus of the poem changes from whether the competing Churches are the true Church to a consideration somewhat different and more basic: given the fact that none of the rival Churches can be identified with Christ's spouse, how can the true Church be found?

The question "Dwells she with us, or like adventuring knights / First travaile we to seeke and then make love?" (ll. 9–10) acknowledges the Spenserian quest and introduces the sexual imagery that dominates the poem's conclusion, but it does so with a literal-mindedness calculated to render the earlier quest and its suppositions more than slightly ridiculous. The disingenuous question reduces the allegorical to the literal, a practice that Donne will develop even further in the final lines of the poem. Of crucial significance, the question of lines 9 and 10 also implies the possibility that true religion may not be found in an earthly institution at all, that it may rather reside in a realm beyond the visible. Rather than a physical reality to be embraced in this world, true religion may be a heavenly ideal to be sought through restless travel and great travail. The quest for Christ's spouse may be an arduous pilgrimage, the sweet consummation of which is to be achieved only after the dangers and difficulties of life.

The concluding plea, requesting the "kind husband" Christ to "Betray . . . thy spouse to our sights" (l. 11), daringly takes literally the metaphor of Christ the bridegroom: "let myne amorous soule court thy mild Dove, / Who is most trew, and pleasing to thee, then / When she'is embrac'd and open to most men" (ll. 12–14). These lines express Donne's passionate longing for a truly catholic Church free of division and strife, a "mild Dove . . . embrac'd and open to most men." But the explicitly sexual imagery here has understandably shocked many readers and has led to William Kerrigan's charge that "The last passage [of the sonnet], beautiful as it is, nearly crumbles. Donne almost loses control of his reader's imagination and therefore of his intentional meaning."[6] It seems to me, however, that Donne's conclusion is deliberately shocking and that its shock value is part of its intentional meaning. Donne's unsettling anthropomorphism here intentionally recoils on itself and intentionally subverts the very tradition it simultaneously evokes. In so doing, it resolves the question at the heart of the poem: how does one discover the true Church?

Donne's anthropomorphism reflects, of course, the traditional interpretation of the Song of Songs as a love song anticipating in the language of desire the union of Christ and his Church at the end of time. This traditional interpretation views the eroticism of the Song of Songs as a particularly gratifying instance of God's graceful condescension to human understanding. For example, one early seventeenth-century commentator, John Dove, marvels that God "stoopeth so low as to accommodate himself to the *fleshy terms and words of carnall love for us*, and by how much the more by speaking he is humbled, by so much we by understanding are exalted."[7] Donne's sonnet

---

6. "The Fearful Accommodations of John Donne," *English Literary Renaissance* 4 (1974): 359. Cf. the comment of Frank Kermode in *John Donne*, Writers and Their Works, no. 86 (London: Longmans, 1957): "Perhaps we dislike this metaphor (Christ as *mari complaisant*) because the image of the Church as the Bride is no longer absolutely commonplace; but having accepted the image we are still unwilling to accept its development, even though we see that the main point is the *glorious* difference of this from a merely human marriage. Something is asked of us we can no longer easily give" (p. 39).

7. *The Conversion of Solomon* (London, 1613), p. 169. Quoted in Heather A.

evokes the Song of Songs in the phrase "mild Dove" and in the image of openness, which echo Song of Songs 5:2: "Open unto me, my sister, my love, my doove, my undefiled." But, as David Novarr notes, even as Donne incorporates the imagery of the Song, he "plays down typological interpretation . . . and, taking advantage of the stereotype of the earthly jealous husband, startles us with a Christ-as-husband whose magnanimity and generosity extend to sharing his wife."[8] Thus, although the anthropomorphism of the Song of Songs may license Donne's eroticism, it does not account for the sonnet's shocking literalism.

The sonnet's conclusion is uncomfortable precisely because the "pseudo-logical exactitude" of its imagery, to use Kerrigan's apt phrase, translates heavenly love into earthly love in a peculiarly graphic manner.[9] Christ is implored to "Betray"

R. Asals, *Equivocal Predication: George Herbert's Way to God* (Toronto: University of Toronto Press, 1981), p. 87.

8. *The Disinterred Muse*, p. 141. Two discussions of the poem stress heavily the typological imagery: Stanley Stewart, *The Enclosed Garden: The Tradition and the Image in Seventeenth-Century Poetry* (Madison: University of Wisconsin Press, 1966), pp. 19–21; and Robert S. Jackson, *John Donne's Christian Vocation* (Evanston, Ill.: Northwestern University Press, 1970), pp. 146–80. However, Stewart's interesting discussion is vitiated by his assumption that "the speaker is himself the Bride of Christ" (p. 20), while Jackson's reading of the poem is so burdened by frequently inappropriate biblical analogues as to be incoherent. Arthur Pollard, on the other hand, attempts to explain the poem's eroticism in terms of Donne's depiction of the Church as "a spiritual mystery expressed through the most tender but also ineluctable of human relationships, a mystery whose greatness is emphasized in that, for Donne, it can only be adequately expressed by inverting the normal order of that relationship, by substituting for a jealously protected exclusiveness a comprehensive inclusiveness" ("John Donne: 'Show me deare Christ, thy spouse, so bright and cleare,'" *Critical Survey* 6 [1973]: 19). But Pollard's explanation fails to confront the central issue of the poem's shock value.

9. "The Fearful Accommodations of John Donne," p. 358. The deliberately graphic and shocking quality of the sonnet's conclusion may be illustrated most clearly by comparing the expression in the sonnet with the more decorous expression of similar ideas in Donne's sermons, where the preacher frequently dwells on the relationship of human marriage and divine marriage, depicting the former as a "type" of the latter. See especially the sermon preached at the wedding of Mistress Margaret Washington on 30 May 1621, where Donne imagines the heavenly marriage: "I shall see all the beauty, and all the glory of all the Saints of God, and love them all, and know that the Lamb loves them too, without jealousie, on his part, or theirs, or mine, and so be maried *in aeternum*, for ever, without interruption, or diminution, or change of affections" (*The Sermons of John Donne*, ed. George R. Potter and Evelyn M. Simpson, 10 vols. [Berkeley: University of California Press, 1953–1962], 3:254). On Donne's the-

his spouse who is "most trewe" when she is most promiscuous; Christ finds her especially "pleasing" when she, striking a pornographic pose, is immodestly open and embraced by multitudes. But there is method to Donne's deliberately shocking anthropomorphism. The force of the sonnet's paradoxes is to juxtapose the sacred and the profane and thereby to point up the difficulty of imagining heavenly love in terms of earthly love and, by analogy, of conceiving the Church Triumphant in terms of any visible Church. Donne's plea "Show me deare Christ, thy spouse" can finally not be answered by reference to any of the rival women, but only by reference to a heavenly love that becomes deeply shocking when translated into its earthly equivalences. Just as Donne's passionate literalization of the notion of Christ as bridegroom betrays its own excess, so the attempts to identify the competing Churches with Christ's spouse are similarly revealed as ludicrous. The daring and moving conclusion to the sonnet beautifully expresses Donne's sincere desire for communion with Christ's spouse the Church, but the extended sexual conceit simultaneously exposes the poet's recognition of the preposterous irony involved in any quest for true religion that identifies Christ's spouse with a temporal institution. The courtship of the "amorous soule" and the "mild Dove" can take place only in some future time and place: "then / when she'is embrac'd and open to most men."

The apocalyptic reading of "Show me deare Christ," locating true religion in the life to come, is strengthened by the poem's association with "Since she whome I lovd," the Holy Sonnet occasioned by the death of Donne's wife. Neither poem was published in the seventeenth century, and each survives in a single manuscript, the Westmoreland.[10] Tied together by their

---

ology of marriage, see Kathryn R. Kremen, *The Imagination of the Resurrection: The Poetic Continuity of a Religious Motif in Donne, Blake, and Yeats* (Lewisburg, Pa.: Bucknell University Press, 1972), pp. 97–107.

10. The poems were discovered by Sir Edmund Gosse and first published in Gosse's *The Life and Letters of John Donne*, 2 vols. (London: Heinemann, 1899). If "Since she whome I lovd" and "Show me deare Christ" are companion pieces, then both poems may have been written fairly soon after the death of Anne Donne in August of 1617, though—as Gardner observes—the sonnet occasioned by her death may have been written somewhat later. For a brief discussion of the relationship of the two sonnets and an argument that links them to the other Holy Sonnets, see Don M. Ricks, "The Westmoreland Manuscript and the Order of Donne's 'Holy Sonnets,'" *Studies in Philology* 63 (1966): 187–202.

common contrast of human and divine love and by the longing for union with spouses, the poems may well be companion pieces: "Since she whome I lovd" mourning the loss of an earthly love, "Show me deare Christ" yearning for a heavenly courtship. Read in concert with "Since she whome I lovd," "Show me deare Christ" might be seen as expressing a plaintive death-wish. God having prematurely taken his spouse, the poet pleads to be shown Christ's spouse, an event that will also occasion a mystical reunion with his dead wife, whose soul has been "early into heaven ravished" (l. 3).

Whatever the relationship of "Since she whome I lovd" and "Show me deare Christ," Donne in the latter poem resists the tendency of both Roman Catholics and Protestants to confuse the Church Militant with the Church Triumphant. His refusal to identify the Church Triumphant with a temporal institution is characteristic of what Dominic Baker-Smith describes as Donne's "acute awareness of the human and his intuitive grasp of history" and his reluctance "to parade the human as the divine, the temporal as the eternal."[11] In regard to the claims of the rival Churches of the sonnet, Donne takes his own advice in "Satyre III" to "doubt wisely" (l. 77). As he says in a christening sermon, the earthly Church "is in a pilgrimage, and therefore here is no setling." In contrast is the heavenly Church, which grows "by continuall accesse of holy *Soules*": "to setle such a glorious Church, without spot, or wrinkle, holy to *himselfe*, is reserved for the Triumphant time when she shall be in possession of that beauty, which Christ foresaw in her, long before when he said, *Thou art all faire my love, and there is no spot in thee*."[12] In Donne's sonnet as well, the consummation of the Christian's love for Christ's spouse may be attained only in the Triumphant time, when the "kind husband" Christ will reveal his glorious bride "to our sights."

One of the most striking aspects of "Show me deare Christ" is that although Donne disputes the claims of the competing Churches to identity with Christ's spouse, he does not deny that they are legitimate Churches. This tolerance is consistent with the anti-authoritarian position he takes in "Satyre III" and

11. "John Donne's *Critique of True Religion*," in *John Donne: Essays in Celebration*, ed. A. J. Smith (London: Methuen, 1972), p. 415.

12. Donne, *Sermons*, ed. Potter and Simpson, 5:126.

in numerous sermons, and it is at one with other liberal positions that he espoused, including, for example, the humanist beliefs that the virtuous ancients may be saved and that unbaptized children are not damned. His conviction that all Churches have some share in the divine light is expressed in a letter to Henry Goodyere. "You know," Donne writes, "I never fettered nor imprisoned the word Religion; not straightening it Frierly, *ad Religiones facititias*, (as the *Romans* call well their orders of Religion) nor immuring it in a *Rome*, or *Wittemburg*, or a *Geneva*; they are all virtuall beams of one Sun."[13] In another letter to Goodyere, Donne acknowledges that both the Roman and Protestant Churches are "diseased and infected," but affirms that they are nevertheless "channels of God's mercies . . . sister teats of his graces." He gives voice to his longing for a universal Church in the *Essays in Divinity*, where he declares,

> I do zealously wish, that the whole catholick Church, were reduced to such Unity and agreement, in the form and profession Established, in any one of these Churches (though ours were principally to be wished) which have not by any additions destroyed the foundation and possibility of salvation in Christ Jesus; That then the Church, discharged of disputations, and misapprehensions, and this defensive warr, might contemplate Christ clearly and uniformely.[14]

Donne's refusal in his sonnet to identify either of the rival women with Christ's resplendent spouse is a negative expression of this positive desire for a unified Church that transcends sectarian and national boundaries.

Helen Gardner sees Donne's liberalism as quintessentially Anglican, for, she remarks, "The Anglican, at this period, differed from the Roman Catholic and the Calvinist in not holding a doctrine of the Church which compelled him to 'unchurch' other Christians."[15] But, as Novarr points out, while Gardner's

13. *Letters to Severall Persons of Honour (1651)*, intro. by M. Thomas Hester (Delmar, N.Y.: Scholars' Facsimiles and Reprints, 1977), p. 29. The quotation immediately following is from p. 102 of this edition.
14. *Essays in Divinity*, ed. Evelyn M. Simpson (Oxford: Clarendon Press, 1952), pp. 51–52. On Donne's religious tolerance, see—in addition to the essay by Dominic Baker-Smith cited above and the discussions by Gardner and Novarr—David Chanoff, "The Biographical Context of Donne's Sonnet on the Church," *American Benedictine Review* 32 (1981): 378–86.
15. *John Donne: The Divine Poems*, p. 122.

description of Anglican tolerance does characterize some liberal Anglicans like Donne, "others of them thought that a wise and goodly reformation called for an assertive claim for exclusivity and a doctrinal and ecclesiastical dogmatism very different from Hooker's stance in the *Laws of Ecclesiastical Polity*."[16] Indeed, Donne's liberalism may have been an impediment to his rise in the hierarchy of the Church of England, explaining why, despite his manifest abilities, he was not elevated to a bishopric. In the sonnet, the extent (and limits) of Donne's latitudinarianism is indicated by his vision of an Apocalyptic Church open to most (though not all) men. In any case, the increasingly bitter division of the Church of England into Anglican and Puritan factions in the 1620s and 1630s led to a marked rise in rhetorical heat and in intolerance. As the battle lines between conservative Anglicans and Puritans and separatists became firmly drawn on the grounds of Church order and government, the religious debate in England became more and more rancorous. This intolerance can be found even in the work of George Herbert, who has persistently been seen as a sweet-tempered, otherworldly contemplative, isolated from the bitter ecclesiastical and political turmoil of his day.

Herbert's "The British Church" is often regarded as merely a graceful celebration of the Church of England as the *via media* and as simply expressing one individual's preference in liturgy and form. What has generally been overlooked, however, is the network of biblical allusions that condemn Rome and Geneva and establish the British Church as simultaneously a temporal institution and the New Jerusalem of the apocalyptic future.[17]

16. *The Disinterred Muse*, p. 137.

17. This network of biblical allusions was first discussed in Claude J. Summers and Ted-Larry Pebworth, "Herbert, Vaughan, and Public Concerns in Private Modes," *George Herbert Journal* 3 (Fall 1979/Spring 1980): 1–21, especially pp. 4–8. The present discussion of "The British Church" is heavily indebted to the earlier essay and to the discussion of the poem in Claude J. Summers and Ted-Larry Pebworth, "The Politics of *The Temple:* 'The British Church' and 'The Familie,'" *George Herbert Journal* 8 (Fall 1984): 1–14. For conventional readings of the poem as merely a playful celebration of the *via media*, see, for example, Joseph H. Summers, *George Herbert: His Religion and Art* (Cambridge: Harvard University Press, 1954), p. 189; and Edmund Miller, *Drudgerie Divine: The Rhetoric of God and Man in George Herbert* (Salzburg: Institut für Anglistik, 1979), pp. 190–92. For the most extreme reading of the poem as merely expressing one individual's preference in liturgy and form, see Richard Strier, "History, Criticism, and Herbert: A Polemical Note," *Papers on*

Herbert's poem is similar to Donne's Holy Sonnet (and to *The Faerie Queene*) in that both use the image of the Bride of the Apocalypse and both conceive of competing Churches in terms of rival women. But they are finally very different, for whereas Donne questions whether either of the rival women in the sonnet can be identified with Christ's spouse, Herbert begins with the assumption that Christ's spouse is the British Church. And whereas Donne and Spenser associate the Church of England with Protestantism generally and create a binary opposition of Protestantism and Roman Catholicism, Herbert contrasts three visible Churches—Anglican, Genevan, and Roman—and locates the British Church as far from Geneva as from Rome, double-moated and protected from the peril posed by each. Herbert's conception of Anglicanism as significantly different from Genevan Protestantism reflects a crucial difference in the religio-political climate in which his and Donne's poems were composed. Beneath the calm and playful surface of Herbert's apparently innocuous aesthetic evaluation of the rival women is a forceful condemnation of both the Roman and the Genevan Churches. While Donne's skeptical "Show me deare Christ" is an expression of liberal tolerance, Herbert's affirmative "The British Church" is a statement of conservative reaction.

Like Una in *The Faerie Queene* and Christ's spouse in Donne's sonnet, Herbert's British Church is depicted as a conspicuously beautiful woman. "Beautie in thee takes up her place," Herbert declares, "And dates her letters from thy face / When she doth write" (ll. 4–6).[18] But Herbert sublimates the eroticism implicit in Spenser and unsettlingly explicit in Donne by presenting the British Church as a maternal figure. "I Joy, deare Mother," he writes, "when I view / Thy perfect lineaments and hue / Both sweet and bright" (ll. 1–3). This description of the maternal Church is reminiscent of both Spenser's and Donne's (and St. John's) emphasis on the Bride's brightness. In addition, the phrase "perfect lineaments" may intentionally

---

Language and Literature 17 (1981): 347–52. Strier's reading of the poem as condemning Rome but not Geneva is unconvincing.

18. All quotations from Herbert's English works are from *The Works of George Herbert*, ed. F. E. Hutchinson (1941; corrected rpt. Oxford: Clarendon Press, 1945). The quotations are cited parenthetically in the text, the poems by line numbers, the prose works by page numbers.

echo Spenser's reference to Una's "heauenly lineaments," and thus may deliberately betray Herbert's specific indebtedness to *The Faerie Queene*.

   The notion of the Church as mother was deeply resonant for Herbert. When, according to Walton, Herbert received a death-bed visit from Edmund Duncon, the poet requested Duncon to pray with him: "which being granted, Mr. *Duncon* asked him, *what Prayers?* to which, Mr. *Herberts* answer was, *O Sir, the Prayers of my Mother, the Church of* England, *no other Prayers are equal to them!*"[19] One reason the concept of the Church as mother was so meaningful for Herbert is that, as Heather Asals points out, Magdalene, the namesake of his mother Magdalene Herbert, "had been throughout the Middle Ages an image of the Church."[20] But the depiction of the British Church as "deare Mother" also reflects a concerted Anglican strategy of advocating devotion and submission to the Established Church and its ceremonies by characterizing it as a maternal figure. Some years after Herbert's use of the phrase, this conservative Anglican strategy was scathingly attacked by Milton in *Animadversions.* Complaining of prelatic use of the metaphor, Milton accuses the Anglican bishops of trying "to impresse deeply into weak, and superstitious fancies the awfull notion of a mother, that hereby they might cheat them into a blinde and implicite obedience to whatsoever they shall decree, or think fit."[21] No less than the bishops' metaphor, Herbert's gentle trope is also calculated to urge obedience to the Established order.

   Herbert's "deare Mother" Church is identified with Christ's spouse by means of the allusion to Revelation 19:7–8 in the description of the Church's attire: "A fine aspect in fit aray, / Neither too mean, nor yet too gay" (ll. 7–8). Like the description of the British Church, the raiment of the Bride of the Apocalypse is of "fine" workmanship, and it is costly, having been purchased with blood—both the blood of the sacrificed Lamb and the blood of those who have been martyred for belief in Him. Yet the garment is of essentially modest material, linen,

   19. *The Life of Mr. George Herbert*, in *The Compleat Walton*, ed. Geoffrey Keynes (London: Nonesuch Press, 1929), p. 442.
   20. *Equivocal Predication*, p. 97.
   21. In *Complete Prose Works of John Milton*, ed. Don M. Wolfe (New Haven: Yale University Press, 1953), 1:728.

rather than of a showy, exotic fabric like silk; and it is adorned not with gold or silver or precious stones, but only with the dazzling whiteness of its dearly purchased purity. In suggesting the biblical passage in his description of Anglicanism, Herbert ingeniously but unmistakably identifies the localized and historical British Church with the universal and eternal Church Triumphant.

The "Outlandish looks" (l. 10) of the foreign Churches may not compare with the "fine aspect in fit aray" of the British Church, for, Herbert says, "they either painted are, / Or else undrest" (ll. 11-12). In these lines, Herbert echoes commonplace Anglican objections to the gaudiness of Roman ritual and the indecorous plainness of Genevan worship. Donne's sonnet similarly presents the Roman Church as "richly painted" and the Protestant Church as dishevelled, and in his sermons Donne speaks of Rome as "*a painted church*" and of Geneva as "*a naked church.*"[22] But "The British Church" goes far beyond "Show me deare Christ" when Herbert, again by means of biblical allusion, connects Rome and Geneva with apocalyptic destruction. Whereas Donne's sonnet deflects identification of the rival women with biblical analogues by placing the suggestive descriptions in the hypothetical form of questions, Herbert's poem encourages such identifications by its straightforward present-indicative statements. Moreover, although Herbert's allusions are fairly subtle, they gain added force by virtue of their structural importance to the poem, which, like many poems in *The Temple*, reflects a double perspective, being rooted in the present but also transcending the temporal to refer to Last Things. By contrasting Christ's spouse with the earthly Churches, Donne's sonnet incorporates a dual perspective as well, but in "Show me deare Christ" these two perspectives are carefully delineated: it is clear that the earthly institutions are merely temporal—indeed, their temporality is the point of their contrast with the Church Triumphant. In "The British Church," however, the earthly Churches are seen—and judged—simultaneously from the aspects of history and eternity.

The description of Roman Catholicism as a painted tempt-

22. *Sermons*, ed. Potter and Simpson, 1:246, 6:284.

ress emphasizes the commonplace Reformation charge of idolatry:

> She on the hills, which wantonly
> Allureth all in hope to be
>   By her preferr'd,
> Hath kiss'd so long her painted shrines,
> That ev'n her face by kissing shines,
>   For her reward. (ll. 13–18)

But Herbert's account also identifies Roman Catholicism with the Whore of Babylon as described in Revelation 17. That temptress sits on a seven-headed beast representing, according to an angel exegete, the "seven mountaines" of the city (Rev. 17:9) and is lewdly arrayed in rich colors and precious stones. An angelic doomsayer expounds on her allurements, stressing the earthly rewards of power and wealth that she offers: "the Kings of the earth have committed fornication with her, and the marchants of the earth are waxed riche of the abundance of her pleasures."

In identifying Roman Catholicism with the Whore of Babylon, Herbert subscribes to an established and popular Protestant tradition, one that the militantly Protestant Spenser incorporates into *The Faerie Queene* and one that Herbert explicitly evokes in "The Church Militant" (ll. 156–236). The annotators of the Geneva Bible, first issued in 1560, make the connection unmistakably clear. Although they identify the beast on which the Whore sits as ancient Rome, they interpret the richly dressed temptress as "the newe Rome which is the Papistrie, whose crueltie and blood sheding is declared by skarlat . . . . the Antichrist, that is, the Pope with the whole bodie of his filthie creatures . . . whose beautie onely standeth in outwarde pompe & impudencie and craft like a strumpet" (Rev. 17, notes *d* and *f*). What is remarkable about Herbert's picture of Roman Catholicism in "The British Church" is that without indulging in the vitriol of sectarian polemic, it nonetheless damns its subject as thoroughly as the Genevan annotators had done. Moreover, by situating the Roman Church within the context of St. John's apocalyptic vision, Herbert is able, without sacrificing the calm sweetness of his poem's surface, not only to criticize that institution in his own day but also to look forward to its utter destruction in an age to come. In the

Last Days, the Whore will be judged by God and her fate will be terrible: "Therefore shal her plagues come at one day, death, and sorowe, and famine, and she shalbe burnt with fyre" (Rev. 18:8).

While Herbert shares with Genevans a scorn of Rome as a painted temptress, he convicts Calvinism in its turn for an inverted pride in deliberate bareness:

> She in the valley is so shie
> Of dressing, that her hair doth lie
> > About her eares:
> While she avoids her neighbours pride,
> She wholly goes on th' other side,
> > And nothing wears. (ll. 19–24)

Herbert's characterization here is vaguely reminiscent of Donne's description of Geneva in "Satyre III" as "plaine, simple, sullen, yong, / Contemptuous, yet unhansome" (ll. 50–51). The condemnation of Geneva's nakedness is similarly reminiscent of Lancelot Andrewes's contention that worship ought not to be an "uncovered and bare-faced religion."[23] Herbert's attack on Geneva in "The British Church" is further illuminated by *Musae Responsoriae* 25, his epigram "On the use of rites," which employs clothing imagery to a similar purpose:

> Long ago, when Caesar
> First set foot from his ships
> Upon our isle,
> Noting all the natives of the place
> Living without clothes, he cried,
> "O victory is mine!
> It will be simple,
> It is assured!"
>
> And so the Puritans,
> While they are covetous of a
> Lord's bride bare of sacred rites,
> And while they wish
> All things regressed
> To their fathers' barbaric state,
> Lay her, entirely

---

23. *Ninety-Six Sermons*, 5 vols. (Oxford: J. H. Parker, 1841–1843), 1:162.

> Ignorant of clothing, bare to conquest
> By Satan and her enemies.[24]

In "The British Church," naked Geneva's neglect of ritual and authority similarly constitutes a dangerous regression to barbarism that exposes her to Satan's ravishment.

St. John's Revelation offers no apposite context for Herbert's picture of Geneva as the underdressed woman of the valley, but one of Christ's parables referring to Last Things does. Significantly, this parable—recounted in Matthew 22:1-14 and concerned with the feast that a king prepares to celebrate his son's marriage—is connected by marginal cross-references to St. John's account of the wedding of the Lamb in the most popularly used Bibles of Herbert's day: the Geneva translation, the 1590 edition of the Vulgate, and the Authorized Version of 1611. Concerned with the Second Coming, the parable speaks primarily to the rejection of Christ by the Jewish nation and his acceptance by Gentile nations; but one of its incidents is stated in terms of human grooming and is apropos to Herbert's poem. While presiding over his son's marriage feast, the king is angered by the appearance of a guest not properly attired in "a wedding garment" (v. 11). The improper dress of the wedding guest is perceived as a mark of disrespect toward both the host and the occasion, a dramatic context that perfectly fits Herbert's attitude toward Geneva in "The British Church." Again, without sacrificing his calm and sweet tone, Herbert is able through allusive context to convey an authoritative rebuke. Just as the identification of Roman Catholicism with the Whore of Babylon inevitably looks forward to that Church's divinely appointed destruction, so the linking of Genevan Calvinism with the improperly garbed wedding guest of Christ's parable also implies that Reformed Church's equally unpleasant fate. The judgment against the disrespectful guest is swift and terrible: "Then said the king to the servants, Binde him hand and fote, and take him away, and cast him into utter darkenes, there shal be weping and gnasshing of teeth" (v. 13).

24. In *The Latin Poetry of George Herbert*, trans. Mark McCloskey and Paul R. Murphy (Athens: Ohio University Press, 1965), pp. 36–39. Subsequent quotations and translations of *Musae Responsoriae* are from this edition and are cited parenthetically by page numbers in the text.

Herbert's antipathy toward Geneva in "The British Church" may seem surprising in light of the recent studies that discover Calvinist doctrine in Herbert's work.[25] But the fact that Herbert was influenced by Calvinism ought not to qualify the poet as a closet Puritan. Nearly every religious thinker of the English Renaissance felt the influence of Calvin to some degree, and the Established Church—though purposely vague on those questions such as election, predestination, and the nature and extent of grace that divided continental Protestants, including Geneva itself—may fairly be described as Calvinist in its dominant theology. As Charles H. and Katherine George note, "the nature of the division between an Anglican and a 'puritan' party within the Church of England was . . . not doctrinal but almost entirely ecclesiastical or institutional."[26] It therefore simply is not the case that to hold Calvinist doctrinal beliefs is necessarily to favor Puritanism or to be sympathetic toward the Genevan Church. Although the differences between conservative Anglicans and Genevan Calvinists were largely ecclesiological, they were not on that account unimportant. Indeed, the ecclesiastical and political revolution of the 1640s in England was sparked preeminently by a liturgical controversy, not by doctrinal differences. Although the customs of worship were considered things external and indifferent to salvation, nevertheless conformity to such customs—according to conservative Anglican Robert Sanderson, for example—is "so necessary, that neither may a man without sin refuse them, where Authority requireth; nor use them, where Authority restraineth the use."[27] However Calvinist Herbert may be in his theology, he consistently rebukes Puritan attacks on the Established Church in such works as *Musae Responsoriae* and *A Priest to the Temple*, and in such poems in *The Temple* as "Divinitie,"

25. See, for example, Ilona Bell, "'Setting Foot into Divinity': George Herbert and the English Reformation," *Modern Language Quarterly* 38 (1977): 219–41; Barbara K. Lewalski, *Protestant Poetics and the Seventeenth-Century English Lyric* (Princeton, N.J.: Princeton University Press, 1979); Jeanne Clayton Hunter, "'With Wings of Faith': Herbert's Communion Poems," *Journal of Religion* 62 (1982): 57–71; and Richard Strier, *Love Known: Theology and Experience in George Herbert's Poetry* (Chicago: University of Chicago Press, 1983).

26. *The Protestant Mind of the English Reformation, 1570–1640* (Princeton, N.J.: Princeton University Press, 1961), p. 354.

27. *XXXVI Sermons* (London: Joseph Hindmarsh, 1689), p. 412.

"Church-rents and schismes," "Conscience," and "The Familie."[28] His attack on Geneva in "The British Church" is consonant with his pervasive support for the ecclesiastical authority of the Church of England.

Herbert concludes "The British Church" by locating the Established Church as the middle way between the equally dangerous extremes of Genevan Calvinism and Roman Catholicism:

> But, dearest Mother, what those misse,
> The mean, thy praise and glorie is,
>   And long may be.
> Blessed be God, whose love it was
> To double-moat thee with his grace,
>   And none but thee. (ll. 25–30)

Herbert's presentation of the British Church as "The mean" is reminiscent of his celebration of the Established Church in *Musae Responsoriae* 39 for enduring "With greater confidence as Puritans / And Roman Catholics arouse the waves / Between which you, the Shepherd, drive your sheep, / Safest in a *via media*" (p. 59). And it is similar to the statement in *Musae Responsoriae* 30 that the British Church knows "With equal care to pass by" both the Charybdis of Roman Catholicism and the Scylla of Puritanism (p. 45).

In his conclusion to "The British Church" Herbert presents the Established Church as double-moated, again reflecting the work's dual perspective. In the poem's present, the Church, like the nation it ministers to, is protected by—in Shakespeare's words—"the silver sea, / Which serves it in the office of a wall / Or as a moat defensive" (*Richard II*, 2.1.46–48). The belief that the sea shields England from the Continent's religious wars is also stated in *Musae Responsoriae* 39, where Herbert asserts that when the Seed of God shaped the world, he "Set aside for

28. See, for example, Summers and Pebworth, "Herbert, Vaughan, and Public Concerns in Private Modes"; Summers and Pebworth, "The Politics of *The Temple*"; and Sidney Gottlieb, "Herbert's Case of 'Conscience': Public or Private Poem?" *Studies in English Literature* 25 (1985): 109–26. For an excellent study that links the surface simplicity of Herbert's verse to a conservative Anglican tradition of plain style, see Leah S. Marcus, "George Herbert and the Anglican Plain Style," in *"Too Rich to Clothe the Sunne": Essays on George Herbert*, ed. Claude J. Summers and Ted-Larry Pebworth (Pittsburgh: University of Pittsburgh Press, 1980), pp. 179–93.

him these sea-divided lands of old, / And shut them like a jewel in his jewel box" (p. 57). But the British Church is *double-*moated because it is also protected by the walls of the New Jerusalem of the apocalyptic future. That this protection is exclusive to the British Church is emphasized by Herbert's final line. The conviction that Christ double-moats "none but thee" is stated as well in *Musae Responsoriae* 39, where Herbert writes that Christ himself, "Taking in the houses of the world at a glance / Says that only England offers a finished worship" (p. 57).

It would be rash to extrapolate from "The British Church" an image of Herbert as a narrow sectarian. The unflattering depictions of the Roman and Genevan Churches and the implied predictions of their ultimate chastisement are not presented with the vitriol common in seventeenth-century religious debate. If the playfulness of the poem's surface plot is seriously qualified by the apocalyptic perspective of the counterplot, it nevertheless remains the fact that the surface plot is sweet-tempered and humane. "The British Church" enacts the advice to the parson given in *A Priest to the Temple* to be "voyd of all contentiousnesse" while using "all possible diligence" in reducing those in his congregation who hold "strange Doctrines" to "the common Faith" (p. 262). By cloaking his denunciation of Rome and Geneva in a subtle rhetoric of allusion, Herbert neatly avoids the appearance of contentiousness. What needs emphasis is neither the vehemence of the poem's denunciation of the rival Churches, nor the apparent trivialization of the differences between them and the personification of Anglicanism, but the poem's serious celebration of the British Church as simultaneously the historical and transcendent Spouse of Christ. It is clear that Herbert believed the Church of England and "none but thee" to be particularly blessed and indeed to be the temporal manifestation of the Bride of the Apocalypse.

Donne's "Show me deare Christ" and Herbert's "The British Church" are both probably indebted to Spenser's contrast of Una and Duessa in *The Faerie Queene* and to Spenser's revelation of Una as the Bride of the Apocalypse. But their differences are as telling as their similarities. All three poems enact quests for true religion, but each resolves its quest quite differently.

Spenser confidently locates England's true religion in Protestantism and more specifically in the accession of Elizabeth. Donne discovers true religion in none of the temporal institutions, finding it expressed only in the love song between his "amorous soule" and Christ's "mild Dove," a union that may be consummated only in a realm beyond the visible world. Donne's attitude toward the competing Churches is both skeptical and tolerant; or, perhaps more accurately, his tolerance is at one with his skepticism. Herbert, on the other hand, finds in his "dearest Mother" British Church both the only truly pleasing historical institution and the Bride of the Apocalypse. Herbert's religio-political position is, thus, a conservative one, and it is probably prompted by the divisions within Protestantism that threatened the unity of the Established Church in England.

Clearly, the different resolutions to these poets' quests for true religion reflect changing historical realities as well as different individual perspectives. Writing at a time when England seemed besieged by Roman Catholic powers, Spenser conflates history and sacred myth to celebrate both Protestantism and Elizabeth. Donne, who was born a Catholic and had carefully studied the claims and counterclaims of the competing religions before entering the Anglican priesthood, expresses a vision that is at once skeptical of the rival temporal institutions and also tolerant of them, juxtaposing their dubious historical records against a transcendent image of unity and love jarringly difficult to accept in human terms and impossible to equate with the unbridelike personifications of Roman Catholicism and Protestantism. Herbert, writing in the midst of a rancorous ecclesiastical debate that was eventually to divide Anglicanism, sees the opposing claimants for the mantle of the Bride of the Apocalypse as not merely Protestantism and Roman Catholicism, but the Roman, Genevan, and British Churches. Herbert's conception of a triple rivalry speaks eloquently of the way in which the religious debate had evolved by the late 1620s and early 1630s. He conceives the Established Church in its "perfect lineaments and hue" as the divinely favored compromise between Roman Catholicism and Genevan Calvinism, as in fact the temporal reality of the Church Triumphant. For all three poets, the image of the Bride of the Apocalypse functions as a litmus by which to test the spiritual claims of the visible

Churches. And by measuring the earthly Churches against the apocalyptic image, the poets express their own religio-political positions.

It is interesting to note that less than twenty years after the publication of *The Temple* another major seventeenth-century religious poet also wrote a poem entitled "The Brittish Church." In Henry Vaughan's bitter work, written in the midst of the Parliamentarian transformation—Vaughan would say, desecration—of Anglicanism, Christ's spouse is neither Spenser's gloriously bright courtly lady nor Donne's mild Dove nor Herbert's fitly arrayed maternal figure, but a ravished bride who urges the Bridegroom to flee lest He be recrucified by their ascendant enemies. And the imagery of apparel in Vaughan's poem centers not on the bridal raiment that informs the earlier works, but on "That seamlesse coat" of Christ, the symbol "of love and hence of unity in the Church,"[29] which the victorious Parliamentarians "dare divide, and stain."[30]

29. Rosemond Tuve, *A Reading of George Herbert* (Chicago: University of Chicago Press, 1952), p. 130.

30. Vaughan, "The Brittish Church," in *The Works of Henry Vaughan*, ed. L. C. Martin, 2d ed. (Oxford: Clarendon Press, 1957), p. 410. I acknowledge with gratitude the support and encouragement of my friend and frequent collaborator Ted-Larry Pebworth.

6

ARS PRAEDICANDI IN GEORGE HERBERT'S POETRY

William Shullenberger

Preaching is rooted in the same Latin verb as predication: *Praedicare*, "to cry in public, proclaim: to declare, state, say" (*OED*). *Ars praedicandi*, the art of preaching, entails the act of predication, the proclamation of the word of God as it orders human existence. Like poetry, preaching creates "predicaments": literally, states of being articulated through language. But insofar as, in both sermon and poem, the word itself is a living action, and the whole of life may be transfigured through language, "predicaments" as logical elements of discourse become something less remote, the very substance of our lives. In the seventeenth century, the procedures of Baconian empiricism, the Ramist streamlining of the logical process and attention to irreducible "simples" as the basis of argument, and the Calvinist desire for a rigorously simple declaration of the plain meaning of a text, all seem to conspire in pressuring speech toward a kind of linguistic positivism. But a preaching poet like George Herbert would nevertheless find himself facing double jeopardy: a scriptural text that is inherently metaphoric, and the ruin, through the Fall, of the human power of naming. After Adam, who forfeited along with Eden the possibility of naming essences, the act of proclamation, the speaking of things as they are, was bound to be a predicative crisis. Whatever the "plain style" might be, it could never be simply achieved. Thus the problem for Herbert as plain speaker is not the often-discussed problem of poetic artifice, but the problem of how to use language at all without betraying himself or his audience:

> My words take fire from my inflamed thoughts,
> Which spit it forth like the Sicilian Hill.
> They vent the wares, and passe them with their faults,
> And by their breathing ventilate the ill.
> But words suffice not, where are lewd intentions:
> My hands do joyn to finish the inventions. ("Sinnes round")[1]

In his own brief notes on *ars praedicandi*, chapter 7 of *A Priest to the Temple*, Herbert appears more sanguine and practical about the handling of language than he tends to be as a poetic speaker. Nevertheless, Herbert's *ars praedicandi* is clearly an *ars poetica* as well. Joseph Summers has shown how Herbert's prose provides a descriptive model of his poetic activity, elaborating an implicitly sacramental theory of language and a rhetorical discipline for a speaker in the "plain style."[2] Herbert counsels a studied simplicity, "a plaine and evident declaration of the meaning of the text" (*PT*, p. 235).[3] The text to be proclaimed must be "moving and ravishing," and the parson responds to it with the sincerity that comes from deep personal experience: "dipping, and seasoning all our words and sentences in our hearts, before they come into our mouths, truly affecting, and cordially expressing all that we say; so that the auditors may plainly perceive that every word is hart-deep" (*PT*, p. 233). The parson preaching must acknowledge a twofold audience, divine and human, and so must direct his speech in two directions at once: by "many Apostrophes to God," he directs the thoughts of his human audience heavenward, and by making his speech open to the power of the Spirit, he makes it a

1. All citations from Herbert's poetry are drawn from *The Works of George Herbert*, ed. F. E. Hutchinson (1941; corrected rpt. Oxford: Clarendon Press, 1945).

2. *George Herbert: His Religion and Art* (Cambridge: Harvard University Press, 1954), pp. 95ff. On sermon theory as background to seventeenth-century English devotional poetry, see Barbara K. Lewalski, *Protestant Poetics and the Seventeenth-Century Religious Lyric* (Princeton: Princeton University Press, 1979), pp. 213–31. Lewalski's attention to Herbert is focused less on his *ars praedicandi* than on his adaptation of biblical genre theory and his place in the tradition of attitudes toward "sacred art."

3. Quotations from *A Priest to the Temple, or, The Country Parson*, are also drawn from the Hutchinson edition, and are cited parenthetically in my text.

site in which God speaks, and the human audience hears, the inspired Word. The felicitous completion of the sermon, the closing of the circuit between the human and the divine, is marked by the preacher's "Holiness," a condition not so much to be defined as to be felt—a condition of complete simplicity, costing not less than everything, to which any of us who have spent much time reading Herbert's poetry can testify.

Herbert thus describes, in his sermon theory, a model of ethical rather than rational persuasion, and the central feature of the ethos is its "Holiness": "he is not witty, or learned, or eloquent, but Holy" (PT, p. 233). The preaching persona achieves "Holiness" by yielding to the holiness of the heart's affections rather than to the affectation of learnedness.[4] Doctrine is transfused with affection rather than justified by eloquence, and the mastery of intelligence yields to the humility of experience: the parson thus makes of himself an exemplary figure, and he demonstrates the meaning of his text by the way in which it is made flesh in him.

Herbert stresses the mediatory role of the "Holy" preacher; as an example of an apostrophe, he says, "Oh my Master, on whose errand I come, let me hold my peace, and doe thou speak thy selfe; for thou art Love, and when thou teachest, all are scholers" (PT, p. 233). Saussurean linguistic theory can help us understand how the divine inhabitation of the speaking voice here does not cancel it. In Saussurean theory, the signifier is the acoustic image, the signified the conceptual presence.[5] In effect, when the speaker gives over to God the burden of instruction, and God himself speaks his self, the preacher becomes his signifier, his acoustic image. This renovated voice achieves in turn a universal instruction: "when thou teachest, all are scholers."

4. Keats's naturalistic honoring the "holiness of the heart's affections" is not quite appropriate to Herbert's understanding of the wayward human heart; but the phrase does render the tone of Herbert's poetry, which presses toward and celebrates the possibility of that heart's renovation. See Richard Strier, *Love Known: Theology and Experience in George Herbert's Poetry* (Chicago: University of Chicago Press, 1983), especially pp. 198–202, for a discussion of Herbert's doctrine of sincerity and his commitment, as preacher and poet, to the experience of the heart as a source of knowledge.

5. Ferdinand de Saussure, *Course in General Linguistics*, trans. Wade Baskin (New York: McGraw-Hill, 1966), p. 66.

If the direction of speech toward God is charged by devotion, by a willingness of the speaking self to hold his peace, the direction of the speech toward its human auditors carries the burden of persuasion. Paradoxically, "Holiness," in this remarkable prose mixture of the sublime and the practical, takes its place as a *strategy* in the context of effective persuasion. In his advice on how to procure attention, Herbert suggests "earnestness of speech, it being naturall to men to think, that where is much earnestenesse, there is somewhat worth hearing; and by a diligent and busy cast of his eye on his auditors, with letting them know, that he observes who marks, and who not; and with particularizing of his speech now to the younge sort, then to the elder, now to the poor, and now to the rich" (*PT*, pp. 232–33). The projection of a "Holy" persona and the "diligent and busy cast of his eye on his auditors" ought in particular to inform our reading of Herbert's poems. If his intention, in sending them to Nicholas Ferrar, was like his intention as a preacher, to "turn to the advantage of any dejected poor Soul,"[6] then the poems ought not to be read so much as private devotions, prototypical confessional poems that the reader is privileged to overhear, but as speech acts like sermons that sustain and transform a particular human community.[7]

Herbert's confidence in the parson's rhetorical strategies, his certainty about the serviceability of rhetoric to the divine intention, is based in his explication of the parson's handling of the text: "first, a plain and evident declaration of the meaning of the text; and secondly, some choyce Observations drawn out of the whole text, as it lyes entire, and unbroken in the Scripture it self. This he thinks naturall, and sweet, and grave" (*PT*, p. 235). Rather than "crumbling" and parsing the text in a demonstration of human interpretative mastery, Herbert's exemplary sermon, like his poems, would become transparent to and coextensive with the Scripture. Insofar as the Scripture thus

6. Izaak Walton, "The Life of Mr. George Herbert," in *The Lives of John Donne, Sir Henry Wotton, Richard Hooker, George Herbert, and Robert Sanderson*, intro. by George Saintsbury (London: Oxford University Press, 1973), p. 314.
7. See Leah S. Marcus, "George Herbert and the Anglican Plain Style," in *"Too Rich to Clothe the Sunne": Essays on George Herbert*, ed. Claude J. Summers and Ted-Larry Pebworth (Pittsburgh: University of Pittsburgh Press, 1980), pp. 179–93, for a discussion of Herbert's community of readers.

comes to speak and interpret itself through the speaker, and the speaker reveals that Scripture is the very text of his own heart, by his ethical example interpreting the hearts of his auditors, the ultimate effect of the parson preaching must be the collection of the private identities of the human participants in the sermon into the body of Christ. Herbert's instructional text periodically becomes sermonic, as it both describes and enacts the way in which human action is inhabited by God: "Oh, let us all take heed what we do, God sees us, he sees whether I speak as I ought, or you hear as you ought, he sees hearts, as we see faces: he is among us; for if we be here, hee must be here, since we are here by him, and without him could not be here" (*PT*, p. 234).

Divine indwelling like this is the experience to which Herbert's poetry gives witness, and we would not be hard pressed to find in the poems the very speaker, rhetorical strategies, and approach to Scripture that Herbert counsels in his pastoral handbook. The first stanza of the first poem in *The Temple* suggests the continuity between sermons and poems as speech acts that put the same sorts of claims upon their audience; in fact, the "bait" of poetry may lead to the renovation of those who can shrug off sermons: "A verse may find him, who a sermon flies, / And turn delight into a sacrifice" ("The Church-porch"). My intention here is to study one of the ways in which Herbert's poems, like honeyed homilies, "turn [poetic] delight into a sacrifice." I wish to suggest that Herbert's lyrics appeal to, and force a crisis in, his reader's penchant for clear predication, the desire to "tell it like it is." Herbert's *ars praedicandi* rests ultimately on his tightrope acts of predication.

All complete sentences in English require a predicate, of course, but Herbert's poems make frequent use of a predicate formed by the copula. The copula nails meaning down, speaks of things as they are; it establishes semantic and metaphoric stability. Herbert's extensive, variegated, and striking use of the copula makes him perhaps the best exemplar of the strategy of definition which Earl Miner has stressed as central to metaphysical poetry: "Whether with ideas alone, with images, or with the two mixed, definition is the commonest Metaphysical way of making single and dual ideas work."[8] Predication of this

8. "Wit: Definition and Dialectic," in *Seventeenth-Century English Poetry: Modern Essays in Criticism*, ed. William R. Keast (Oxford: Oxford University Press, 1962; rev. ed., 1971), p. 50.

sort is central to Herbert's poetic structures. He uses the copula for brief and often climactic metaphoric assertion: "Love is swift of foot, / Love's a man of warre . . ." ("Discipline"); "Childhood is health" ("H. Baptisme [II]"). Metaphoric definition may be extended and complicated to the point of metaphysical paradox: "Love is that liquor sweet and most divine, / Which my God feels as bloud; but I, as wine" ("The Agonie"); "The bloudie crosse of my deare Lord / Is both my physick and my sword" ("Conscience"). Often the closing prayer of a poem, in which the speaker gives over any ambition to define his own existence, securely places the metaphoric definition, by means of an optative form of the copula, in the hands of God: "That, as the world serves us, we may serve thee, / And both thy servants be" ("Man"); "Yet, Lord, instruct us so to die, / That all these dyings may be life in death" ("Mortification"); "Such a heart, whose pulse may be / Thy praise" ("Gratefulnesse").

Herbert's poetic intention, to "plainly say, *my God, my King,*" without loss of rhyme ("Jordan [I]"), is often achieved only at the close of a poem, and the fact that many of the lyrics arrive at a successful predication only as they conclude suggests the impossibility of avoiding the pitfalls of fallen speech by speaking plainly. The plain uncomplicated predication may find itself in need of immediate revision: "For man is ev'ry thing, / And more: He is a tree, yet bears more fruit; / A beast, yet is, or should be more . . ." ("Man"). The attempt to define "The Quidditie" of verse pursues a *via negativa* to arrive at an extraordinarily complex statement, not of an essence either of poetry or of the self spoken in the poetry, but of an inclusive subordinating relationship which alone intricately sustains the "quiddity" of self and verse: "But it is that which while I use / I am with thee, and *Most take all.*" Herbert foregrounds the crisis in predication that the devoted language user must feel. He stresses the contrast between the fullness of being of the divine Word and the untutored contingency of the human speech that longs to give it utterance: "Lord, how can man preach thy eternal word? / He is a brittle crazie glass . . ." ("The Windows"); "We say amisse, / This or that is: / Thy word is all, if we could spell" ("The Flower"). The crisis unfolds in certain poems when an initial copula proves to be insecure or in need of revision. The speaker's longing for a predicative certainty that human speech alone can never achieve thus finds itself exposed and broken. In the recognition of his brokenness the speaker gives over all the signs of his resistance, which he had taken to be signs of his devotion, to the divine Word, which has been waiting to be spoken all along. The poems become then rites of linguistic purification, acts of conversion: the conversion of experience from the humanly predicated to the divinely dictated; the conversion, through that experience, of speaker and auditor from a state of contra-diction to a state of divine instruction; the conversion of language itself from the conjugations of finitude which perpetuate human insufficiency to "a kind of tune which all things heare and fear" ("Prayer [I]"), capable of attuning human speech to the infinitive "eternal word":

> Yet if thou shunnest, I am thine:
> I must be so, if I am mine.
> There is no articling with thee.
> I am but finite, yet thine infinitely.
>
> ("Artillerie")

Relating human conditionality to the infinite "I AM" of God, Herbert indicates that self-possession is a grammatical illusion; the "I" becomes enduring essence only when it gives up its distinctions between definite and indefinite ("no articling with thee") and articulates itself in terms of divine possession. Predicative attunement is the sign of atonement, the making of the human voice a transparency through which the divine Word becomes audible. The original "authour of this great frame" ("Love I") solves the human predicament when the poet and preacher resolves all claim to predicate himself.

If I court catachresis here by speaking of a transparent voice, I do so to indicate the linguistic predicament that opens Herbert's poem explicitly about the art of preaching, to which I wish to give closer attention now: "Lord, how can man preach thy eternal word? / He is a brittle crazie glass" ("The Windows"). The strong opening stresses, the piling up of spondees and trochees, reveal the speaker's frustration that man is particularly unsuited to preach the "eternal word," and outrage that he nevertheless presumes to do so. The emotional stress seems to determine an impossible metaphor. Helen Gardner's explanation of a metaphysical conceit as a comparison "whose ingenuity is more striking that its justness" is appropriate here,[9] for

9. "The Metaphysical Poets," in Keast, ibid., p. 36.

the act of predication seems impossibly flawed. As a preacher, man would be a vocal medium; but here he is predicated as visual slag, "crazie glass," shot through with spiritual flaws, with no capacity for language of any sort.

"Yet . . ." the reformation of the image begins at once. In the final lines of the stanza, God turns contradiction into paradox by claiming and transfiguring the image, redeeming the faulty predication from the finite indicative, *is*, to the infinitive condition: "Yet in thy temple thou dost him afford / This glorious and transcendent place, / To be a window, through thy grace." The allusion to the larger text of *The Temple* in which this poem has been graciously placed makes the poem characteristically self-referential at the same time that it is self-effacing, as its mood changes from bewilderment to gratitude. Helen Vendler interprets the self-referential hints in the poem as signs of Herbert's personal ambivalence about the task of proclamation: the poem "hides its personal origin in generalized language."[10] But Herbert's persona here, as in other poems, is not the Romantic persona that Vendler seems to disclose. Identification is appropriately generalized to stress that this speaker is typologically related to "man" in general; he is not the type of the modern self-conscious individual. Not that man, this speaker or the fallen species whom he typifies, claims any glory unto himself. His "transcendent place" in the temple is of ultimate expense to God, the same "rich Lord" whose sacrificial generosity affords a place for human claims in "Redemption." Light passes through a window; one would expect the initial conceit to be elaborated through this natural pattern, so that man becomes the window "through" which God's grace passes. But the preposition *through* veers away from the metaphor of direction toward the metaphor of agency; it stresses not the human medium but the divine prevenient action that makes human mediation a possibility: man is made what he is by means of grace. The preposition thus moves us from the visibility of windows in a temple to the invisibility of grace, absorbing what can be seen into what can more clearly be heard. The "grace" which seals the stanza where we expect the word *light* is associated with light, yet connotes more than our under-

10. *The Poetry of George Herbert* (Cambridge: Harvard University Press, 1975), p. 83.

standing of light. The word *grace* sanctions the visual image even as it includes it in the nonvisible activity of a divine reality that presents itself first as a Word.

Without quite cancelling the visual image, then, the poem nevertheless moves us inward by its Protestant stress upon verbal over iconic apprehension.[11] In the second stanza, the divine artificer of reality combines word and picture in a not-quite-visible stained-glass image: "But when thou dost anneal in glass thy storie, / Making thy life to shine within / The holy Preachers . . . ." Grace by fire in-structs the holy Preachers in a Christ-like life. As the once-brittle crazie glass is hardened, its colors fixed, by annealing fires, the holy preachers are strengthened, their true colors flash out, by the suffering of this life, which is the discipline of God. Yet what they show forth is nothing of their own; they manifest "thy storie," the life of Christ, which is the true proclamation. These lines solve the contradiction posed by the opening: man can preach the "eternal word" because the "eternal word" became a man; God annealed himself in the brittle slag of human mortality, covered the stain of Adam with the atoning stain of his blood, which showed forth not spots and cracks but light and glory. "The holy Preachers" thus appear in the central line of the poem as what Barbara Lewalski, discussing Herbert's typological patterns, refers to as "the Christic fulfillment of [imperfect] types."[12] They constitute the completed image that resolves the apparent contradictions of the first half, for they show forth God's "storie" in the *visibilia* of their lives as well as in their preaching: language and life reveal the renovated image of God. Now glass can tell a story, and life can be visibly displayed: verbal and visible patternings begin to "combine and mingle," manifesting the "light and glorie" with an intensity neither word nor image could suggest alone.

Beginning after the strong stress on the pivotal "then," the second half of this perfectly symmetrical poem describes what God brings about through the image he has perfected in the first half:

11. The epic paradigm of such a pattern is the speech of the Father in book 3 of *Paradise Lost*, which will continue to be denigrated by readers hungry for sense data, but which, read on its own terms, approaches a kind of pure poetry.

12. *Protestant Poetics*, p. 312.

then the light and glorie
More rev'rend grows, & more doth win;
Which else shows watrish, bleak & thin.

Doctrine and life, colours and light, in one
When they combine and mingle, bring
A strong regard and aw . . . .

What one notices in this passage are the qualities and effects of the preachers; what one looks for without success is a recognizable image. In a poem about stained-glass windows, we are not given a single particular color. As the medium through which God reveals his "eternal word," the preachers remain throughout the poem anonymously instrumental to that revelation. Herbert's strategy is thus to refuse us a recognizable icon, and thereby to deny us the opportunity to make an idol of an image and confusedly admire the image rather than the ultimately imageless presence that sanctions it. The syntactic architecture of this closing indicates something of the vital symbolic geometry of Herbert's "plain style," providing a verbal equivalent to the ordered complexities of great stained glass. In the effortless yoking of apparently irreconcilable opposites, we are confirmed in understanding that all virtue, light, and glory is from God, and that man, if he is anything, is what God makes of him. Life inexpressible marries articulate doctrine, a light too bright for human eyes irradiates visible and rhetorical "colours" to make the eternal word shine out to humanity; but the divine elements combine and mingle by a life of their own, and the "one" in whom they meet is but "watrish, bleak, & thin," until his life becomes theirs. "Strong regard and aw" is not due to him, but to the original "One" who shines within and through him.

From this "transcendent place" in which apparently distinct orders of reality are fused by the annealing fire of God, the poem issues a stern judgment against "speech alone." Mere proclamation or predication, typologically un-instructed, is an ephemeral action, appealing only to the ear of sense and dying out as that organ and all that it apprehends as real must die. The poem thus closes with a disproportionate antithesis between the radiant fullness of the holy preacher as a sign of Christ completed in Christ and the dying fall of an acoustic image bereft of significance.

It might be suggested that Herbert sets up a contrast here between "holy" and "unholy" preachers. Vendler sets them up as alternative possibilities indicating Herbert's "qualms of conscience over preaching religion without exemplifying it."[13] The poem does not seem to split this way; rather, it makes a matter-of-fact Calvinist acknowledgment of the natural depravity and insufficiency of even the best of men. Human speech alone is a brief candle too weak to anneal a lasting and glorious image in glass. But by creating images that become transparent to the eternal word they proclaim, by speaking words resplendent with divine light—by thus instructing the eye to hear what it cannot see, and the ear to see what it cannot hear—God speaks through the awakened senses to the conscience. "The Windows" is thus a poetic text whose process of incarnation both exemplifies and interprets the act of preaching, even as Herbert's notes on preaching in *A Priest to the Temple* interpret his art of verse.

But the circuit of performative speech in Herbert's work cannot be a closed system in which poetry and preaching continuously refer to each other: "Resort to sermons, but to prayers most: / Praying's the end of preaching" ("The Church-porch"). Walton's account encourages us to place "Prayer (I)" as an example of Herbert's predicative art in the same relation to "The Windows" as Herbert placed the reading pew in relation to the pulpit: "by his order, the Reading Pew, and Pulpit, were a little distant from each other, and both of an equal height; for he would often say, 'They should neither have a precedency or priority of the other: but, that Prayer and Preaching being equally useful, might agree like Brethren, and have an equal honor and estimation.'"[14] If Herbert as poet counseled that "praying's the end of preaching," he demonstrated, in too many poems to count, that praying's the end of poetry. "Prayer (I)" is peculiar, however, because as E. B. Greenwood notes, it is simultaneously evocation, invocation, and incantation: "In a way it contrives to be a prayer at the same time as being about prayer."[15] Prayer, like preaching, carries the possibility of

13. *The Poetry of George Herbert*, p. 82.
14. *Lives*, p. 278.
15. "George Herbert's Sonnet 'Prayer': A Stylistic Study," *Essays in Criticism* 15, no. 1 (January 1965): 31, 29.

atonement for speaker and for auditor because of Christ's typological inhabitation of the human speech act. And "Prayer (I)," like "The Windows," enacts the verbal event whose conditions and effects it defines. Whereas "The Windows" begins with a metaphoric predicament that the poem proceeds to resolve, "Prayer (I)" evades predicament by refusing completed predication. The poem thus seems written both to encourage and to tease us out of predicative thought; its sequence of appositive phrases is a series of virtual predications that suggest the inexhaustible generative power of prayer by never arriving at the closure marked by a main finite verb. Although Greenwood is right in suggesting that the poem's syntactic structure thus "marks the fact that prayer is literally a thing of *infinite* preciousness and meaning to the poet,"[16] Mario Di Cesare is most persuasive in his explanation of the necessary absence of the verb: "it would take a daring reader of this poem to install a particular verb. 'Is,' the most likely candidate, specifies a rigid one-to-one relationship. But why that instead of some other? No, the absence of the verb is deliberate privation. We can only speculate, not know for sure. The relationships that replace straightforward predication are fluid and uncertain."[17] With the lack of finite closure—and the sequential order it could supply—the poem unfolds through a floating series of conceits, each of which proposes a new meditative threshold. It thus develops exponentially to achieve a power of infinite suggestion, a condition of timelessness in which all its elements occur simultaneously, as if under the eye of God.

If the surface structure of the poem's syntax works against sequential ordering of event and subordinating of ideas, the very activity of free association, and the emotional rhythms it generates, registered both in patterns of stress and in clusters of image, suggest that the poem may be the working through of a spiritual crisis, which so frequently provides the "plot" of Herbert's poems. The poem is such an echo chamber of biblical, patristic, liturgical, and meditative suggestions that any number of interpretative maps might explain it in part; for the sake of economy I shall explore those images that take part in

16. Ibid., p. 28.
17. "Image and Allusion in Herbert's 'Prayer (I),'" *English Literary Renaissance* 11, no. 3 (Autumn 1981): 310.

the drama of a poetic speaker at first easy with, then struggling with the consequences of, his desire to predicate. The drama of a conversion of understanding may be more covert in "Prayer (I)" than elsewhere in Herbert, but it provides a latent design that accounts for what sequence there may be in the profusion of images.

Not that there is anything inadequate about the initiatory images of the poem. Their full implication does not make itself felt until we have arrived at the understanding of the end of the poem. By then, we can read in them meanings of which the speaker does not seem fully appreciative:

> Prayer the Churches banquet, Angels age,
>   Gods breath in man returning to his birth,
>   The soul in paraphrase, the heart in pilgrimage,
> The Christian plummet sounding heav'n and earth.

With proper stress accorded the first beat in "Prayer" and the name of God, the opening lines fall into an otherwise iambic regularity that highlights a sense of confidence and serenity in the expansive and nourishing powers of prayer. Helen Vendler suggests that there is something bookish and dogmatic about these lines.[18] They move too easily in their implicit faith, as if their assertions were not personally felt. The easy flow of the meter seems to gloss over the potential of the images, which seems to emerge only in retrospect, as if the human predicative intention is redeemed preveniently before it can realize its own failure. After all, the poem's end is in its beginning: the "Churches banquet" is the Eucharistic feast, the celebration of and participation in the sacrificial body of Christ.[19] But the way in which the voice of the poem breezes past this initial and potentially climactic recognition suggests that the banquet may be, to this speaker at this point, no more than the "light snack" (OED) that the word denoted in Herbert's time.

The assurance that prayer can accomplish such astonishing feats as measure the age of angels or the dimensions of heaven and earth—and by "sounding" them, to set them ringing— buckles suddenly under the following violent ruptures of stress and image: "Engine against th'Almightie, sinners towre, / Reversed thunder, Christ-side-piercing spear . . . ." Everything seemed to be going so smoothly; what happened? The fourth line perhaps provides a clue, the latent spring which releases this association of prayer with aggression, with the instruments of Christ's Passion. The claim that prayer can "sound" heaven and earth is evidence of the pride figured in the "sinners towre" of Babel. It is a "Christian plummet" without Christ, for it omits the descent into Hell which Christ, the true "Christian plummet," also sounded. The psychological detour around those regions of death and despair is a symptom of a spiritual amnesia that interferes with a full prayerful identification with Christ: true prayer must, like Christ, enter and harrow Hell, perhaps especially the hell of one's own fallen heart in hiding, or else becomes a site in which hell revives its power, a "plummet" destructively cast, a missile or weapon (*OED*) aimed at God which reenacts the tormenting of Christ on the antitype of all sinners' towers, the Cross. The opening diction of "Deniall" supports this reading with its hint that self-absorbed devotion may become an unconsciously wielded weapon against God: "When my devotions could not *pierce* / Thy silent eares" (emphasis supplied).[20]

Another unexpected shift takes place before the second quatrain is completed: the nightmare of Crucifixion yields, in the seventh line of the poem, to the prospect of the world recreated; tortuous syntactic and metric compression opens out into the deep breathing of a syntactic unit congruent with the poetic line: "the six-days world transposing in an houre." Paradoxically, as in "The Agonie," the "Christ-side-piercing spear" becomes an instrument of grace that sets flowing the blood which redeems the world. The original creation, blessed by God with a seventh day of rest and transposed by Adam to a state of decay and death, is transposed by the second Adam to a new creation, opening into the eternal Sabbath. The final seven lines of the sonnet intimate and celebrate this Sabbath.

If the poem does split into two seven-line units, the first of which climaxes in a seventh line that, like the seventh day,

20. Di Cesare treats the violence of the imagery but avoids the implication that prayer may be the instrument of violence.

"transposes" all which led up to it, and opens into the timelessness of the second unit, then the surface structuring of the sonnet by its rhyme scheme is itself transposed by a higher order of imaginative organization. When the hour comes to transpose the six-days world, human schemes to parcel out existence become transparent to the activity of a pure naming that takes us as close to the divine presence as language can make possible while still reminding us of how distant we remain. In contrast to the discreet geographies of cosmos and soul in the first part of the poem—hours, days, earth, heaven, heart, soul, breath—the sublime yet homely imagery of the final seven lines is free floating:

> A kinde of tune, which all things heare and fear;
> Softnesse, and peace, and joy, and love, and blisse,
>   Exalted Manna, gladnesse of the best,
>   Heaven in ordinarie, man well drest,
> The milkie way, the bird of Paradise,
> Church-bels beyond the starres heard, the souls bloud,
>   The land of spices; something understood.

The passage opens and closes with deliberate vagueness—"a kinde of tune," "something understood"—to mark the thresholds of a condition that language can infinitely suggest but never denote. And yet there is no soupy transcendentalism here: Herbert uses his indefinites with syntactic precision to represent divine inexhaustibility. Existence provides an infinite reserve of images for the experience of the divine presence, yet any particular image can only be a faint and provisional suggestion of that experience, an approach but not a closure. Of the final phrase of the poem, Earl Miner writes, "in the end the full meaning of prayer cannot be defined. Definition is shown to be impossible only after its resources are fully exhausted."[21] Similarly, Helen Vendler writes, "The final definition of prayer as 'something understood' abolishes or expunges the need for explanatory metaphors. Metaphor, Herbert seems to say, is after all only an approximation: once something is understood, we can fall silent; once the successive rethinkings of the definition have been made, and the truth has been arrived at, the poem is

21. "Wit: Definition and Dialectic," p. 51.

over."[22] It seems to me that "something" works very differently from what Miner and Vendler suggest about it. It does not close the poem off or indicate the exhaustion of metaphor; rather, it keeps the poem open by its very indefiniteness, and suggests that prayer may be the endless generation of metaphor. The truth, for Herbert here, is not something that "has been arrived at," but is, as in Wordsworth, "something evermore about to be."

The very indefinability of that which must be approached through the word generates the invention process that for Herbert is both prayer and poetry, atonement and attunement. Perhaps this passage is Herbert's sweet plain style in its purest form, especially the ninth line, with its crescendo of radiant and gentle nominations intimating a Protestant equivalent to the rings of light concentered in God, wherein Dante found all desire simultaneously wakened, intensified, purified, quieted, and consumed. Verbal action grows quiet here. The remote soundings of past passive participles replace the present actives of the poem's first half, and in those past passives subject and object do not so much recede from each other as recede into each other in a moment of spiritual apprehension that settles all differences. Plainness makes sublimity possible, for the passage evocatively combines and mingles what we readily understand—food, stars, church-bells—with what we usually only faintly and fitfully apprehend—Heaven, Paradise, providence.

These ghostly demarcations hint at a Sabbath celebration, perhaps the apocalyptic Marriage of the Book of Revelation, the wedding of the Church or the redeemed Soul with God. Di Cesare has previously stressed the poem's sources in the Gospel of John.[23] Although we tend not to think of Herbert as an apocalyptic poet, the subject of "Prayer (I)" pulls him toward the apocalyptic drama of Revelation. Here the six-days world is transposed by a "new heaven and a new earth" (Revelation 21:1), and "a kind of tune" of judgment and of joy is sounded: "The voice of harpers harping with their harps: And they sung as it were a new song" (14:2–3). Here the spices of the Song of Songs

22. *The Poetry of George Herbert*, p. 39.
23. In addition to the article previously cited, see Di Cesare's "Prayer (I) and the Gospel of John," in "*Too Rich to Clothe the Sunne*," ed. Summers and Pebworth, pp. 101–12.

are poured forth, and here man is at last well dressed: "Let us be glad and rejoice, and give honor to him: for the marriage of the Lamb is come, and his wife has made herself ready. And to her was granted that she should be arrayed in fine linen, clean and white: for the white linen is the righteousness of saints" (19:7-8). Herbert mutes the eschatological thunder and quietly transposes the sacrament to the homely simplicity of a wedding feast in Cana, or in Bemerton: "Heaven in ordinarie, man well drest." And if this marriage is intimated, the "houre" into which the six-days world has been transposed is also an "Our," which the poet can claim with humility, because God has made it so. The "something understood," which provides a kind of pause in a ceaseless movement of human speech toward God, is something shared by man and God. For the poem leads its human prayers, poet and reader, to understand that God understands, stands under and transposes, all that he creates, including human understanding. And in that understanding, all acts of predication—prayer, preaching, poetry—find their origin and end.

In "Prayer (I)" the implied yet withheld copula thus acts as a pulley to draw human speaker and speech toward God. A predicative closure indefinitely both promised and forestalled registers God's presence as the essential condition for authentic human speech just as clearly as the neat closures elsewhere in Herbert, whose final copulas are like a seal of the divine indwelling. Syntactic formation in Herbert's poetry thus reveals God drawing man to himself through the "crooked winding wayes" of human speech ("A Wreath"), and flawless closure becomes the sign of that atonement. In the atonement of the human speaker with the Word, the speaker's life is folded into the rhetorical artifice of his proclamation, and the poem becomes in its dramatic and exemplary effect a miniature sermon, a homily whose attributes correspond to the features of the *ars praedicandi* sketched in Herbert's priestly handbook. An extended study of predicative closure in Herbert would continue to pursue his use of the copula, which modern grammarians tend to describe as a syntactic link, a semantic cypher, yet which a biblically instructed poet like Herbert, meditating on the enigma of the divine name, would discover to be the very word of power, whose semantic basis is in the imperturbable and uncontingent Being of God himself. The biblical God identified himself to

Moses as Yahweh, "I am who I am," or "I will be who I will be" (Exodus 3:14), and this revelation authenticates the theological and poetic privilege of the verb *to be*.[24]

The stress in this essay on predicative crisis and closure in Herbert's poetry might help to clarify the strengths as well as resolve some of the differences between major interpretative approaches to Herbert in recent years. For predication is, for the poet and preacher, both a dramatic and a theological issue, and if we can discern in the syntactic formation of the poems both dramatic intensity and theological integrity, then we need not sacrifice the dramatic complexity of the poems as Stanley Fish has taught us to read them in order to acknowledge in them the theological structures of a fundamentally Protestant poetics. The differences between affective stylistics and Protestant poetics as ways of reading need not obscure the similarities between their conclusions. If one attempts a close reading of Herbert's lyrics as dramatic events, acts of conversion, one is bound to be affected by Fish's powerful and suggestive analysis. Barbara Lewalski and others are correct in criticizing Fish's Augustinian paradigm as anachronistic and inadequate in explaining the spiritual dynamics of the Protestant conscience. Fish's central insights, and deeper syntactic attention, can nevertheless be aligned with a more properly Calvinist explanation of what happens in Herbert's poetry. Lewalski remarks of Herbert,

> Poem after poem recognizes that the poet's praises (like the preacher's sermon) must emanate from a renewed heart and must be in some sense God's work and not his own; God hews the stony altar of the heart and fits the stones for praise; God must tune the poet's breast as an instrument of praise, must mend him, and must relieve his griefs and miseries before he can praise; God must indeed complete his praises when he cannot. And the poet-speaker must relinquish any claim to his praises as his own work, even as he must to any other spiritual accomplishment.[25]

This sounds very like the conclusion Fish reaches about Herbert's poetry:

24. See my essay "The Power of the Copula in Milton's *Sonnet VII*," *Milton Studies* 15 (1981): 201–12, for theological and linguistic backgrounds to Milton's use of the verb *to be*. The same conclusions about the theological implications of poetic grammar inform my discussion here.

25. *Protestant Poetics*, p. 227.

> it is characteristic of these poems that at precisely those points where we are most aware of them as formal structures, we are aware of them as formal structures that have been mended or completed or given meaning by God. The moment of highest artfulness always coincides with the identification of the true source of that art; the wit and ingenuity are referred to that source rather than to the poet, who in losing title to his poem also loses (happily) the presumption of its invention, and is known for what he always was, a discoverer, one who copies out.[26]

For both Fish and the students of Protestant poetics, the human self and all its work are given over to God; but whereas Fish suggests that this conversion experience involves ultimately the silencing of the human speaker at the moment that he is "absorbed into the deity,"[27] Lewalski and others (including her precursor, Summers) reckon the impossibility of such beatific closure for the Calvinist conscience in this life, and they demonstrate the ways that the self and the work stand because they are under-stood by God.

Heather Asals builds on earlier research by detailed and extensive attention to the theological basis of Herbert's strategies of predication. But Asals stresses the role of the poet as *priest* who must "break the host of language itself" so that poetic action tends toward "equivocation," the multiplication of possibilities that ruptures the ordinary habits of predication that divide us from God.[28] What Asals tends to interpret as symbolic gesture I tend to interpret as predicative crisis, for the poet is a *preacher* in Herbert's work, and the poem as speech act is more effectively to be aligned with the proclamation of the Word than with the mysteries of the Eucharist. Thus Herbert's poetry often registers the moment of the word's indwelling by a climactic predication, not, as Asals suggestively argues, by "a method of predication which transcends the usual grammatical subject-predicate format."[29] Asals's concern with the nominative category which supports her investigation of punning leads her to divide her subject by declensions. The stress in this

26. *Self-Consuming Artifacts: The Experience of Seventeenth-Century Literature* (Berkeley: University of California Press, 1972), p. 203.

27. Ibid., p. 157.

28. *Equivocal Predication: George Herbert's Way to God* (Toronto: University of Toronto Press, 1981), p. 11.

29. Ibid., p. xi.

essay on predicative action leads me to study conjugations, in particular the conjugations of the verb *to be*, as the crux of Herbert's art of predication.

The architectural solidity of Herbert's achievement, both in the large edifice of *The Temple* and in the individual lyrics, is the mark of a poetic that ultimately claims and renovates the signs and the forms of this world as the sites of divine encounter. The poet and his readers are not led by the dialectic of the poems to a condition of timeless and silent beatitude; rather, they find themselves and their language typologically renovated by the power of the indwelling Word. This may be what we mean when we speak of Herbert's "plain style": not that the acts of the mind or the syntax which expresses them are uncomplicated, but that the world which the poetry in-vents, discovers, has the phenomenological freshness of a new world naked, "plain" in its absence of distortions, made new by a predicative style which, with its stress on the power of the copula, comes to participate in the sublime simplicity of the fiat of Genesis: "Let there *be* . . . and there *was.*"

7

STANDING ON CEREMONY: THE COMEDY OF MANNERS IN HERBERT'S "LOVE (III)"

Michael C. Schoenfeldt

> Etiquette is a kind of dance, dance a kind of ritual, and worship a form of etiquette.
>
> —Clifford Geertz[1]

In his "Notes on Herbert's Temple," Coleridge suggests that a complete appreciation of Herbert's poems requires "a constitutional predisposition to ceremoniousness, in piety as in manners."[2] In no poem is the conjunction of piety and manners more important than in "Love (III)." But because "Love (III)" comes at the end of a sequence of poems about the "last things"—"Death," "Dooms-day," "Judgement," and "Heaven"—criticism has focused on its otherworldly piety at the expense of its involvement in worldly manners. The power of the poem, however, lies in its ability to manifest its strenuous piety through the complex politics of Renaissance hierarchical relationships. By representing God as an affable lord and man as an unworthy guest, Herbert amplifies the overtones of hospitality already implicit in Reformation discussions of the

---

1. "Person, Time, and Conduct in Bali," in *The Interpretation of Cultures* (New York: Basic Books, 1973), p. 400.
2. *Coleridge on the Seventeenth Century*, ed. Roberta F. Brinkley (Durham, N.C.: Duke University Press, 1955), p. 534.

Eucharist.[3] But this act of amplification also entangles the discourse between God and man in the strategically submissive yet subtly coercive vocabulary of courtesy.[4] When read as a part of this vocabulary, both the host's gracious invitation and the speaker's equally gracious protestations of unworthiness register an intense concern with propriety, precedence, and prestige. In "Love (III)," Herbert employs a situation fraught with great social anxiety and political importance in the Renaissance—dining at the table of the great—to reveal the immense difficulty of responding properly to God's overwhelming beneficence.[5]

"Love (III)" is based upon the common Renaissance concept of the Lord's Supper as an actual meal to which one is invited by a lord. In a pun that the poem never mentions, the Eucharistic host is incarnated in a worldly and courteous host who makes the speaker an offer he cannot, finally, refuse.[6] By depicting the sacrament in social terms, Herbert draws upon a rich cultural

3. I agree with Louis Martz, *The Poetry of Meditation* (New Haven: Yale University Press, 1962), p. 319, and Chana Bloch, *Spelling the Word: George Herbert and the Bible* (Berkeley: University of California Press, 1985), p. 100, that "Love (III)" represents *both* the soul's reception of the Eucharist and heaven's reception of the soul.

4. On Herbert's use of the language of secular supplication in his devotional discourse with God, see my "Submission and Assertion: The 'Double Motion' of Herbert's 'Dedication,' " *John Donne Journal* 2, no. 2 (1983): 39–49.

5. On the political and social ramifications of the Renaissance anxiety about proper behavior, especially when dining, see Norbert Elias, *The History of Manners*, vol. 1 of *The Civilizing Process*, trans. Edmund Jephcott (New York: Urizen, 1978), pp. 84–129. In *Ambition and Privilege: The Social Tropes of Elizabethan Courtesy Theory* (Berkeley: University of California Press, 1984), Frank Whigham argues persuasively that the acute attention to conduct represented by Renaissance courtesy literature was a reaction to the troubling phenomenon of social mobility. My sense of the social nuances of deferential expressions is indebted to Whigman's powerful article, "The Rhetoric of Elizabethan Suitors' Letters," *PMLA* 96 (1981): 864–82.

6. In his edition of *Shakespeare's Sonnets* (New Haven: Yale University Press, 1977), pp. 488–89, Stephen Booth has a provocative note on the capacity of puns to structure a poem in which they do not appear. Anne Williams has recently explored the two kinds of accommodation inherent in this pun on *host* in "Gracious Accommodations: Herbert's 'Love (III),' " *Modern Philology* 82 (1984): 13–22. Stanley Fish, *The Living Temple: George Herbert and Catechizing* (Berkeley: University of California Press, 1979), pp. 131–34, describes eloquently the difficulty of refusing Love's hospitality, and suggests that the host's repetition of his invitation makes it "an offer you can't refuse." Similarly, Richard Strier, *Love Known: Theology and Experience in George Herbert's Poetry* (Chicago: University of Chicago Press, 1983), pp. 82–83, views the host's coercive power as a manifestation of the Lutheran doctrine of the irresistibility of divine grace, and depicts God as "a host Who will not take no for an answer."

treasury of images and associations. Heinrich Bullinger, for example, observes that "as often as thou comest unto the supper of ye lord, thou sittest down at the lords table, thou art made Christs guest."[7] Similarly, the "Homily of the worthy receiving . . . of the Sacrament" speaks of the Lord's "heavenly Supper, where every one of us must be ghestes," and compares the presumption of entering unworthily "into this presence of our Lord and Judge" to the behavior of servants who dare "presume to an earthly masters table, whom they have offended."[8] In "Love (III)" Herbert exploits these traditional associations of the Lord's Supper with earthly hospitality, disposing the discourse between God and man according to the strategies and ceremonies of courtesy.

The first line encapsulates the pattern of gracious invitation and polite deferral, thrust and counterthrust, which runs throughout the poem: "Love bade me welcome: yet my soul drew back."[9] Helen Vendler aptly compares the poem to "some decorous minuet . . . a pace forward, a hanging back, a slackening, a drawing nearer."[10] The speaker's initial withdrawal from Love's invitation is countered by Love's definitively hospitable and courteous question about whether the speaker lacks anything. Yet the speaker's witty response to this question—"A guest . . . worthy to be here"—supplies the verbal equivalent of his initial impulse to draw back from his Lord's threshold.

Within the guest-host metaphor, the speaker's protestation of unworthiness provides a courteous response to the offer of honor from a superior. In *The Civile Conversation*, a popular courtesy book praised by Edward Herbert (George Herbert's eldest brother), Stefano Guazzo observes that "it is the parte of him whiche receiveth these outwarde honours, first, modestly to refuse them, shewing thereby that hee looketh not for them,

7. *Commonplaces of Christian Religion*, trans. John Stockwood (London, 1572), p. 200v.

8. *Certaine Sermons or Homilies Appointed to be Read in Churches In the Time of Queen Elizabeth I (1547–1571): A Facsimile Reproduction of the Edition of 1623*, ed. Mary Ellen Rickey and Thomas B. Stroup, 2 vols. in 1 (Gainesville: Scholars' Facsimiles and Reprints, 1968), 2:197, 205.

9. *The Works of George Herbert*, ed. F. E. Hutchinson (Oxford: Clarendon Press, 1945). All citations of Herbert's works are from this edition.

10. *The Poetry of George Herbert* (Cambridge: Harvard University Press, 1975), pp. 275–76.

otherwise hee shall shewe to bee somewhat proude."[11] Similarly, Baldassare Castiglione suggests that a man ought

> alwaies to humble his selfe somewhat under his degree, and not receive favor and promotions so easily as they be offered him, but refuse them modestly, shewing he much esteemeth them . . . that he may give him an occasion that offereth them, to offer them with a great deale more instance.
>
> Because the more resistance a man maketh in such manner to receive them, the more doth he seeme to the prince that giveth them to be esteemed.[12]

The modest denial of worth thus offers an occasion for the expression of ingratiating humility; at the same time, it furnishes praise of the superior in the recognition that what one is about to receive has not been earned, but is instead a gift, an act of grace. Such a ceremony of first refusal serves to underscore the fact that the recipient is about to enter into a debt, an obligation he can never fully repay. The modest initial deferral of the speaker of "Love (III)" thus is not necessarily a rejection of his superior's judgment but can be seen as an attempt to enhance that superior's status.

Yet the speaker does not stop there. Instead, he continues to stand on ceremony, to cling to the issue of his inability to merit such an honor. To his host's assertion that "You shall be [a guest worthy to be here]," the speaker protests his own unworthiness for the favor which his superior has chosen to bestow upon him, replacing his general statement of man's unfitness—"Guiltie of dust and sinne"—with a declaration of his own particular sinfulness—"I the unkinde, ungratefull"—and a confession of the shame this sinfulness engenders in him—"Ah my deare, / I cannot look on thee." Love counters with a question—"Who made the eyes but I"—that stresses his own prerogative of judgment

11. Trans. George Pettie, ed. Edward Sullivan, Tudor Translations, 2d ser., nos. 7–8, 2 vols. (London: Constable, 1925), 1:166. In his autobiography, Edward Herbert states: "I could say much more . . . concerning That discreete Civillity which is to bee observed in Communication either with freinds or strangers but that this worke would growe too bigg, And that many precepts conducing thereunto may bee had in Guazzo della Civile Conversatione . . ." (*The Life of Lord Herbert of Cherbury*, ed. J. M. Shuttleworth [London: Oxford University Press, 1976], p. 36).

12. *The Book of the Courtier*, trans. Thomas Hoby (London: Dent, 1928), p. 109.

derived from his status as creator of the speaker's eyes as well as his "I," his sense of an integral and independent self. The speaker concedes this point, but his concession only gives him material for a further deferral, as he proceeds to assert his own unworthiness on the grounds that he has corrupted these gifts from his Lord: "Truth Lord, but I have marr'd them: let my shame / Go where it doth deserve." Love responds to this deferral with another question—"And know you not . . . who bore the blame"—this time emphasizing not his creative but his redemptive powers. The speaker then offers to meet his Lord halfway, entering into his house, but only as a servant, not as an honored guest: "My deare, then I will serve." In offering to serve, the speaker is still declaring his unworthiness to be served, still attempting to avoid the gracious invitation his Lord has extended. Love's final response cleverly appropriates the speaker's proffer of service; Love commands him, as one orders a servant, to behave as an esteemed guest: "You must sit down, sayes Love, and taste my meat." The speaker, realizing that he has been beaten at his own game, is compelled by his own tender of submission to submit to a position of honor. He finally surrenders, performs as he is told: "So I did sit and eat."[13]

The speaker of "Love (III)" obviously goes far beyond the ceremony of first refusal recommended by Guazzo and Castiglione as the proper response to a superior's favors. What begins as a gesture of modest denial quickly becomes a "contest in courtesy and humility"[14] in which guest and host battle for the superiority inherent in the capacity to do someone service. The initially ingratiating gestures by which the speaker avows his unworthiness are supplanted by the speaker's stubborn insistence on the impropriety of his presence at his Lord's table. Deference and submission, normally expressions of one's willingness to adapt to the will of another, thus become vehicles for self-assertion and intransigence. The very terms by which one

13. As M. Thomas Hester suggested to me, the speaker here demonstrates a rudimentary lesson of table manners: don't talk with your mouth full.
14. Arnold Stein, *George Herbert's Lyrics* (Baltimore: Johns Hopkins University Press, 1968), p. 194. Leah S. Marcus, *Childhood and Cultural Despair: A Theme and Variations in Seventeenth-Century Literature* (Pittsburgh: University of Pittsburgh Press, 1978), p. 117, similarly terms the poem "a playful contest of wit and courtesy."

indicates subordination of self and respect for another contain an adverse impulse.

The Mirrour of Complements, a seventeenth-century courtesy book, discloses the manner in which such deferential expressions can become occasions for social aggression. The following dialogue, entitled "To entertaine a friend that comes to visit us," suggests that the contest of courtesy between the speaker and host of "Love (III)" is actually a battle for political superiority:

> You are very welcome, good Sir, you honor me a thousand times above my merit . . . .
>
> Pardon mee Sir, it is I that have received the honour . . . .
>
> Sir, you oblige me too much, I have not merited these favors from you.
>
> Sir, this is but a part of my respect, for I owe you much more in things of greater consequence.
>
> Sir, there is no need that you should use these terms to your obliged servants . . . . I wish to serve you in all that I am able, and I should more willingly expresse it in action than in speech.
>
> Sir, you have already expressed it very amply, and I were worthy to be thought ingratefull if ever I should faile to make acknowledgement that I am much beholding to you . . . .
>
> I see that you will conquer me with courtesie, but if it please you to sit, wee shall discourse more at leisure.
>
> I thanke you sir, it needs not; besides, it were undecent for mee to be first in place, but if it please you to sit, I shall keepe you company.
>
> Then I pray you sit there.
>
> It shall be then to obey you.
>
> Sir, I am your servant.
>
> Sir, it is I that am yours, and the most affectionate of all your servants.[15]

In this dialogue, the seemingly simple matter of inviting a friend to dinner becomes charged with questions of social status and political power. Like the guest and host of "Love (III)," the two interlocutors engage in an elaborate fencing match, employing

15. London, 1635, pp. 27–29. For a similar dialogue on the ceremonies surrounding the process of sitting down to meat, see Philomusus, *The Academy of Complements* (London, 1640), pp. 108–10.

expressions of deference, obligation, and service as foils. Victory is achieved not by mastery but by submission. He who wins is he who most effectively serves and obeys the other, since in doing so he places the other in his debt. Expressions of obligation, unworthiness, and respect thus exclude the self from further obligation and provide for the symbolic acquisition of real social power.

So the speaker of "Love (III)," by asserting his unworthiness and declaring his desire to serve rather than to be served, attempts to shun the acknowledgment of his complete dependence upon his superior. His "avoidance of Love" is, in essence, a rejection of the obligation that his superior's beneficence imposes upon him, an obligation which Milton's Satan calls "The debt immense of endless gratitude, / So burthensome still paying, still to owe."[16] To receive beyond desert is to be hampered with a debt that can never be repaid. As Denys de Refuges observes in his *Treatise of the Court*, "we are . . . shame fac'd before those whom we are oblig'd and beholding, without having had the meanes to requite."[17] Like Satan, the speaker of "Love (III)" finds it easier to confess his own ingratitude and shame than to express the infinite gratitude necessary to begin to recompense his Lord. In declaring his unworthiness and subordination, the speaker is, paradoxically, attempting to avoid a recognition of his own complete unworthiness and subordination. His expressions of self-deprecation comprise an elaborate "avoidance ritual" by which he attempts to mark off some part of himself as "sacred," inviolable, not subject to his superior.[18]

16. I borrow the phrase "avoidance of love" from Stanley Cavell's powerful essay, "The Avoidance of Love: A Reading of *King Lear*," in his *Must We Mean What We Say?* (Cambridge: Harvard University Press, 1976), pp. 267–353. Strier, *Love Known*, p. 79, discusses the relevance of Cavell's comments on shame to "Love (III)." The citation from Milton is to *Paradise Lost*, ed. Scott Elledge (New York: Norton, 1975), 4.52–53.

17. Trans. John Reynolds, 2 vols. in 1 (London, 1622), 1:80. Herbert's collection of gnomic wisdom, *Outlandish Proverbs*, includes an adage (no. 805) asserting that "God, and Parents, and our Master, can never be requited" (*Works*, p. 348).

18. Erving Goffman, "The Nature of Deference and Demeanor," in his *Interaction Ritual: Essays on Face-to-Face Behavior* (Garden City: Anchor, 1967), p. 62, defines "avoidance rituals" as "those forms of deference which lead the actor to keep at a distance from the recipient and not violate . . . the 'ideal sphere' that lies around the recipient." In "Love (III)," though, the speaker employs forms of deference not so much to prevent his violation of his host's

Because of the subjugation inherent in accepting the favor of a superior, Henry Peacham recommends the complete avoidance of dining at the table of the great. When "a great man inviteth you to dinner to his table," Peacham observes, "the sweetness of that favor and kindness is made distasteful by the awe of his greatness."[19] For Peacham, the experience, although in itself an honor, is inherently humiliating: "in his presence not to be covered, to sit down and to be placed where and under whom he pleaseth, to be tongue-tied all the while . . . you must endure to be carved unto many times of the first, worst, or rawest of the meat." Superiors, he remarks, revel in doling out scraps from their tables to subordinates, because "they love you should have a kind of dependency of them, that they might make use of you at their pleasure." Like Jonson in "To Penshurst," Peacham differentiates himself from those "faine to sit . . . At great mens tables," declaring: "I had rather dine even at a threepenny ordinary, where I may be free and merry, than to be a dumb tenant for two hours at a lord's table."[20] Similarly, in *The Diall of Princes*, Antony de Guevara warns: "that day the Courtyer graunteth to dyne with any man, the same day hee bindeth himselfe to be beholding to him that bids him."[21]

The speaker of "Love [III]" indeed attempts to elude with all his verbal resources the subordination inherent in the acceptance of his superior's invitation to supper. Yet his Lord demonstrates even greater dexterity and courtesy, countering every move of the speaker and displaying a hospitality that is truly overwhelming. Like Peacham's lord, the host of "Love [III]" acts in a manner that emphasizes his guest's dependency upon him. By right of creation, redemption, and sustenance, the host of "Love [III]" asserts his authority to compel others to sit and be served in his house. But unlike Peacham's lord, the host of "Love [III]" does not carve the "worst of the meat" for his guest. Rather, like the hospitable

---

"ideal sphere" as to protect his own "ideal sphere" from violation by his host.

19. *The Truth of Our Times* (1638), in *The Complete Gentleman, The Truth of Our Times, and The Art of Living in London*, ed. Virgil B. Heltzel (Ithaca: Cornell University Press, 1962), p. 203.

20. Ibid., p. 196; "To Penshurst," ll. 65–66, in *Ben Jonson*, ed. C. H. Herford, Percy Simpson, and Evelyn Simpson, 11 vols. (Oxford: Clarendon Press, 1925–1952), 8:95. David Riggs of Stanford University called my attention to the relationship between "To Penshurst" and "Love [III]."

21. Trans. Thomas North (London, 1619), p. 619.

lord of Penshurst, Sir Robert Sidney, he offers to his guest the "lords owne meate" ("To Penshurst," 1. 62), and even stoops to serve the meat himself.

Yet such gestures of condescension by the powerful can be more coercive than outright commands. As Guazzo remarks, inferiors "are marvellous wel apaid when they see a Gentleman, notwithstanding the inequalitie, which is betweene them, to make him selfe their equall. Whereby they are induced to love him, to honor him, and to doe him service."[22] By deigning to approach their inferiors on apparently equal terms, social superiors reward their inferiors. This reward, moreover, encourages inferiors to further acts of subservience. In the *Discoveries*, Jonson also identifies the persuasive power of such acts of social abasement. Jonson, however, finds not reward but a cause for resentment in those moments when superiors stoop to serve their servants: "I *have* discovered, that a fain'd familiarity in great ones, is a note of certaine usurpation on the lesse. For great and popular men, faine themselves to bee servants to others, to make those slaves to them."[23] To Jonson, the act of social condescension accomplishes a kind of inverted usurpation that results in the covert enslavement of those who are ostensibly being rewarded by familiarity with the powerful. This enslavement is all the more binding for the veil of beneficence it dons.[24]

By descending the social hierarchy in order to serve his dusty and unworthy guest, the host of "Love (III)" reinforces that hierarchy by acting in a way that induces his inferior "to love him, to honor him, to do him service." He makes himself a servant in order to make the speaker a kind of slave. When he says to the speaker, "You must sit down . . . and taste my meat," the coer-

---

22. *The Civile Conversation*, 1:192.
23. *Ben Jonson*, 8:597–98. On Jonson's enigmatic relationship to the authorities to whom his poems are addressed, see Stanley Fish's provocative essay, "Authors-Readers: Jonson's Community of the Same," *Representations* 7 (1984): 26–58.
24. Pierre Bourdieu, *Outline of a Theory of Practice*, trans. Richard Nice (Cambridge: Cambridge University Press, 1977), p. 191, asserts that "when domination can only be exercised in its *elementary form*, i.e. directly, between one person and another, it cannot take place overtly and must be disguised under the veil of enchanted relationships . . . . in order to be socially recognized, it must get itself misrecognized." Jonson astutely exposes both the domination inherent in acts of social condescension and the enchantment with which this domination is disguised.

cive power of the Lord's own act of submission is made manifest. He offers the finest fare from his table, but compels the speaker to accept. It is not just that "the polite form [of 'must'] is the thinnest of coverings for the naked command," as Stanley Fish observes.[25] Rather, the request obliges the speaker precisely because of the politeness and social abasement through which it is expressed. Love's gentle behest is a much more subtle—and therefore more constraining—version of the decree by which a host ends a dispute over seating arrangements in a sixteenth-century dialogue: "You shall sit there," he tells his guest, "have I not power to commaunde in my house?"[26]

The Country Parson, Herbert's manual of conduct for rural clergy, displays great sensitivity to the manipulative power of such acts of social condescension. "The poor," Herbert observes, "are welcome also to [the Country Parson's] table, whom he sometimes purposely takes home with him, setting them close by him, and carving for them, both for his own humility, and their comfort, who are much cheered with such friendliness" (p. 243). The Parson's hospitality and courtesy, like his displays of charity, "causeth [his poor parishioners] still to depend on him; and so by continuall, and fresh bounties, unexpected to them, but resolved to himself, hee wins them to praise God more" (pp. 244–45). Similarly, the host of "Love (III)" enforces dependence through gestures of humility, through stooping to serve his subordinate, surprising his guest with his unexpected bounty and hospitality. Such is the essence of courtesy: manipulating the behavior of others through words and gestures that manifest beneficence and declare subordination.

Such hierarchical condescension is also the essence of the sacrifice which the Lord's Supper commemorates: God becoming man, offering himself to and for man. After the Last Supper, Jesus asks his apostles: "For whether is greater, hee that sitteth at meat, or hee that serveth? Is not he that sitteth at meat? But I am among you as he that serveth" (Luke 22:27, AV). Like the host of "Love

25. *Living Temple*, p. 134. Strier, *Love Known*, p. 83, correctly asserts that "In the courtesy framework, the graciousness of grace is one with its irresistibility." *Outlandish Proverbs*, no. 589, observes: "There is great force hidden in a sweet command" (*Works*, p. 341).

26. *The Elizabethan Home Discovered in Two Dialogues by Claudius Hollyband and Peter Erondell*, ed. Muriel St. Clare Byrne (London: Westminster, 1925), p. 25.

(III)," Jesus consciously violates the principles of hierarchical decorum, making his inferiors sit at meat while he serves. In the Christian framework, normal status indicators such as the equation of service and subordination are inverted, so that "every one that exalteth himselfe, shall be abased; and he that humbleth himselfe, shall be exalted" (Luke 18:14). Just as the Son's greatness is measured by the degree to which he is willing to humble himself for man, so is man's ultimate greatness measured by the degree to which he is willing to humble himself for God: "Humble yourselves in the sight of the Lord, and he shall lift you up" (James 4:10).

This is exactly what the speaker of "Love (III)" attempts to do. He engages in forms of self-deprecation that allow his host the opportunity to perform the beneficent action of lifting him up. This conjunction of courteous self-deprecation and Christian humility is far from coincidental. In the passage from Castiglione advocating the initial refusal of honor from a superior, one of the interlocutors suggests that "me thinke ye have this clause out of the Gospel, where it is writen: When thou art bid to a mariage, goe and sit thee down in the lowest roome, that when he commeth that bid thee, he may say, Friend come higher, and so it shall bee an honour for thee in the sight of the guestes."[27] The Christian inversion of earthly hierarchies intersects the language by which a social supplicant addresses his superior. A humble persona is appropriate to social and devotional performances because it demonstrates the supplicant's recognition of the system of hierarchical differences into which he is attempting to insinuate himself; at the same time, such a persona disguises his ultimate desire to rise. Both the Christian supplicant and the social subordinate must approach their respective superiors in a posture of submission. The Christian's response to God's grace enjoys a common language and a common set of behavioral imperatives with a social inferior's response to his superior's beneficence because they share analogous political pressures. As Stefano Guazzo remarks, gentlemen should behave "according to that philosophical and Christian saying, That the more loftie we are

27. *Book of the Courtier*, p. 109. Sir Fredericke refers here to the parable of the wedding feast, Luke 14:7–10. Bloch, *Spelling the Word*, pp. 99–112, identifies the many biblical precedents for "Love (III)," including this parable.

placed, the more lowly wee ought to humble ourselves: which is in deed, the way to ryse higher."[28]

Herbert's portrait of man's relationship to God in terms of a social transaction between an inferior and a superior releases the linguistic energy inherent in this fusion of social and sacred behavior in the Renaissance. But it also demonstrates the potential duplicity of any display of one's own humility. If humility is indeed "the way to ryse higher," can any expression of it remain uncontaminated by the inverted forms of pride and self-exaltation it entails? Herbert's own sense of himself, we need to remember, was quite fully invested in the very forms of humility and subordination by which the speaker of "Love (III)" attempts to avoid divine grace. According to Nicholas Ferrar, Herbert's "Motto, with which he used to conclude all things that might seem to tend any way to his own honour," was "Lesse then the least of Gods mercies." Ferrar also records that Herbert "in his ordinarie speech" would refer to Jesus as "My Master."[29]

Yet in "Love (III)" these same qualities—self-deprecation and subordination—are revealed to be impertinent and inadequate accounts of man's relationship to God. It is as if in "Love (III)" Herbert is exposing the incipient pride of his characteristic humility while revealing the close relationship between insolence and submission that the formulae of courtesy intend to conceal. In a sermon on Genesis 32:10 (the verse from which Herbert's motto is taken), Donne observes, "We are not worthy as to profess our unworthiness . . . . even humility it self is a pride, if we think it to be our own."[30] The speaker of "Love (III)," in stubbornly professing his unworthiness and thus contradicting his Lord's declaration that "You shall be he," is asserting a kind of worthiness and pride—the worthiness to judge his own unworthiness, the pride of thinking humility to be his own.[31]

28. *The Civile Conversation*, 1:192.

29. The quotations are from Ferrar's preface to *The Temple*, "The Printers to the Reader," in *Works*, pp. 4–5.

30. *The Sermons of John Donne*, ed. George Potter and Evelyn Simpson, 10 vols. (Berkeley: University of California Press, 1953–1962), 1:271.

31. The arrogance implicit in the speaker's protestations of humility is discussed by Michael McCanles, *Dialectical Criticism and Renaissance Literature* (Berkeley: University of California Press, 1975), p. 76; Fish, *Living Temple*, pp. 131–36; A. D. Nuttall, *Overheard by God: Fiction and Prayer in Herbert, Milton,*

Even his sincere offer to serve suggests, quite presumptuously, that he has something of his own that he may present to God. Like his pledge of service, his desire to go where he deserves implies that service and worth and desert are the criteria by which God dispenses his grace. But such criteria defy the very essence of grace; as Edwin Sandys asserts, "It is called grace, because it is given gratis; freely and undeservedly on our parts, to whom it is given."[32]

In *The Saints Humiliation*, Samuel Torshell reveals the theological pride inherent in the rejection of God's hospitality because of a conviction of unworthiness:

> Let not our unworthinesse discourage us, to maintaine these or the like Scruples: Will God looke upon such poore abject worthlesse Wretches? If I should offer any Service, would he not contemne both it and me? If I were more worthy, I would then draw neare him: as I am I dare neither sue for entertainment nor expect it. Away with such proud reasonings, such shewes of humilitie: would wee be challengers rather than beggars?[33]

For Torshell, the objections by which the speaker of "Love (III)" asserts his unworthiness are only "shewes of humilitie" which cloak "proud reasonings"; they are challenges to a God from whom we may only beg. A genuine awareness of our unworthiness, Torshell argues, would lead us not to dispute with or withdraw from God but to approach him and pray for acceptance.

In like manner, John Wing asserts in *Jacobs Staffe* that although you should judge yourself unworthy,

> if the Lord thinke you worthy it is well enough, you are bound to the one, he is free to the other, though it be your duty to account meanely of your self, yet it is his mercy to accept you as worthy of his best favours, and your estate must be conceived of, according to his, not

Dante and St. John (London: Methuen, 1980), pp. 65–68; and Strier, *Love Known*, p. 80.

32. *Sermons*, ed. John Ayre (Cambridge, 1841), p. 297. Sandys is paraphrasing Augustine on the Psalms. On the issue of grace in Protestant theology and literature, see William Halewood, *The Poetry of Grace: Reformation Themes and Structures in English Seventeenth-Century Poetry* (New Haven: Yale University Press, 1970), pp. 33–70; Barbara Kiefer Lewalski, *Protestant Poetics and the Seventeenth-Century Religious Lyric* (Princeton: Princeton University Press, 1978), pp. 3–27; and Strier, *Love Known*, passim.

33. London, 1633, p. 115.

your owne estimate . . . they who alledge [unworthiness] . . . doe make the favour and love of God farre inferiour to mans.[34]

To contend with God about one's unworthiness is to invert the very hierarchy that one's expressions of unworthiness are intended to assert. Although one's duty is to account oneself unworthy, one must also accept God's estimate of one's worth; to do otherwise is to elevate one's own judgment above God's.

At the moment of divine invitation, the speaker of "Love (III)" is torn between the necessary assertion of his own unworthiness and the duty such unworthiness entails of yielding to the judgment of his superior. This dilemma is inherent in the two rubrics prefacing the service of the Eucharist in the Book of Common Prayer. When the parishioners have been negligent to attend the Lord's Supper, the minister is to beseech the congregation

> that ye will not refuse to come thereto, being so lovingly called and bidden of God himself. Ye know how grievous and unkind a thing it is, when a man hath prepared a rich feast . . . and yet they which be called without any cause most unthankfully refuse to come . . . . When God calleth you, be you not ashamed to say you will not come? . . . what thing can this be accounted else, than a further contempt and unkindness unto God? Truly it is a great unthankfulness to say nay when ye be called.[35]

The very language by which the speaker of "Love (III)" attempts to justify his refusal to partake of his Lord's meat ("I the unkinde, ungratefull," "let my shame / Go where it doth deserve") is here used to describe the effect of such refusal. An authentic sense of unkindness, ungratefulness, or shame should not discourage the communicant from approaching but encourage him to approach even more fervently.

Yet when the parishioners have been receiving the Eucharist negligently and without proper reverence, the minister's duty is not to encourage them to communicate but to "exhort" them

> to consider the dignity of the holy mystery, and the great peril of the unworthy receiving thereof . . . so that in no wise you come but in

---

34. Flushing, 1621, pp. 126–30.

35. *The Book of Common Prayer 1559: The Elizabethan Prayer Book*, ed. John E. Booty (Washington, D.C.: Folger Shakespeare Library, 1976), pp. 254–56. Bloch, *Spelling the Word*, pp. 102–4, examines the biblical background of this passage in her discussion of "Love (III)."

the marriage garment, required of God in Holy Scripture, and so come and be received as worthy partakers of such a heavenly table . . . . For otherwise the receiving of the Holy Communion doth nothing else but increase your damnation.[36]

It is an unkind and ungrateful act to refrain from partaking of the rich feast the Lord has prepared; but it is an extremely perilous venture to approach such a table unworthily. One cannot approach confident of one's own worth because to do so would be the worst form of presumption, and a sign that one was indeed unworthy. But to approach in full awareness of one's unworthiness is to risk damnation. The approach to the Eucharist, like the approach to figures of political power, is dangerous, full of great peril and potentially great rewards: "as the benefit is great, if with a truly penitent heart and lively faith we receive that holy Sacrament . . . so is the danger great if we receive the same unworthily."[37] Correspondingly, Guazzo observes of communication with princes: "though this conversation be daungerous . . . yet being well used, bringeth estimation and profite."[38]

Herbert's Country Parson, like the speaker of "Love (III)," experiences "great confusion" about how to behave at the table of his Lord. Discussing the much-debated point of the proper posture for the reception of the Eucharist, Herbert initially concedes that "The Feast indeed requires sitting, because it is a Feast," apparently aligning himself with Puritan controversialists who saw elements of Catholic superstition and idolatry in the kneeling required in the Book of Common Prayer, and who argued that sitting was more appropriate because it signified "rest, that is, a full finishing through Christ of all the ceremonial law and a perfect work of redemption wrought, that giveth rest forever."[39] Herbert, though, immediately distances himself from this view, asserting that although the decorum of a feast requires sitting, "man's unpreparednesse asks kneeling. Hee that comes to the

36. Ibid., pp. 256–57.
37. Ibid., p. 258.
38. *The Civile Conversation*, 1:210.
39. *Works*, p. 259. Donald J. McGinn, ed., *The Admonition Controversy* (New Brunswick: Rutgers University Press, 1949), p. 211. McGinn, pp. 209–13, collects the major texts by Whitgift and Cartwright on the issue of the proper posture for reception of the Eucharist.

Sacrament, hath the confidence of a Guest, and hee that kneels, confesseth himself an unworthy one, and therefore differs from other Feasters: but hee that sits, or lies, puts up to an Apostle: Contentiousnesse in a feast of Charity is more scandall then any posture" (p. 259). Paradoxically, one is to approach the Sacrament with "the confidence of a Guest," but in a posture by which he "confesseth himself an unworthy one." To sit with the confidence of a guest and without a confession of unworthiness is to presume to the status of an apostle.[40]

The speaker of "Love (III)" inverts this presumption. He does not approach his Lord's table with the confidence of a guest; instead, he confesses himself unworthy to be there. Yet this confession provides him with the occasion for a contentiousness and presumption as scandalous as that precipitated by non-Conformist arguments about sitting as the proper posture for reception. In contending with his Lord about his own worthiness to be invited, the speaker "puts up to" his Lord, assumes for himself the Lord's prerogative to determine whether or not the speaker indeed belongs there. He expresses not the confidence of a guest, but the confidence of one who can know for certain that he is unworthy to be a guest. When told by his host that he "must sit down . . . and taste my meat," the speaker is compelled in a complex gesture of complete surrender to presume to the status of an apostle. He gives up his proud and stubborn claims to unworthiness and receives in return a feast for which no man can be worthy.

As Chana Bloch asserts, in "Love (III)" Herbert "explores, with sympathy and without censorship, the painful contradictions of the human condition."[41] The poem uncovers the pride inherent in the speaker's protestations of unworthiness; yet in doing so, the poem reveals the full nature of his unworthiness. The poem manifests God's overwhelming love for man, but at the same time it compels man to accept an ontology of complete dependence upon God. The thrust of the poem is to deny any possibility of reciprocity between God and man; yet the form of the poem—a dialogue between God and man—suggests at least the prospect of verbal reciprocity. The poem's tone is that of a playfully courteous social encounter. But the language of courtesy

40. In contrast, Strier, *Love Known*, p. 78, n. 41, sees the fact that the speaker sits as proof that "Love (III)" is not primarily a Eucharistic poem.

41. *Spelling the Word*, p. 109.

also provides the medium in which the two interlocutors maneuver for political power.

These dilemmas have proved divisive for discussions of the poem. Vendler, Bloch, and Marcus, for example, focus on the sweetness of the reward the speaker receives and on the gentleness with which it is offered.[42] Stein, Fish, and Strier, on the other hand, emphasize Love's coercive force and the psychological costs of accepting this beneficence.[43] Yet the power of the poem lies in its ability to comprehend such apparently contradictory perspectives on man's relationship to God. Humility is revealed to be both the last refuge of a proud mind and a necessary response to the beneficence of a superior. Divine love is depicted as both a coercive social superior and a gentle host. With remarkable brevity and grace, the poem displays the extreme anxiety and immense rewards of the Christian devotional life.

Throughout *The Temple*, Herbert's various speakers struggle to find a way to serve God, to achieve a status based upon desert.[44] But here, in the last lyric of "The Church," the speaker is instructed to "sit and eat," to display his status as the undeserving and unilateral recipient of God's beneficence. The poem is, finally, a comedy of manners, concluding the divine comedy of "The Church" on a note of gentle mirth.[45] But like most good

42. Vendler, *Poetry of Herbert*, pp. 54–55, 58–60, 232, 274–76; Marcus, *Childhood and Cultural Despair*, pp. 116–17; Bloch, *Spelling the Word*, pp. 99–112.

43. Stein, *George Herbert's Lyrics*, pp. 190–95; Fish, *Living Temple*, pp. 131–36; Strier, *Love Known*, pp. 74–80. However, Strier, *Love Known*, p. 77, n. 37, does suggest a similarly synthetic account of the poem: "Both Fish and Bloch are right—the divine voice does have an edge of toughness and the poem *is* truly sweet. The toughness makes for the sweetness."

44. The most explicit expressions of Herbert's recurrent desire to serve his God include "The Dedication," "The Altar," "The Thanksgiving," "Affliction (I)," "Employment (I)," "Praise (I)," "The Windows," "Employment (II)," "Submission," "Obedience," "Dialogue," "Providence," "Love Unknown," "The Priesthood," "The Crosse," "The Odour. 2 Cor. ii. 15," and "The Elixir."

45. Vendler, *Poetry of Herbert*, p. 275, sees the poem in terms of a "social comedy," and Strier, *Love Known*, p. 74, refers to the poem as a "comedy of manners." In *The Country Parson*, Herbert explores the rhetorical power of the self-deprecating humor that contributes to the comic ambiance of "Love (III)." "A pleasantness of disposition," he observes, is "of great use," because men will "sell the interest, and ingagement of their discourses for no price sooner, then that of mirth . . . even to the losse of honour" (p. 252). Similarly, the Country Parson "condescends to humane frailties both in himselfe and others; and intermingles some mirth in his discourses occasionally, according to the pulse of the hearer" (p. 268).

comedies, it is also a problem comedy, containing deep political tensions, and requiring coercion by a figure of superior power in order to achieve a successful resolution.[46] In "Love (III)," Herbert conjoins the ceremonies of piety and courtesy in order to reveal how astonishingly complex, and how unutterably simple, are the dynamics of the conjunction between God and man. As it fuses theological and social definitions of *grace*, "Love (III)" discloses the gentleness and the force of God's love for man, despite man's unworthiness, and the necessity and presumption of man's protestations of unworthiness. It is a feast for which we are not worthy.

46. Fish, *Living Temple*, p. 136, asserts that the sense of completion communicated by "Love (III)" is "a closure which, rather than being earned, is imposed."

8

CRASHAW'S EPIPHANY HYMN: FAITH OUT OF DARKNESS

Lorraine Roberts

Of all the important English religious poets of the seventeenth century, Richard Crashaw has generally received the least sympathetic response from readers and critics. He is likely to be attacked on three grounds: his use of ingenious imagery allegedly operates at the expense of thought, his development of themes is often found wanting in logic or dramatic progression, and his expression of emotion is thought to be too flamboyant.[1] But when one examines the critical commentary on Crashaw's sacred poetry, one discovers that these three negative judgments arise from a consideration of only a few poems, rather than from a consideration of all. Thus, the comments may apply to "The Weeper" or some of the sacred epigrams; they do not, however, apply to excellent poems such as the Nativity or Epiphany Hymns. The latter poem in particular serves well to discredit the three negative generalizations about Crashaw's poetry, for it

1. Marc F. Bertonasco, appendix 1, "Crashaw Scholarship in the Twentieth Century, Survey and Assessment," in his *Crashaw and the Baroque*, pp. 123–43 (University: University of Alabama Press, 1971), assesses Crashaw criticism and notes where it is deficient in understanding Crashaw's intellectual content, his use of emblem, and his use of Salesian meditative structure. Albert R. Cirillo in "Recent Studies in Crashaw," *English Literary Renaissance* 9 (1979): 183–93, attests to other deficiencies when he says, "The most notable exception to the common treatment of Crashaw as not genuinely English in spirit and sensibility and therefore deficient as a poet in some way has been Ruth Wallerstein's classic study. There appears to be a trend in recent studies to get beyond facile and clichéd preconceptions of Crashaw as 'baroque' in order to deal directly with the poetry in a critical and analytical manner" (p. 188).

demonstrates that Crashaw is consciously in control of the poem's structure, imagery, and theme, and that his intent is not only emotional but rational as well.

Not all readers agree, however, that a conscious control of structure and theme is manifested in the Epiphany Hymn. While the four-part division that George Walton Williams outlines for the poem elicits no disagreement, the logic underlying the four parts has not gone unquestioned. The choral poem opens with the arrival of the Magi to worship Christ, the new day in night (ll. 1–41); it then moves to a rejection of former pagan religions that falsely worshiped the sun as God (ll. 42–133); from this past time it projects into the future to the moment of the Crucifixion and the sun's eclipse, interpreted as a sign of the sun's reparation for having accepted the false worship of men (ll. 134–233); the poem closes with the conversion and the obeisance of men and nature, represented by the figures of Dionysius the Areopagite, the Magi, and the sun (ll. 234–54).[2]

One is not surprised by the convergence of all planes of time in the poem—past, present, future, eternity—for the liturgical basis of the poem naturally allows for it. Nor is one surprised by the section that banishes religions that falsely worshiped the sun, for Milton anticipated Crashaw with such an account in his Nativity poem. Nor in fact is one surprised by the presence of the Passion in a poem about the manifestation of Christ to the Gentiles. Rosemond Tuve has reminded us that this alignment had its inception in Scripture and its flowering in poets and painters through the ages.[3] The presence of the Crucifixion in a poem about the Epiphany completes the theological significance of the Incarnation, a significance one would expect to be the climactic moment of the poem. Yet in the Epiphany Hymn more action follows this moment, namely, the conversion of Dionysius the Areopagite, and it is his presence in the third division that has elicited questions about the structure and the theme of the poem.

Ruth Wallerstein, for example, believing there is a disjunction between the light-dark imagery of the first part of the hymn

2. *Image and Symbol in the Sacred Poetry of Richard Crashaw* (Columbia: University of South Carolina Press, 1963), p. 70.

3. *A Reading of George Herbert* (Chicago: University of Chicago Press, 1952), p. 65.

and the attention given to Dionysius later, declares that "the statement of the concept [of the *via negativa*] does not flower from the vision of the poem as a whole, but seems added to it."[4] Austin Warren sees a disjunction between Crashaw's earlier interest in Teresian mysticism, with its emphasis on "picture thinking" about the spiritual world, and his seemingly radical shift to the *via negativa* of Dionysian mysticism, with its emphasis on the voiding of sense perceptions and intellect in order to apprehend God.[5]

If the Epiphany Hymn were primarily about mysticism, as both Warren and Wallerstein—indeed, most critics—presume, then their questions and objections would inevitably follow. But the Epiphany Hymn is not primarily about the mystical way; it is about faith—about the way of belief that exists for those beyond the time of the historical Christ in the darkened natural world.

In a poem whose scene of action is the manifestation of God in the Christ Child, that is, the spiritual becoming material, why would Crashaw advocate the *via negativa*, the conscious voiding of the material to know the spiritual? Dionysius is not present in the poem primarily as an advocate of the *via negativa*, but rather as one whose example shows us the way to epiphany. The poem contains not just one illumination or epiphany, that is, that of the Magi, but two, that of Dionysius also. The reason for the presence of the great mystic in this poem becomes clearer when one recognizes that the structure of the poem embodies a comparison of sorts between the conversion of the Magi and that of Dionysius, the first taking place in the presence of the human Christ, the second in the darkness of the Crucifixion.

With careful artistry Crashaw emphasizes imagery of the "face" in the first conversion—the face of God as well as the face of the natural sun, along with all the features contained therein—eyes, cheek, lips. Facial imagery is so prevalent that it cannot be ignored, yet only one critic has called attention to it—and merely to suggest that Warren is incorrect in saying the

4. *Richard Crashaw: A Study in Style and Poetic Development* (Madison: University of Wisconsin Press, 1935), p. 143.
5. *Richard Crashaw: A Study in Baroque Sensibility* (University: Louisiana State University Press, 1939), pp. 147–51.

poem lacks sensuous imagery.[6] This frequent use of facial imagery, however, helps to underscore the contrast between the earlier epiphany of the Magi and the later one of Dionysius, and thus the overall theme and intellectual content of the poem.

Perhaps the more obvious and traditional paradoxes of light and dark in the poem obscure the emphasis meant to be placed on the "face" of God as it displaces the "face" of the natural sun as the light of the world. Yet the opening of the poem announces this theme and action:

> (1. Kinge.) Bright BABE! Whose awfull beautyes make
> The morn incurr a sweet mistake;
> (2.) For whom the'officious heavns devise
> To disinheritt the sun's rise,
> (3). Delicately to displace
> The Day, and plant it fairer in thy face. (ll. 1–6)[7]

These lines echo several biblical passages that compare Christ's face with the sun, such as "his face shone like the sun" (Matt. 17:2). It is appropriate, indeed traditional, when speaking of events surrounding the Incarnation to do so in terms of human imagery. God has become man and is manifested to the Gentile world, represented by the Magi. He has thus the physical attributes of man—face, eyes, smile, cheeks, lips, all of which and more are part of the imagery of the face in the hymn.

Yet this concrete imagery is balanced by some very abstract imagery as well. A prime example of this balance is Crashaw's "depiction" of Christ:

> (1.) All-circling point. All centring sphear.
> The world's one, round, AEternall year.
> (2.) Whose full and all-unwrinkled face
> Nor sinks nor swells with time or place;
> (3.) But every where and every while
> Is One Consistent solid smile. (ll. 26–31)

Nothing could be more concrete than for Crashaw to evoke

---

6. Joseph P. Hilyard, "The Negative Wayfarers of Richard Crashaw's 'A Hymn in the Glorious Epiphanie,'" in *Essays on Richard Crashaw*, ed. Robert M. Cooper (Salzburg: Institut für Anglistik, 1979), pp. 174–75.

7. All quotations of the poem are from *The Complete Poetry of Richard Crashaw*, ed. George Walton Williams (Garden City, N.Y.: Anchor Books, Doubleday, 1970).

God's "full and all-unwrinkled face," his "One Consistent solid smile," lines reminiscent of one in Herbert's "To all Angels and Saints": "See the smooth face of God without a frown" (l. 2).[8] On the other hand, nothing could be more abstract than "All-circling point. All centring sphear." This technique of balancing the concrete and the abstract is appropriate for, even emblematic of, the God-Man being described. Ultimately, however, in this most metaphysical of Crashaw's poems,[9] the conceit or intellectual idea, not the visualization of images, is important. Thus, this passage asserts that God is changeless and loving, unlike the sun, which—the poem emphasizes—changes daily and yearly and leads men astray. When Christ is no longer in men's presence, his changelessness, his love continue as sources of illumination.

The ways that men find God are central to the poem. As Robert V. Young has noted, the word *way* is used as a rhyme in the Epiphany Hymn seven times, underscoring this concept.[10] In the opening of the poem the Magi are fortunate to see the "glory of God in the face of Christ" (2 Cor. 4:6). After a life spent in the false worship of the sun, the Magi are "illuminated" by a star that directs them to the manger, where they have the privilege of seeing God in the flesh.

> (1.) We, who strangely went astray,
>   Lost in a bright
>   Meridian night,
> (2.) A Darkenes made of too much day,
>   (3.) Becken'd from farr
>   By thy fair starr,
> Lo at last have found our way. (ll. 15–21)

Both the natural and spiritual worlds—that is, the human Christ and the "illumination" produced by the star, a star less material than spiritual—combine to produce their epiphany, although one could say the natural dominates, because the Magi have before them the human figure of Christ. This somewhat greater emphasis on the human Christ parallels the liturgy from

---

8. *The Works of George Herbert*, ed. F. E. Hutchinson (Oxford: Clarendon Press, 1941), p. 77.

9. Warren, *Richard Crashaw*, p. 148.

10. *Richard Crashaw and the Spanish Golden Age* (New Haven: Yale University Press, 1982), p. 105.

Christmas up to Epiphany, which also stresses Christ's humanity. The feast of the first Epiphany celebrates equally Christ's humanity and his divinity, while the following four epiphanies of the liturgical calendar emphasize Christ's divinity, recounting, in fact, some of his first miracles.[11] This same movement from an emphasis on Christ's humanity in the epiphany of the Magi to a greater emphasis on his divinity in the epiphany of those who live after the death of the historical Christ is reproduced in the Epiphany Hymn.

This movement is provided for us by the wise men, who have visionary powers that allow them to foresee the eventual death of Christ on the cross and the darkening of the natural world in response. The sun, guilty of having accepted the worship of men, is glad to be free of its sin and does penance by bowing its head at midday for three hours. Crashaw describes the eclipse in sensuous "face" imagery:

> (3). That forfeiture of noon to night shall pay
> All the idolatrous thefts done by this night of day;
> And the Great Penitent presse his own pale lipps
> With an elaborate love-eclipse
> > To which the low world's lawes
> > Shall lend no cause
> (Cho.) Save those domestick which he borrowes
> From our sins and his own sorrowes. (ll. 149–56)

The human attributes of the sun serve to connect the subservience and obeisance of nature to those of men. For in doing penance for its past sins, the sun, the world of nature, becomes a means of leading men to God:

> (2.) And as before his too-bright eye
> Was Their more blind idolatry,
> So his officious blindnes now shall be
> Their black, but faithfull perspective of thee. (ll. 168–71)

The natural world of the sun—transformed by the supernatural eclipse—will lead men to a belief in the supernatural world, for they will be unable to explain the eclipse by natural laws.

11. A. B. Chambers, "Christmas: The Liturgy of the Church and English Verse of the Renaissance," in *Literary Monographs*, vol. 6, ed. Eric Rothstein and Joseph Anthony Wittreich, Jr. (Madison: University of Wisconsin Press, 1975), pp. 111–18.

The power of God to become man on the one hand or to subdue the natural world on the other is the means to produce epiphany. Thus, when the wise men foresee the darkening of the sun at the Crucifixion, they predict the relationship of the sun and the future believers in these words:

> (1.) Three sad hour's sackcloth then shall show to us
> His penance, as our fault, conspicuous.
> (2.) And he more needfully and nobly prove
> The nations' terror now then erst their love.
> (3.) Their hated loves changd into wholsom feares,
> (Cho.) The shutting of his eye shall open Theirs. (ll. 157–62)

Dionysius himself says, in an account of his conversion after witnessing the eclipse,

> . . . both of us at that time, at Heliopolis, being present, and standing together, saw the moon approaching the sun, to our surprise (for it was not appointed time for conjunction); and again from the ninth hour to the evening, supernaturally placed back again into a line opposite the sun . . . . So great are the supernatural things of that appointed time, and possible to Christ alone, the Cause of all, Who worketh great things and marvellous, of which there is not number.[12]

The Magi in Crashaw's Epiphany Hymn contrast their experience in the presence of the new-born Christ with the spiritual illumination of Dionysius. Whereas the Magi are led to Christ by the light of the star, Dionysius will find illumination in darkness at the supernatural eclipse of the sun:

> (2.) By the oblique ambush of this close night
>   Couch't in that conscious shade
> The right-ey'd Areopagite
> Shall with a vigorous guesse invade
> And catche thy quick reflex; and sharply see
>   On this dark Ground
>   To descant THEE.
> (3.) O prize of the rich SPIRIT! with what feirce chase
>   Of his strong soul, shall he
>   Leap at thy lofty FACE,
> And seize the swift Flash, in rebound
> From this obsequious cloud. (ll. 189–200)

This difference in arriving at the same faith—to see "face to

12. As quoted in Williams, *Image and Symbol*, p. 80.

face" or "through a glass darkly"—is of ultimate importance to the theme of the poem.

Most critics emphasize the contrast between the sun-son worship and the banishment of paganism by the new faith, but then fail to see the comparison between the illumination of those present at Christ's birth and of those who come after his death. It is this comparison that occasions the figure of Dionysius in the poem, not the *via negativa*; it is his example as one who saw in darkness and believed, who saw the natural world controlled by the supernatural, rather than his method of contemplation, that fulfills the poem's theme. Just as the sun's darkness taught men to see the true god—"The shutting of his eye shall open Theirs"—so too shall Dionysius's example of conversion teach the rest of mankind how to know God in darkness:

> (1.) Thus shall that reverend child of light,
> (2.) By being scholler first of that new night,
> Come forth Great master of the mystick day;
> (3.) And teach obscure MANKIND a more close way
> By the frugall negative light
> Of a most wise and well-abused Night
> To read more legible thine originall Ray,
> (Cho.) And make our Darknes serve THY day. (ll. 205–12)

I do not deny that this passage is charged with terms and concepts suggestive of Dionysian mysticism. But I do not believe that it functions as an advocacy of this mysticism, that is, as it is understood by many, a rejection of the material world. Rather, the passage functions as a symbol of submission and faith for those who are left with only this material world, but who see in its darkness a sign of divine power and divine love. To Crashaw, mystical union with God is of course the acme of Christian experience, yet he does not seem to suggest that such union is beyond the sincere Christian's spiritual ken. Life on earth for Crashaw is always related to life in heaven. The Epiphany Hymn makes this connection explicit. Asking for a "commerce" between "thy world and ours," "A mutual trade / 'Twixt sun and SHADE" (ll. 215–16), the Magi, as representatives of mankind, wish to make their darkness serve God's day.

Having been taught by Dionysius's example that their

"noble powres" of sight and intelligence will not bring them "the blissfull PRIZE" of "fastening on Thine eyes," they offer to all mankind an alternative to dependence on human faculties. Like the sun, they submit themselves to God: "(Cho.) Now by abased liddes shall learn to be / Eagles; and shut our eyes that we may see" (ll. 231–32). This passage does not suggest the descriptions of mystical experience given by the saints or even by Crashaw in other poems; this is no "luminous trance" or "divine annihilation." It is mystical only in the sense that any epiphany or conversion or spiritual illumination is mystical. The emphasis in the passage is on the "confederacy" of man and God in Christian time. But it is not a confederacy of equals.

Thus in the last stanza, the poem elaborates on the correct order of the natural world and of man in relationship to the heavenly one. The sun bows in adoration to God at the same time that it is to be the "golden index" to man, "Pointing us Home to our own sun / The world's and his HYPERION" (ll. 252–53). Man must use the natural world and its right order to see through it to the divinity of Christ. Even Dionysius in *The Divine Names* speaks to this role of the sun:

> this great, all-bright and ever-shining sun, which is the visible image of the Divine Goodness, faintly re-echoing the activity of the Good, illumines all things that can receive its light while retaining the utter simplicity of light, and expands above and below throughout the visible world the beams of its own radiance . . . . I say not (as was feigned by the ancient myth) that the sun is the God and Creator of this Universe, and therefore takes the visible world under his special care; but I say that the "invisible things of God from the creation of the world are clearly seen, being understood by the things that are made, even His eternal power and Godhead."[13]

The fact is that Dionysius did not write only of a negative way to God, that is, the shutting down of human eyes and mind as a means of knowing God in exchange for passive emptiness that hopefully is filled by the divine presence. Dionysius also wrote of an affirmative way, suggested by the passage quoted above. That way stresses the use of human eyes and mind in experienc-

13. Dionysius the Areopagite, *On the Divine Names and the Mystical Theology*, ed. C. E. Rolt (London: Macmillan, 1957), pp. 92–94.

ing God (imperfectly of course), for both natural and eccle-
siastical signs and symbols are present in the universe to testify
to the presence of the divine.[14] While this way does not lead to
mystical ecstasy, it can lead to faith in Christ, as Dionysius him-
self so effectively shows us by his own example. Christ is the
supreme representation of the affirmative way, the material sign
of a higher divinity, even more, the perfect union of the human
and the divine. Surely the affirmative way is more appropriate
than the negative way in a poem that celebrates the Incarnation
and the manifestation of Christ to all mankind.

The theme of the Epiphany Hymn is, thus, very carefully
structured around the illumination of the Magi and of
Dionysius the Areopagite. The refrain that ends both the sub-
mission of the sun and the submission of the ordinary believer
serves to tie together these different conversions. The fact that
we are dependent on the world of nature, as well as God's inter-
vention in that world through the supernatural star and the
unnatural eclipse of the sun, teaches what faith is. With a con-
sciously and artistically crafted imagery meant to emphasize
the humanity of God and the limitation of human knowledge,
Crashaw works out with great control the paradoxes and the full
significance of the Epiphany. At no point in the poem are our
emotions engaged excessively; what strikes us instead is the
intellectual depth and the consummate control of the poet over
all aspects of his poem.

If Crashaw's Epiphany Hymn is not representative of *all* his
work, it is representative of a larger portion than is popularly
supposed. A number of the poems have been analyzed struc-
turally and thematically with profitable results: we need only
remind ourselves of Louis L. Martz's study of "Hymn to the
Name of Jesus," of Kerby Neill's analysis of the three versions of
"Hymn in the Holy Nativity," of A. R. Cirillo's examination of
the whole cycle of Christmas-tide poems, of Marc Bertonasco's
defense even of "The Weeper."[15] The present-day reader should

14. Rufus M. Jones, *Studies in Mystical Religion* (London: Macmillan,
1909), pp. 105–8.
15. Martz, *The Poetry of Meditation* (New Haven: Yale University Press,
1954), pp. 331–52; Neill, "Structure and Symbol in Crashaw's 'Hymn in the
Nativity,'" *PMLA* 63 (1948): 101–13; Cirillo, "Crashaw's 'Epiphany Hymn': The
Dawn of Christian Time," *Studies in Philology* 67 (1970): 67–88; Bertonasco,
Crashaw and the Baroque, pp. 94–117.

not forget that Crashaw is in fact a very learned poet, aware of classical forms, biblical tradition, meditative methods, liturgical rites, and Continental trends—all of which to some degree inform his poetry. Some recent critics who have not ignored this fact—Diana Benet, Eugene R. Cunnar, Paul A. Parrish, and Robert V. Young, Jr.—have all argued successfully for a rationality behind a number of the poems.[16] Thus to approach Crashaw's poetry free of the popular censures and aware of its intellectual dimension undoubtedly elicits new insights as well as lends a more balanced assessment of his work as a whole.

16. Benet, "The Redemption of the Sun: Crashaw's Christmastide Poems," in *Essays on Richard Crashaw*, ed. Cooper, pp. 129–44; Cunnar, "Crashaw's Hymn 'To the Name Above Every Name': Background and Meaning," in ibid., pp. 102–28; Parrish, "Crashaw's Two Weepers," *Concerning Poetry* 10, no. 2 (1977): 47–59; Young, "Truth with Precision: Crashaw's Revisions of *A Letter*," *Faith and Reason* (The Journal of Christendom College) 4, no. 3 (1978): 3–17.

9

"THE CORONET": MARVELL'S "CURIOUS FRAME" OF ALLUSION

James Andrew Clark

In his devotional poem "The Coronet," Andrew Marvell takes some garlands once woven for a pastoral love and sets out to rework them into a crown for Messiah:

> When for the Thorns with which I long, too long,
>   With many a piercing wound,
>   My Saviours head have crown'd,
> I seek with Garlands to redress that Wrong:
>   Through every Garden, every Mead,
>   I gather flow'rs (my fruits are only flow'rs)
>   Dismantling all the fragrant Towers
> That once adorn'd my Shepherdesses head. (ll. 1–8)[1]

In the midst of his craft, however, he finds desolation:

> And now when I have summ'd up all my store,
>   Thinking (so I myself deceive)
>   So rich a Chaplet thence to weave
> As never yet the king of Glory wore:
>   Alas I find the Serpent old
>   That, twining in his speckled breast,

1. *The Poems and Letters of Andrew Marvell*, ed. H. M. Margoliouth, 3d ed., rev. by Pierre Legouis, 2 vols. (Oxford: Clarendon Press, 1971), 1:14. Unless otherwise stated, the poetry of Marvell will be quoted from this edition, line numbers being given parenthetically in the text.

> About the flow'rs disguis'd does fold,
> With wreaths of Fame and Interest. (ll. 9–16)

Finally, as Marvell abandons ragged indentation for a justified left-hand margin, the devotional artistry that began in diligence ends in self-reproach and an urgent prayer to Christ:

> Ah, foolish Man, that would'st debase with them,
> And mortal Glory, Heavens Diadem!
> But thou who only could'st the Serpent tame,
> Either his slipp'ry knots at once untie,
> And disentangle all his winding Snare:
> Or shatter too with him my curious frame:
> And let these wither, so that he may die,
> Though set with Skill and chosen out with Care.
> That they, while Thou on both their Spoils dost tread,
> May crown thy Feet, that could not crown thy Head. (ll. 17–26)

The New Critic John Edward Hardy, in a still-luminous reading of Marvell's poem, advances the claim that "critical emphasis must be, not upon what materials Marvell has used, and where he got them . . . but upon what he has, here, wrought with them."[2] Rejecting the mere labeling of poetic sources, Hardy wishes to focus on workmanship rather than on filiations.

Such attention to the text, of course, was the central strength of the New Criticism. In the case of Marvell, however, such an emphasis has two unfortunate consequences. First, it obscures recognition of Marvell the "alchemical ventriloquist," as Joseph Summers has called him, the wide reader and frequent imitator of verse, major and minor, by his predecessors and contemporaries. Summers's work, like that of J. B. Leishman, has shown that study of Marvell's materials need not detract from practical appreciation of his craft.[3]

Hardy's emphasis on the self-sufficient work also isolates his discussion of "The Coronet" from a theory of intertextuality, whether one beginning from what Rosalie Colie labeled "the resources of kind" or one convinced of what Roland

2. "Andrew Marvell's 'The Coronet': The Frame of Curiosity," in *The Curious Frame: Seven Poems in Text and Context* (Notre Dame: Notre Dame University Press, 1962), p. 59.
3. See Leishman, *The Art of Marvell's Poetry* (London: Hutchinson, 1966); and Summers, *The Heirs of Donne and Jonson* (New York and London: Oxford University Press, 1970), pp. 130–55.

Barthes has called the *"irreducible* plurality" of texts.[4] In their distinct ways, both Colie's focus on genres and Barthes's on plurisignification lead back at least to this: while Marvell's poem may be seen as an individual's completed work, it may also be felt as a texture, a *weaving* of quotations, echoes, and allusions that stand in default of a work yet to be framed. By examining "The Coronet" in light of the theory of allusion, I wish to describe as a function of intertextuality Marvell's odd mixture of confidence in and disdain for his own poetic offering, an ambivalence only heightened when the proposed recipient is God.

"The Coronet" poses a problem for any understanding of intertextuality. From one point of view, the poetic filiations of this lyric are tangled and undecidable. The flowers that Marvell speaks of having "set with Skill" represent a generic code of pastoral verse, a set of elegances not ascribable to any particular origin.[5] His four sentences condense and displace the already symbolic discourses of previous lyrics. In good Barthesian fashion, Marvell's poem is "completely woven with quotations, references, and echoes."[6] We should thus be cautious about assigning poetic affinities to Marvell, for, as Harold Bloom says, "No poem has sources." Yet, as Bloom also says, "Criticism is the art of knowing the hidden roads that go from poem to poem."[7] Some, at least, of Marvell's "flow'rs" are specific quotations, utterances literally "chosen out with Care" from

4. See Colie, *The Resources of Kind: Genre-Theory in the Renaissance,* ed. Barbara K. Lewalski (Berkeley and London: University of California Press, 1973), pp. 3–31; Barthes, "From Work to Text," in *Textual Strategies: Perspectives in Post-Structuralist Criticism,* ed. Josué V. Harari (Ithaca: Cornell University Press, 1979), p. 76.

5. Discussions of the genre of "The Coronet" include Colie, *"My Ecchoing Song": Andrew Marvell's Poetry of Criticism* (Princeton: Princeton University Press, 1970), pp. 41–42; Hardy, *Curious Frame,* pp. 58–60; Lewalski, "Marvell as Religious Poet," in *Approaches to Marvell: The York Tercentenary Lectures,* ed. C. A. Patrides (London and Boston: Routledge & Kegan Paul, 1978), p. 256; and Annabel M. Patterson, "'Bermudas' and 'The Coronet': Marvell's Protestant Poetics," *ELH* 44 (1977): 490.

6. Barthes, "From Work to Text," p. 77.

7. Harold Bloom, *The Anxiety of Influence: A Theory of Poetry* (Oxford and New York: Oxford University Press, 1973), pp. 43, 96. With reference to influences on Marvell, see especially the caution by C. A. Patrides, "'Till Prepared for Longer Flight': The Sublunar Poetry of Andrew Marvell," in *Approaches to Marvell,* p. 32.

the texts of identifiable predecessors and applied to his own purposes. I will take up the allusiveness of Marvell's poem from each perspective in turn.

The diction of "The Coronet" illustrates well how an intertextual lexicon may supply the poet with prior codes or what Jonathan Culler has called "anonymous discursive practices."[8] For example, the phrase "curious frame" (l. 22), which I will call a quotation, is also teasingly intertextual in this anonymous sense. Annabel Patterson traces this image of the human body to Psalm 139:15: "My substance was not hid from thee, when I was made in secret, and curiously wrought in the lowest parts of the earth."[9] Both "curious" and "frame" belong to the common store of sixteenth- and seventeenth-century poetic diction, however. Spenser uses both words frequently, though never together. In *Venus and Adonis*, Shakespeare first describes how the Destinies "cross the curious workmanship of nature" by thwarting Adonis's "beauty with infirmities," then, a few lines later, lets Venus command "Nature's death for framing [him] so fair."[10] Even if Marvell read these poems, however, he does not cite "curious frame" from them. They are analogues rather than sources. Better, they are fellow occupants of a shared discursive space.

The poems of George Herbert likewise belong, when we consider "The Coronet," to what Barthes calls the "already read."[11] Marvell's words appear to displace a phrase of Herbert's in "Dulnesse," where "The wanton lover" sings a "curious strain" to his "fairest fair," and "with quaint metaphors her curled hair / Curl[s] o're again."[12] By a similar displacement,

---

8. *The Pursuit of Signs: Semiotics, Literature, Deconstruction* (Ithaca: Cornell University Press, 1981), p. 103. A fuller definition of the term *intertext* is offered by Michael Riffaterre: "An intertext is a corpus of texts, textual fragments, or textlike segments of the sociolect that shares a lexicon and, to a lesser extent, a syntax with the text we are reading" ("Intertextual Representation: On Mimesis as Interpretive Discourse," *Critical Inquiry* 11 [1984]: 142).

9. "Protestant Poetics," p. 492.

10. Hardin Craig and David Bevington, eds., *The Complete Works of Shakespeare*, rev. ed. (Glenview, Ill.: Scott, Foresman, 1973), p. 434 (lines 734–35, 744).

11. "From Work to Text," p. 77.

12. *The Works of George Herbert*, ed. F. E. Hutchinson (Oxford: Clarendon Press, 1941), p. 115 (lines 5–8). In subsequent references, line numbers will be cited parenthetically in the text.

"The Coronet" shares textual space with Herbert's "Home," where we read a prayer, like Marvell's, for dissolution. "Oh loose this frame, this knot of man untie!" (l. 61), Herbert pleads. Marvell, one might say, turns Herbert's twin metaphors for the body into discrete substances, requesting God to "untie" the serpent's "slipp'ry knots" or to "shatter" his own "curious frame" (ll. 20–22).

If we start from other words in "The Coronet," we can again have the uncanny sense that Herbert had already written Marvell's poem. The phrase "winding Snare," for example, may displace and echo by rhyme a central question in Herbert's "Jordan (I)": "Is all good structure in a winding stair?"[13] Again, three central words in "The Coronet" appear first in a stanza of Herbert's "Affliction (V)":

> Affliction then is ours;
> We are the trees, whom shaking fastens more,
> While blustring windes destroy the wanton bowres,
> And ruffle all their curious knots and store. (ll. 19–22)

The words *curious*, *knot*, and *store* are woven into Marvell's text, and yet we can identify no deliberate quotations.

It is not surprising, of course, that Marvell's poem should echo *The Temple*. Marvell the student and Herbert's volume appeared in Cambridge together in the same year, 1633. Moreover, Marvell is considering the way in which curiosity, ambition, and self-interest wind themselves into devotion, a problem that Herbert often considers too. Their shared concerns appear most vividly, perhaps, when we recall "Jordan (II)." There Herbert recounts how in the "joyes" of first religious writing he "sought out quaint words, and trim invention" (ll. 1, 3), just as Marvell later seeks old garlands. But Herbert says that the thoughts and metaphors that "began to burnish, sprout, and swell" (l. 4) within him would not quite serve. He concludes the lyric by depicting vividly his plight and the manner of its removal:

> Nothing could seem too rich to clothe the sunne,
> Much lesse those joyes which trample on his head.

13. A connection between these poems is suggested by Donald M. Friedman, *Marvell's Pastoral Art* (Berkeley: University of California Press, 1970), p. 82.

> As flames do work and winde, when they ascend,
> So did I weave my self into the sense.
> But while I bustled, I might heare a friend
> Whisper, *How wide is all this long pretence!*
> *There is in love a sweetnesse readie penn'd:*
> *Copie out onely that, and save expense.* (ll. 11–18)

Herbert here sums up a store of images. A few of them Marvell does not employ in "The Coronet," especially images that bear strongly Herbert's signature—the flames, the bustle, the whispering friend, the accounts book. Others—clothing, trampling, winding, weaving—reappear in Marvell's poem, deliberately or otherwise. Herbert's religious verse was so paradigmatic that it would have been difficult for Marvell not to sound like him.

And yet no more than Marvell himself is Herbert the only occupant of what Culler has called "the general discursive space that makes a poem intelligible."[14] Outside of *The Temple*, there are many other intertexts for "The Coronet." In stanza 31 of "Saint Mary Magdalene, or The Weeper" (the 1652 version), sometimes called a source for Marvell's "Eyes and Tears," Richard Crashaw, like Marvell, crowns his poem with self-abasement. Mary's tears refuse, Crashaw says,

> to trace
> The Fortune of inferior gemmes,
> Preferr'd to some proud face
> Or pertch'd upon fear'd Diadems.
> Crown'd Heads are toyes. We goe to meet
> A worthy object, our lord's FEET.[15]

In Marvell's own "Horatian Ode" it is Oliver Cromwell who "to the *Commons Feet* presents / A *Kingdome*, for his first years rents" (ll. 85–86) and who "has his Sword and Spoyls ungirt, / To lay them at the *Publick's* skirt" (ll. 89–90). Poems published in *Lucasta* (1649) by Richard Lovelace, Marvell's "Noble Friend," afford other intertexts for "The Coronet." In "The Scrutinie," for example, Lovelace anticipates Marvell's return from a progress "Through every Garden, every Mead" (l. 5):

14. *The Pursuit of Signs*, p. 106.
15. *The Complete Poetry of Richard Crashaw*, ed. George Walton Williams (New York: New York University Press, 1972), p. 137. The references to "fear'd Diadems" and "Crown'd Heads" are lacking in the versions of 1646 and 1648, written before the execution of Charles I. See *Complete Poetry*, p. 136.

Then, if when I have lov'd my round,
   Thou prov'st the pleasant she;
With spoyles of meaner Beauties crown'd,
   I laden will returne to thee,
Ev'n sated with Varietie. (ll. 16–20)[16]

Another image from "The Coronet" is anticipated in "To Chloe, Courting Her for his Friend." Acting on behalf of his rival Damas, Lovelace declares unto Chloe,

I'd not be King, unlesse there sate
Lesse Lords that shar'd with me in State;
   Who by their cheaper Coronets know
   What glories from my Diadem flow. (ll. 9–12)

Lovelace even poses for Chloe a choice like the one Marvell poses for Christ: "*Chloe* behold! Our Fate's the same, / Or make me Cinders too, or quench his Flame" (ll. 7–8).

In a dedicatory poem to *Lucasta*, John Hall praises Lovelace's "desire of Glory" and sees on the poet's head "safely set / Both th' *Delphick* wreath and *Civic* Coronet" (ll. 7–8). Marvell's own dedicatory poem comes just before Hall's and, in some well-known lines, uses similar imagery to a much different end. In Lovelace's "candid Age," "Twas more esteemd to give, then weare the Bayes" (ll. 5, 8).

Modest ambition studi'd only then,
To honour not her selfe, but worthy men.
These vertues now are banisht out of Towne,
Our Civill Wars have lost the Civicke crowne.
He highest builds, who with most Art destroys,
And against others Fame his owne employs.
I see the envious Caterpillar sit
On the faire blossome of each growing wit. (ll. 9–16)

In "The Coronet" that caterpillar becomes "the Serpent old" (l. 13) sitting among Marvell's own flowers. From only these examples, it is easy to understand why the Barthesian text is plural and why that quality inheres in "the *stereographic plurality* of the signifiers that weave it."[17] Reading "The Coronet" is like

16. *The Poems of Richard Lovelace*, ed. C. H. Wilkinson (Oxford: Clarendon Press, 1930), p. 27. In subsequent references, line numbers will be cited parenthetically in the text.
17. Barthes, "From Work to Text," p. 76.

reading a palimpsest. Marvell's lyric well illustrates the founding power of Barthes's quotations without quotation marks.

In view of this connection between two of Marvell's own poems, however, belief in a total *mise en abîme* becomes more difficult to maintain. As Thomas Greene has argued, some modes of allusion are not "totally aleatory."[18] To stop with the "already read" is to ignore Marvell's salient quotations from other poets. Greene argues powerfully that "When a literary work . . . calls to the reader's attention its own deliberate allusiveness, it can be said to be affirming its own historicity, its own involvement in disorderly historical process."[19] In the special case of self-conscious intertextuality, Greene concludes, "we are able to analyze the function of the subtext in terms of a specific retrospective vision."[20] In "The Coronet" something of that vision may be inferred from Marvell's specific allusions to Herbert, Edmund Spenser, and Sir Philip Sidney.

We may consider first the relation of "The Coronet" to Herbert's own crown-poem, "A Wreath."[21] Immediately, Marvell's phrase for the serpent in his garland—a "winding Snare"—recalls Herbert's description in "A Wreath" of his own "crooked winding wayes" (l. 4). But there is a closer connection between these poems. In his first line, Marvell uses the rhetorical figure of mind-changing. The figure is anadiplosis (what Puttenham calls the "Redouble") if considered as a scheme; if considered as a trope, the figure is metanoia, which Puttenham appropriately labels "the Penitent."[22] Long? (the speaker might be asking himself); no, more that that—*too* long. By a happy accident, the printer of the 1681 folio *Miscellaneous Poems* broke the poem's

18. *The Light in Troy: Imitation and Discovery in Renaissance Poetry* (New Haven and London: Yale University Press, 1982), p. 14. Even a committed structuralist like Culler admits the difficulty of discussing anonymous intertextuality without turning to "particular pretexts with which the work is indubitably wrestling" (*The Pursuit of Signs*, p. 107).

19. *The Light in Troy*, p. 16.

20. Ibid., p. 18.

21. For general comparisons of these two poems, see J. H. Summers, "Marvell's 'Nature,'" *ELH* 20 (1953): 121–35; Margaret Carpenter, "From Herbert to Marvell: Poetics in 'A Wreath' and 'The Coronet,'" *Journal of English and Germanic Philology* 69 (1970): 50–62; and Patterson, "Protestant Poetics," pp. 478–99.

22. George Puttenham, *The Arte of English Poesie* (1589), intro. Baxter Hathaway (1906; rpt. Kent, Ohio: Kent State University Press, 1970), pp. 210, 223.

first line, thus suggesting visually its excessive length and curvature:

> When for the Thorns with which I long, too
> (long . . .[23]

Even unaided by typography, the rhetorical bending or "penitence" of Marvell's line reproduces just that sinuous turn of thought from which Herbert generates "A Wreath," where each new line bends back upon its precursor. By so using the word *winding* in line 21 and Herbert's winding figure of speech in line 1, Marvell nods allusively toward his great predecessor, consciously directing his readers to remember that Herbert had already used this figure and this word.

As others have pointed out, "The Coronet" also reflects Marvell's reading of Spenser and Sidney.[24] From each Marvell takes specific, though unmarked, quotations that evoke by synecdoche their original contexts. Unlike "A Wreath," however, the texts Marvell claims from Spenser and Sidney are generically distant from "The Coronet." Knowingly, it seems, Marvell quotes out of context. The technique is neither pilferage nor vague recollection. Nor is it alchemical transmutation. It is rather a mode of self-conscious and creative errancy.[25]

23. Marvell, *Miscellaneous Poems* (London, 1681), p. 9.
24. Both borrowings I discuss are noted in Elizabeth Story Donno, ed., *Andrew Marvell: The Complete Poems* (Harmondsworth, Middlesex: Penguin Books, 1970), p. 237. Earlier, the quotation from Spenser was noted by Leishman, *Marvell's Poetry*, p. 194. Leishman also points out that "Marvell took hints from . . . many of his immediate predecessors" and singles out especially Thomas Randolph's "Eglogue occasion'd by two Doctors disputing upon predestination" (p. 196).
25. How Milton uses this technique has been shown by Edward Le Comte, *Sly Milton: The Meaning Lurking in the Contexts of his Quotations* (East Meadow, N.Y.: English Studies Collections, 1976). For theoretical treatments of intertextuality, see Culler, *The Pursuit of Signs*, pp. 80–118; and Riffaterre, "Intertextual Representation," pp. 141–62. For discussions of allusion in particular, see Ziva Ben-Porat, "The Poetics of Literary Allusion," *PTL: A Journal for Descriptive Poetics and Theory of Literature* 1 (1976): 105–28; Harold Bloom, *A Map of Misreading* (New York: Oxford University Press, 1975), pp. 125–43; and Michael Wheeler, *The Art of Allusion in Victorian Fiction* (London: Macmillan, 1979), pp. 1–8. Among many discussions of Renaissance intertextuality, see John Guillory, *Poetic Authority: Spenser, Milton, and Literary History* (New York: Columbia University Press, 1983), pp. 139–45; Greene, *The Light in Troy*, pp. 1–53 and passim; and John Hollander, *The Figure of Echo: A Mode of Allusion in Milton and After* (Berkeley and London: University of California Press, 1981), pp. 62–112.

We may begin with the phrase "speckled breast," fetched from book 1 of *The Faerie Queene* and applied by Marvell to "the Serpent old."[26] Spenser uses it of the dragon fought by Redcrosse Knight. This creature is first seen "Forelifting vp aloft his speckled brest, / And often bounding on the brused gras, / As for great ioyance of his newcome guest."[27] Both Spenser's dragon and Marvell's serpent descend, with modification, from "that old serpent, called the Devil, and Satan" and "the great dragon" (Revelation 12:9, AV), but there is more to the resemblance than that. Marvell's quotation from the eleventh canto invites readers to consider "The Coronet" as somehow dependent upon Spenser's legend.

The "winding Snare" involves in each text what Marvell calls the "wreaths of Fame and Interest" (1. 16). A desire for fame first leads Redcrosse Knight "To Faery court," and he wins garlands of fame by defeating the dragon and liberating Una's parents (1.10.66). The young men of her country throw "laurell boughes" (1.12.6) at his feet, while the young women crown Una with "a girland greene" (1.12.8).

Before Redcrosse Knight can win "mortal Glory," however, he must learn to question its worth. This lesson comes home most clearly near the end of book 1 in the vision of New Jerusalem, a sight that makes a due impression on Spenser's hero:

> Till now, said then the knight, I weened well,
> That great *Cleopolis*, where I haue beene,
> In which that fairest *Faerie Queene* doth dwell,
> The fairest Citie was, that might be seene;
> And that bright towre all built of christall cleene,
> *Panthea*, seemd the brightest thing, that was:
> But now by proofe all otherwise I weene;
> For this great Citie that does far surpas,

26. In Randolph's poem "A Pastoral Courtship" (published in 1638), the speaker says to the woman he aims to seduce, "There lurks no speckled serpent here." *Poetical and Dramatic Works of Thomas Randolph*, ed. W. Carew Hazlitt, 2 vols. (1875; rpt. New York and London: Benjamin Blom, 1968), 2:612. Leishman, who cites the poem in connection with *Upon Appleton House*, thinks it "almost certain" that Marvell had read "A Pastoral Courtship" (*Marvell's Poetry*, p. 252, n. 1).

27. *Spenser: Poetical Works*, ed. J. C. Smith and E. de Selincourt (1912; rpt. Oxford and New York: Oxford University Press, 1970), p. 59. In subsequent references, line numbers will be cited parenthetically in the text.

And this bright Angels towre quite dims that towre of glas.

(1.10.58)

Like Marvell's "fragrant Towers" (l. 7), Spenser's glassy Panthea sums up the poet's store. Yet Marvell's question in "The Coronet" is asked first here. In comparison with their supernal patterns—"Heavens Diadem" (l. 18) or an "Angels towre"—what good are earthly cities, towers of glass, winding stairs, withering wreaths?

For Spenser, however, there remains some room for "mortal Glory." The knight's guide, Contemplation, admits that Redcrosse Knight's words are "Most trew,"

> Yet is *Cleopolis* for earthly frame,
> The fairest peece, that eye beholden can:
> And well beseemes all knights of noble name,
> That couet in th'immortal booke of fame
> To be eternized, that same to haunt,
> And doen their seruice to that soueraigne Dame,
> That glorie does to them for guerdon graunt:
> For she is heauenly borne, and heauen may iustly vaunt.
>
> (1.10.59)

Because Redcrosse Knight does wish to be "eternized," he must and can win "famous victorie" before shunning "the suit of earthly conquest" (1.10.60).

This difference in emphasis makes evident one use of Marvell's quotation. By giving his "Serpent old" the "speckled breast" of Redcrosse Knight's opponent, Marvell allows "The Coronet" to be read as a revision of Spenser's legend. Glory is Redcrosse Knight's "guerdon" from the Fairy Queen for slaying the dragon. Marvell, however, resymbolizes glory as the serpent itself. Heaven, for Marvell, may still "iustly vaunt," but his plot lacks a mediator, a Gloriana or Una. Save for Christ himself, there is no "heauenly borne" figure in "The Coronet."

If Marvell's allusive reading of this episode substitutes pastoral for epic romance, his ambivalent quest for poetic glory also diverges from Spenser's own. True, like Marvell, Spenser acknowledges a rift between his matter—the "glorious type" of "Knights and Ladies noble deeds" (1.proem.1)—and his means of expression, what he calls variously his "afflicted style" (1.proem.4), his "couert vele" (2.proem.5), his "homely verse, of many meanest" (6.12.41). Spenser calls his Muse "The Nourse of time, and euerlasting fame" (1.11.15), yet he sometimes seems to feel separated from her power. Many of Spenser's protestations of inability could illustrate the topic of conventional modesty described by Curtius.[28] One could argue that because he has a Gloriana, Spenser retains confidence in the fitness of his poetic offering, however wreathed about with self-interest it may be. Thus, again, Marvell's allusion to *The Faerie Queene* ironically distances "The Coronet" from Spenser.

The other quotation to be considered is the overdetermined phrase "curious frame" (1. 22). The words echo, as I have suggested, a range of other poems, but they are still arguably taken from Sidney's *Astrophil and Stella* 28, where—to make matters more complex—they bear quite a different signification. This quotation, even more than the one from Spenser, gives Marvell an opportunity for creative errancy.

Astrophil and Stella 28 concludes a series of six sonnets (23-28) addressed not to Stella but, polemically, to bad interpreters of Sidney's love. (Evidence that Marvell is borrowing the phrase from Sidney includes resemblances between "The Coronet" and other members of this series.) The butts of his irony Sidney calls "curious" and "dustie wits" or "Rich fooles."[29] These people fail, he claims, though they struggle "with paine," to understand beauty and virtue, for they weigh "each thing in sense's ballance" only (25.5-6). Sidney accuses them especially of hermeneutic excesses: they fancy allusion, they "make speech of speech arise" (27.4), and they read allegorically. In Sonnet 23, Sidney writes that they have failed to discover the true cause of his recent sadness:

> The curious wits, seeing dull pensivenesse
>   Bewray it selfe in my long setled eyes,
>   Whence those same fumes of melancholy rise,
> With idle paines, and missing ayme, do guesse.
> Some that know how my spring I did addresse,

---

28. Ernst Robert Curtius, *European Literature in the Latin Middle Ages*, trans. Willard R. Trask, Bollingen Series, no. 36 (Princeton: Princeton University Press, 1953), pp. 83–85.

29. Sonnets 24.1, 25.1, and 26.1, in *The Poems of Sir Philip Sidney*, ed. William A. Ringler, Jr. (Oxford: Clarendon Press, 1962), pp. 176–79. In subsequent references, line numbers will be cited parenthetically in the text.

> Deeme that my Muse some fruit of knowledge plies:
>   Others, because the Prince my service tries,
> Thinke that I thinke state errours to redresse.
>   But harder Judges judge ambition's rage,
> Scourge of it selfe, still climing slipprie place,
> Holds my young braine captiv'd in golden cage.
> O fooles, or over-wise, alas the race
>   Of all my thoughts hath neither stop nor start,
>   But only *Stella's* eyes and *Stella's* hart.

Aside from the four words it shares with "The Coronet" (*curious*, *fruit*, *redresse*, and *slipprie*), this sonnet knots together with several other strands of Marvell's poem. Here, too, lie images of error, captivity, false surmise, ambition, and more than a suggestion of lost paradise in a "fruit of knowledge" which, plied in verse, produces "fumes of melancholy." Moreover, Sidney's concluding lines resembles Marvell's in wording, imagery, and sentiment. Both castigate folly, and both, in the end, use rhetorical doubling to emphasize their centers of value—Stella's eyes and heart, Christ's head and feet.

In *Astrophil and Stella* 28, Sidney derides readers who insist on turning literal statements into allegories. Marvell quotes from the first line, but, as before, the quotation makes available a larger context, even though Marvell changes the sense of the words *curious frame*:

> You that with allegorie's curious frame,
>   Of other's children changelings use to make,
>   With me those paines for God's sake do not take:
> I list not dig so deepe for brasen fame.
> When I say '*Stella*', I do meane that same
>   Princesse of Beautie, for whose only sake
>   The raines of *Love* I love, though never slake,
> And joy therein, though Nations count it shame.
>   I beg no subject to use eloquence,
>   Nor in hid wayes to guide Philosophie:
> Looke at my hands for no such quintessence;
>   But know that I in pure simplicitie,
>   Breathe out the flames which burne within my heart,
>   *Love* onely reading unto me this art.

Here Sidney criticizes a "frame" of interpretation that is "curious" to a fault. His utterance, "Stella," if interpreted allegorically might yield "eloquence," "Philosophie," or even a kind of "quintessence" of meaning, but such reading would also, he claims, destroy the "pure simplicitie" of Love's art. Dressed up in the "brasen fame" of such overreadings, Stella's beauty would be tarted up, not revealed.

Marvell's quotation from this sonnet makes possible an act of self-interpretation in "The Coronet." Sidney complains that allegorical reading replaces children with changelings. (Such was the birth of Redcrosse Knight himself.) But in "The Coronet," which form of verse, erotic or devotional, should be called Marvell's best piece of poetry? Which is the real child and which the curiously framed simulacrum? Piety insists that erotic verses—those "fragrant Towers"—should be revealed as fakes, thorny trivializations of the rich, simple "Chaplet" of religious poetry. Genuine devotional art, the argument goes, finds its *copia* in copying out "sweetnesse readie penn'd." It says, with Herbert, "My God and King," as plainly as Astrophil says, "Stella."[30]

Such is the argument of Herbert's "Jordan (II)," but it is not exactly what Marvell says here. In "The Coronet," after all, the "curious frame" is the speaker's own construction. Of course, the phrase includes in its field of reference the woven flowers and Marvell's own body, which (perhaps remembering "Lycidas") he prays Christ might "shatter." As quoted from Sidney, however, Marvell's phrase also refers to wrongful transformation, a misguided curiosity that has led him to refashion old garlands into a new crown. Paradoxically, Marvell's real poetic products are, first, those flowers—"my fruits are only flow'rs" (l. 6), he admits—and, second, the crown of thorns with which for too long he has pierced his Savior's head. The emblem of the serpent in the garland is not surprising, as Colie has shown.[31] *Et in Arcadia ego.* Yet Marvell finds the serpent not in pastoral itself but only when, like the overreaders Sidney scorns, he tries to frame from insufficient materials a "quintes-

30. On the contrast within *copia* between production and *re*-production, see Terence Cave, *The Cornucopian Text: Problems of Writing in the French Renaissance* (Oxford: Clarendon Press, 1979), pp. 4–5, 75. Cf. Margaret W. Ferguson, *Trials of Desire: Renaissance Defenses of Poetry* (New Haven and London: Yale University Press, 1983), pp. 27–28.

31. *"My Ecchoing Song,"* p. 80.

sence" of devotional poetry, such a crown "As never yet the king
of Glory wore" (l. 12). His wonted verse, fashioned from thorns
and flowers, may have been ostentatious or cruel. But the spe-
cific problem of "The Coronet" arises when the poet attempts to
fashion a wreath of fame, disregarding these flaws in his mate-
rials and intentions. As Warren Chernaik has written, "'The
Coronet' owes much of its poignancy to the paradox it embod-
ies," a paradox whereby the poem invokes "an ideal simplicity
by means of a complex and carefully woven wreath of lan-
guage."[32] Complex, carefully woven, and—one must add—
abandoned.

In the poem he intended to write, Marvell uses quotation
self-consciously to liken himself to Sidney's "dustie wits," dig-
ging for "brasen fame." But, in the poem he wrote, he claims to
be also, ultimately, like Astrophil, hearing what Love lectures
truly. The difference is that what Astrophil knows to begin
with, Marvell says he learns only in the act of composition; yet
it is just this composition that permits the comparison to begin
with.

From this position, one may see some larger significance in
Marvell's allusive devotional technique. In "The Coronet," it is
an act whereby he may compare himself with Herbert, Sidney,
and Spenser, while at the same time saying, as he wrote even of
Lovelace's day, "Our times are much degenerate from those."[33]
If Sidney is modestly proud and Spenser balances vaunting and
abnegation, Marvell fuses these two attitudes in an
ambivalence that is characteristic of many modes of allusion.
Harold Rosenberg, writing of allusion in modern painting, has
described its mixture of "despondency" and "assurance." It is a
trope, he says,

> through which is asserted the uneasy intuition of this epoch that
> "real" art belongs to other times and places, to communions
> destroyed by our revolutionary age: but through which is asserted
> at the same time the counter-intuition that art is deathless and

32. *The Poet's Time: Politics and Religion in the Work of Andrew Marvell*
(Cambridge: Cambridge University Press, 1983), p. 84. Cf. Friedman, *Marvell's
Pastoral Art*, p. 101.
33. On this poem see Patterson, *Marvell and the Civic Crown* (Princeton:
Princeton University Press, 1978), pp. 17–19. Cf. Chernaik, *The Poet's Time*, p.
16.

that it actually rises to new heights in becoming nothing else than the artist's experience of it. Allusion expresses both the despondency of modern art and its enthusiasm, its awareness of itself as "counterfeit" as well as its clarified assurance of the inferior significance of all less history-conscious productions.[34]

Though describing twentieth-century painting, Rosenberg's terms seem to fit the experience Marvell describes in "The Coronet." There "despondency" and "assurance" are emotions felt first on account of the need to honor Christ and the impossibility of doing so, felt second in the midst of a revolutionary and self-conscious age.

They are also emotions, however, articulated by the structure of allusion. As Colie has suggested, writing of *Upon Appleton House*, an "emblem-symbol works allusively, drawing in a whole area of association not necessarily explored directly in a poem."[35] It is thus one cognitive function of allusion to open what Hollander has called "the portable library shared by the author and his ideal audience."[36] Marvell's devotional poem is certainly emblemlike, and it presupposes acquaintance with at least a slender library of other verse. His reference to "A Wreath" and his quotations from Spenser and Sidney speak of questions Marvell saw himself sharing with his predecessors. The fragments he draws synecdochically from their poems are signs of his commerce with their recorded experiences.

Yet it is not quite enough to describe Marvell's intertextual devotion as an emblem or library. As Hardy saw, one must speak of how Marvell uses his materials. But one must also consider how those materials surprise him, how their meaning slips in translation. In "The Coronet," as in a passage from Dante discussed by Greene, "An errancy is taking place that is not purely random or destructive."[37] But it is an errancy, a "curious frame," still. Marvell's quotations acknowledge that. In his poem "On Mr. *Milton's* Paradise Lost," Marvell recounts his

34. *Arshile Gorky: The Man, the Time, the Idea* (New York: Sheepmeadow Press/Flying Point Books, 1962), p. 62. I am indebted to Hollander, *The Figure of Echo*, p. 72, n. 5, for reference to Rosenberg's stimulating discussion.

35. *The Resources of Kind*, p. 38.

36. *The Figure of Echo*, p. 64.

37. *The Light in Troy*, p. 13.

original fear that Milton's "vast Design" would "ruine . . . /
The sacred Truths to Fable and old Song" (ll. 2, 7–8). The first
element of that design is what he himself first attempts to see in
"The Coronet": a vision of "*Messiah* Crown'd" (l. 3). "Ah,
foolish Man," he tells himself there, "that would'st debase with
them, / And mortal Glory, Heavens Diadem!" (ll. 10–11). Later,
however, seeing the design accomplished, Marvell asks Milton's
pardon:

> Thou hast not miss'd one thought that could be fit,
> And all that was improper dost omit:
> So that no room is here for Writers left,
> But to detect their Ignorance or Theft. (ll. 27–30)

Milton has succeeded where Marvell claims to fail in "The Cor-
onet." Messiah is crowned; Milton's verse stands unrhymed.
For Marvell, though, such success would also cancel the effect
of his allusive devotion, grounded and groundless. Weaving
what he cannot disentangle, quoting what he cannot unquote,
Marvell uses allusion to express, at once, the despondency and
assurance of a poet who attempts to make from other texts an
offering acceptable unto God. That attempt, unlike Milton's, is
a failure. The "Chaplet" is not ever woven. What Marvell gives
us instead is a successfully allusive text about that failure.

10

TIMELY TIMELESSNESS
IN TWO NATIVITY POEMS

Patricia G. Pinka

Nativity poems of the English Renaissance usually contain complicated time schemes, in part because they record both the historical event of Christ's birth and the continuing recurrence of that event both in the Church calendar and in the realm of the eternal present. The complexity of time in these poems also reflects, as A. B. Chambers notes, the intertwining of past, present, future, and eternal present in the Church liturgy of the Christmas season and in the mysteries of the Incarnation lying behind that liturgy.[1] The vacillation of time in these Nativity lyrics ranges from the ambiguity of *now* and *to night* in the past-tense narrative of the first Christmas in Ben Jonson's "A Hymn on the Nativity of My Saviour" to a metaphorical restructuring of providential history to allow for a second Nativity in Robert Herrick's "An Ode on the Birth of Our Saviour."[2] But perhaps no Nativity poems manipulate time more fully and more imaginatively than George Herbert's "Christmas" and John Milton's "On the Morning of Christ's Nativity."

Like the other poems, these two, as James Holly Hanford notes, commemorate "the divine events at their appropriate anniversaries in the church calendar," mark, in other words, the

1. "Christmas: The Liturgy of the Church and English Verse of the Renaissance," in *Literary Monographs*, vol. 6, ed. Eric Rothstein and Joseph A. Wittreich, Jr. (Madison: University of Wisconsin Press, 1975), pp. 111–18.
2. *The Complete Poetry of Ben Jonson*, ed. William B. Hunter, Jr. (1963; rpt. New York: Norton, 1968), p. 120; *The Complete Poetry of Robert Herrick*, ed. J. Max Patrick (1963; rpt. New York: Norton, 1968).

point where history and the cycle of the ecclesiastical year inter-
sect.[3] A mingling of time frames thus undergirds their very pur-
pose. In most Nativity lyrics only the events surrounding the
birth of Christ move through the time frames. In Herbert's and
Milton's poems, however, the speakers participate in the vari-
ous temporal structures; indeed their connections with time
form a singular focus. True, Henry Vaughan's persona in "The
Nativity" does respond to his vision of the Star of Bethlehem
and the Magi by praying for his contemporary Englishmen. But
the poem immediately switches from the supplicant to the
prayer and thus returns both the emphasis and the speaker to
Christmas 1656.[4] Not so in Herbert's and Milton's Nativity
poems. The Nativity Ode begins with Milton's commemora-
tion of Christmas in 1629, moves to his inspiration by the Heav-
enly Muse, which allows him to traverse time, includes his
response to his inspiration, and ends with the poet's brief eval-
uation of his inspired composition. In "Christmas," Herbert's
persona encounters Christ in the allegorical no-time of "one
day," then moves into historical time, which he measures with
a spiritual yardstick, and finally envisions his life in eternity.[5]
Thus time in these two poems not only marks the point where
history and the cycle of the church calendar intersect but also
the moment when the human spiritual experiences of rebirth,
illumination by the Holy Spirit, and sanctification both develop
from the commemoration of Christmas and reflect the time-
lessness implied by the cyclical return of a festal day.

This focus on the individual's developing spiritual state, as
indicated by the time structure of Milton's and Herbert's
poems, parallels contemporary Anglican ideas about how the
proper observance of festival days can build the faith required to

3. *A Milton Handbook*, 4th ed. (New York: Appleton-Century-Crofts,
1946), p. 145.

4. *The Complete Poetry of Henry Vaughan*, ed. French Fogle (1964; rpt.
New York: Norton, 1969), p. 422.

5. *The Works of George Herbert*, ed. F. E. Hutchinson (Oxford: Clarendon
Press, 1941), p. 80. All citations are to this edition. Numerous critics mention an
allegorical dimension in "Christmas," among them R. E. Hughes, "George Her-
bert's Rhetorical World," *Criticism* 3 (1961): 86–94; and Jean Wilkinson, "Three
Sets of Religious Poems," *Huntington Library Quarterly* 36 (1974): 203–26.
Helen Vendler, *The Poetry of George Herbert* (Cambridge: Harvard University
Press, 1975), pp. 57–99, delineates allegory in Herbert's poems, although she
does not include "Christmas" in her discussion.

move a person from time to eternity. Richard Hooker writes that the iteration of festal days

> is a most effectuall meane to bringe unto full maturitie and grouth those seedes of godlines . . . sown in the hartes of manie thousandes duringe the while that such feastes are present . . . the wisdome of God hath commended especiallie this circumstance amongst others in solemne feastes, that to children and novices in religion they minster the first occasions to ask and inquire of God. . . . The daies of solemnitie . . . cannot choose but soone finish that outward exercise of godlines which properlie apperteineth to such times, howbeit mens inward disposition to vertue they both augment for the present and by theire often retournes bringe also the same at the length unto that perfection which wee most desire. (5.71.3)[6]

Hooker, focusing on the celebrant's experience of commemorating feast days, declares that holidays affect each person according to his religious development. But the opportunity to benefit from these commemorations comes only when the celebrant rests, when he leaves those labors that bind him to his physical and earthly existence, to think instead on God. And indeed his festal rest figures forth the blissful eternal rest at the end of time: "festivall rest doth [represent] that coelestiall estate whereof the verie heathens them selves . . . imagin that it needes must consist in rest . . ."(5.70.4; 2:365). Thus Hooker, who begins the sections on festival days with a discussion of time and eternity (5.69.1), attributes the profitable celebration of festival days to a man's leaving his timely concerns to concentrate on eternal matters.

Although John Calvin denies the special significance of any day for the spiritual development of human beings, he, like Hooker, links man's movement to eternity to his withdrawal from timely concerns: "If our sanctification consists in mortifying our own will, then a very close correspondence appears between the outward sign and the inward reality. . . . In short, we must rest from all activities of our own contriving so that,

6. *Of the Laws of Ecclesiastical Polity*, vol. 2 of *The Folger Library Edition of the Works of Richard Hooker*, ed. W. Speed Hill (Cambridge, Mass.: Belknap Press, 1977), pp. 371–72. All citations are to this edition.

having God working in us, we may repose in him, as the apostle also teaches" (2.8.29).[7]

Theologically, then, both Calvin and Hooker tie the Christian's movement from time to eternity with spiritual meditation, although Calvin staunchly argues against the commemoration of any holiday not specified in the Bible. Hooker, on the other hand, specifically associates spiritual meditation on festal days with the Christian's inner development. Young Milton and Herbert follow Hooker poetically by having their speakers' involvement with the various time frames in the poems reflect changing spiritual states as the personae celebrate Christmas.

In the opening lines of Herbert's "Christmas," the allegorical "one day" both delineates the speaker's sinful state and helps to define Christmas in spiritual, not calendrical terms:

> All after pleasures as I rid one day,
>   My horse and I, both tir'd, bodie and minde,
>   With full crie of affections, quite astray,
> I took up in the next inne I could finde.
>
> (ll. 1–4)

The man, "tir'd, bodie and minde," and traveling "quite astray," is an allegorical portrait of the sinner existing without purpose—a portrait poetically supported by the dangling modification and ambiguity of many of the phrases in this quatrain. His lack of connection with time metaphorically details the spiritual limbo of his inner life. Yet, ironically, the narrative cause-and-effect structure of the tale suggests a purpose behind the speaker's purposelessness and helps define the spiritual meaning of Christmas as the moment when Christ is reborn in the heart of a sinner: "There when I came, whom found I but my deare, / My dearest Lord, expecting till the grief / Of pleasures brought me to him . . . ?" (ll. 5–7). The speaker's journey and the inn allude to the events of the first Christmas; yet Christ's anticipation and loving welcome of the man allegorically differentiate the sinner's experience of Christmas from that of the holy family. Indeed, Christ's love for the speaker elicits the

7. *Institutes of the Christian Religion*, trans. Ford L. Battles, ed. John T. McNeill (Philadelphia: Westminster Press, 1960), 1:396.

man's prayers for purification and for the rebirth of Christ in his heart, or, as Richard Strier phrases it, "the entry of Christ into the individual believer's life."[8]

The allusion to the Crucifixion, where Christ experienced the "grief / Of [every man's] pleasures" and where He again proved himself everyone's "most sweet relief," reinforces the spiritual fluidity of the historical events of Christ's life: "Furnish & deck my soul, that thou mayest have / A better lodging then a rack or grave" (ll. 8, 13–14). Here, Christmas and Good Friday merge. The speaker too begins to participate in this timelessness as Christ partially incorporates him by experiencing the "grief / Of [his] pleasures." In addition, by commemorating the anniversary of the historical Nativity, the speaker is reborn, even as Christ is. A secondary reading of Christ as the parent-to-be "expecting till the grief / Of pleasures brought me to him" corroborates the man's experience of beginning regeneration. By the end of the sonnet section, then, the growing identification between the speaker and Christ, which reflects man's rebirth in the image of God,[9] implies the propriety of the speaker's traversing temporal planes from oblivion, to the timely commemoration of an historical event, to a partial participation in spiritual timelessness. As Helen Vendler notes, Herbert often inventively modifies allegory "in the direction of personal inner experience."[10]

Unlike Herbert's persona, Milton from the beginning of the Nativity Ode is very conscious of time, timelessness, and his participation in both, for he begins the poem at a point in his spiritual development far advanced from that of Herbert's persona. Even the ambiguity of the *On* in his title calls attention to Milton's historical point in time, 1629; to the first Christmas; and to the interplay of the two, one instance of which is the poem "On the Morning of Christ's Nativity, Composed 1629."[11] Indeed Milton's ability to write the Nativity Ode, where, inspired by the Heavenly Muse, he crosses boundaries of

8. *Love Known: Theology and Experience in George Herbert's Poetry* (Chicago: University of Chicago Press, 1983), p. 154.

9. Calvin, *Institutes*, 1.4.4 (1:189), following Paul, defines regeneration as Christ's reforming us to God's image. In 3.3.9 (1:600–601) he identifies repentance with regeneration.

10. *Poetry of Herbert*, p. 58.

11. Chambers, "Christmas," p. 142.

time and space, attests to Milton's spiritual illumination. As Calvin remarks: "when we are drawn [by the Spirit of God] we are lifted up in mind and heart above our understanding. For the soul, illumined by him, takes on a new keenness, as it were, to contemplate the heavenly mysteries, whose splendor had previously blinded it" (3.2.34; 1:582). And indeed, according to Calvin the good works that arise from spiritual illumination confirm one's adoption by God: ". . . the grace of good works . . . shows that the Spirit of adoption has been given to us" (3.14.18; 1:785).

Part of Milton's good work in 1629 is to explain divine will to his contemporaries, as he has seen that will in his illumination by the Holy Spirit. His use of time in the poem marks both his identification with his contemporaries and his special position as one adopted by God. Initially he plants himself firmly in 1629 with his fellow Englishmen: "This is the Month, and this the happy morn" on which Christ "did bring" "Our great redemption" (ll. 1, 4).[12] By stanza three, however, Milton has, with the aid of the Heavenly Muse, transcended time to be present at the Nativity: "*Now* while the Heav'n by the Sun's team untrod, / Hath took no print of the approaching light, / And all the spangled host keep watch in squadrons bright" (ll. 19–21, italics supplied). His request for the Heavenly Muse to intervene before the arrival of the Magi at the scene of the Nativity delineates the way in which cycle (Milton's commemoration of Christmas) can modify history in the mind of God. Linear time becomes a human fiction. So does space, for, still under the perspective of the Heavenly Muse, Milton sees both the manger and the "Star-led Wizards" (l. 23) hasting towards Bethlehem; space lies spread before him like a living painting. With this spiritual view of both time and space Milton also foresees his future as a prophetic singer, like Isaiah, as he instructs the Muse to join the "Angel Choir, / From out his secret Altar toucht with hallow'd fire" (ll. 27–28).[13]

12. *John Milton: Complete Poems and Major Prose*, ed. Merritt Y. Hughes (Indianapolis: Odyssey Press, 1957). All citations are to this edition.
13. Lowry Nelson, Jr., *Baroque Lyric Poetry* (New Haven: Yale University Press, 1963), p. 42; John Hill, *John Milton, Poet, Priest, and Prophet: A Study of Divine Vocation in Milton's Poetry and Prose* (Totowa, N.J.: Rowman and Littlefield, 1979), p. 59.

By the end of the narrative sections of both poems, then, each speaker's sense of time reflects his spiritual state. Milton has both a linear, human perspective and the eternal vision because he is illuminated by the Holy Spirit. Herbert's speaker, having moved out of the no-time of spiritual deadness, understands the historical meaning of Christmas as Christ's birthday and some of its spiritual meaning as he begins his regeneration.

To commemorate their spiritual happiness on Christmas, both speakers sing hymns, thus following the pattern for festival celebration Hooker advocates: ". . . generallie offices and duties of religious joy are that wherein the hallowing of festivall times consisteth. The most naturall testimonies of our rejoycinge in God are first his praises sett forth with cheerefull alacritie of minde . . ." (5.70.2; 2:363). Through their poetic structuring of time in the hymn portions, Herbert and Milton give their speakers a glimpse of personal eternal life and thus apply in a specific way the idea that on 25 December, the date of the winter solstice on the Julian calendar and the time at which the sun was said to be reborn, Christ, the *sol verus*, the true sun, came to replace the old sol.[14] Thus the traditional concept that the Nativity marks the beginning of the return to the golden world becomes for these speakers a personal realization that Christmas initiates their having a place in eternity.

As Herbert's persona responds to his love of Christ by singing His praises, he seems to be at the scene of the Nativity and, as Helen Vendler remarks, in competition with the shepherds: "The shepherds sing; and shall I silent be?" (l. 15).[15] Such a reading, however, detracts from the poem's account of the speaker's spiritual development—a detraction clarified by redefining *shepherd* as *soul* and thereby refining the tense of *sing* from the chronological present to the eternal present of lyric, hymn, and spiritual life: "My soul's a shepherd too; a flock it feeds / Of thoughts, and words, and deeds" (ll. 17–18). Because the persona defines himself in terms of his spiritual life, his song this Christmas, like Milton's in the ode, is contemporaneous with that of the shepherds. Even more importantly, the speaker's alliance with the shepherds begins his evolution from an individual

14. J. C. J. Metford, *Dictionary of Christian Lore and Legend* (London: Thames and Hudson, 1983), p. 67.
15. *Poetry of Herbert*, pp. 153–54.

lover of God to a portion of the mystical body of Christ—from an historical personage to a spiritual entity.

As a part of that evolution he both minimizes his life by describing it as a day and commits himself to the service of God: with his thoughts, words, and deeds he "shall sing," indeed "Out-sing the day-light houres" (ll. 21–22). Although he acknowledges the activity of his life as work in praise of God, he realizes that no song, no matter how long, will express his love for God sufficiently. Consequently, he momentarily chides the sun for not providing adequate time; then, recognizing the sun too as a creature of God, promises to join with it to seek a new sun which "Shall stay, till we [the man and the sun] have done" (l. 28). This new sun is, of course, Christ, the *sol verus*, whose birth on Christmas marks the beginning of the end of time and the promise of eternal life. Because of his rebirth on Christmas, the speaker's personal history parallels the eschatology.

Throughout the hymn the speaker's imaginative contemplation of eternity corresponds with his developing spiritual identity from an individual Christian to a member of the mystical body. Late in the poem that union materializes. At first in lovers' terms he says that he and the new sun will "one another pay," that is, gratify, satisfy, and please each other (l. 32). His explanation of that union makes the two almost indistinguishable: "His beams shall cheer my breast, and both so twine, / Till ev'n his beams sing, and my musick shine" (ll. 33–34). Christ will first *cheer*, that is, solace and comfort (*OED*), the man's breast. Then the two will take on, *twine*, each other's qualities. Paul provides a biblical explanation of this transformation: "[In Heaven the Lord Jesus Christ] shall change our vile body, that it may be fashioned like unto his glorious body" (Philippians 4:21, AV).

Paradoxically, as the man envisions his eternal union with Christ, he finds that he has no temporal way of expressing that eternity and resorts to synaesthesia to communicate the magnificence of unmeasurable bliss: "Till ev'n his beams sing, and my musick shine." His language reminds him of his human limitation even as his vision assures him of his salvation. Herbert's persona, then, through his commemoration of Christmas comes to what Calvin calls "certainty of faith": ". . . he alone is truly a believer who, convinced by a firm conviction that God is a kindly and well-disposed Father toward him, . . . lays hold on an undoubted expectation of salvation" (3.2.16; 1:562). Herbert delineates this spiritual development in part through the shifting time frames of the poem, whereby the persona's cyclical commemoration of historical Christmas transports him imaginatively to the eternal realm where history and cycle merge.

Like Herbert, Milton in the hymn portion of his poem gives testimony of his spiritual assurance through his participation in various time frames. However, since one reason for Milton's adoption of the role of prophet in his work is to illuminate the meaning of the Nativity to his contemporaries, he vacillates between the temporal planes, sometimes detailing the historical perspective he shares with his readers, sometimes experiencing the wonders of the Nativity firsthand.

In the first twelve stanzas of the hymn Milton stresses the historical perspective of the Nativity by using the past tense twenty-eight times: "It was the Winter wild"; "Kings sat still with awful eye" (ll. 29, 46). Yet because he mixes time denominators, the scenes he describes vibrate:[16]

> When such music sweet
> Their [the shepherds'] hearts and ears did greet,
>   As never was by mortal finger struck,
> Divinely-warbled voice
> Answering the stringed noise.
>   As all their souls in blissful rapture took . . . . (ll. 93–98)

The ongoing music almost lifts the historic shepherds to response, and the scene becomes a moving tableau. This hovering of tenses captures Milton's perspective of the scene, for the historical events he ponders take life through the illumination of the Heavenly Muse.

The vacillation of time frames around "events" unseeable to human eyes further suggests that Milton is fulfilling his task as prophet by interpreting the Nativity for his readers as intensely as possible. As William Kerrigan notes, Milton understood his role as prophet to be both that of passive vessel into which God poured inspiration and that of rational knower who

---

16. Archie Burnett, *Milton's Style: The Shorter Poems, "Paradise Regained," and "Samson Agonistes"* (New York: Longman, 1981), p. 39.

directed the people of his time.[17] Part of that direction consists of delineating the significance of the birth of Christ as the harbinger of the return of the golden age. Hence Milton consigns natural, historical events to the past tense: "And Kings sat still with awful eye, / As if they surely knew their sovran Lord was by" (ll. 59–60). But he describes occurrences with symbolic significance, such as the Ocean's forgetting to rave, or abstractions come to life, such as Peace's striking "a universal Peace through Sea and Land" (l. 52), in the present tense, thereby using them as prophetic metaphors for the golden world.

Unwilling to remain just an inspired prophet, however, Milton with an even more remarkable manipulation of time seems to jump into the scene of the Nativity to direct the cosmic orchestra and thus speed the return of the golden world: "Ring out ye Crystal spheres, / Once bless our human ears, / (If ye have power to touch our senses so) . . ." (ll. 125–27). Yet even as he urges on the golden age, Milton seems to be marking rather poignantly the difference between his illumined vision and his life. His illumined vision makes him yearn for the kingdom of God. As Calvin declares, the presence of the Holy Spirit in a man makes him wish for eternity: ". . . man's understanding, thus beamed by the light of the Holy Spirit, then at last truly begins to taste those things which belong to the Kingdom of God, having formerly been quite foolish and dull in tasting them" (3.2.34; 1:582). Yet even as he rapturously yearns to be glorified, Milton's persona is painfully aware of his place in time. He implores the spheres to play for him and for us: "*Once* bless our *human* ears" (italics supplied). His plea, the parenthetical "If ye have power to touch our *senses* so" (italics supplied), and his calling the music "unexpressive" (l. 115) make clear that he has not actually heard the notes. Until history is played out, the "holy Song" can enwrap only "our fancy" (ll. 133–34).

Milton's trip through providential history, which undergirds the return of the golden age, continues the dual temporal perspective of most of the hymn except as he approaches either Judgment Day or the golden age. Then he writes in the future

17. *The Prophetic Milton* (Charlottesville: University of Virginia Press, 1974), pp. 103–5.

tense. It seems as if, even as an inspired narrator, he cannot fully assume the eternal vision of the Heavenly Muse: "Truth and Justice then / Will down return to me" and "The dreadful Judge in middle Air shall spread his throne" (ll. 141–42, 164). Yet this limitation gives way to Milton's most personally profound realization as he proclaims: "And then at last our bliss / Full and perfect is, / But now begins . . ." (ll. 165–67). Although *at last* and *now* convey temporal distinctions, Milton, by envisioning "our bliss" in the present tense, expresses his assurance of salvation even as he returns to diurnal time.

At the end of the poem Milton instructs the Heavenly Muse, "Time is our tedious Song should here have ending . . ." (l. 239). The admonition is a reminder of the necessity to resume daily activities. His word *tedious*, however, seems an insult if it refers to the Muse's creation. In the Renaissance as now, it meant "wearisome by continuance" and was usually applied to speakers or writers. But it also meant "tired or exhausted" (*OED*). If *Song* is a metonymy for Milton—and Quintilian lists the substitution of the invention for the inventor as an exemplary form of metonymy in poetry (8.6.23)—then *tedious*, meaning exhausted, describes the young poet as he completed his poem at dawn on Christmas 1629.[18] Although his illumination gives evidence of his adoption and his work offers proof of the presence of the Holy Spirit within him, Milton remains for the time being a human, subject to weariness and exhaustion.

Time in both Milton's and Herbert's Nativity poems, then, reflects the changing spiritual states of the speakers. As they commemorate the historical birth of Christ in its return on the church calendar, they move outside of time themselves into the spiritual present of eternity.

---

18. Marcus Quintilian, *Institutes of Oratory*, trans. H. E. Butler (Cambridge: Harvard University Press, 1976), 3:313–15.

11

THE SEVENTEENTH-CENTURY RELIGIOUS ODE AND ITS CLASSICAL MODELS

Stella P. Revard

Poets of the middle third of the seventeenth century, following in the tracks of Donne and Herbert and faced with their crowning achievement in the short personal lyric, had either to imitate them and their highly introspective I-centered poems or to cast about for different models for the religious lyric, models that might range from the psalms, often considered in the Renaissance the only true paradigm for the religious poem, to the classical hymns and odes that Continental poets such as Ronsard had been attempting to adapt for other subjects.[1] For Milton, Crashaw, and Cowley—Cambridge-educated poets who had been steeped since childhood in Latin and Greek—the attraction of the classical model was particularly strong, although certainly for Milton the choice of classical model did not mean neglect of the psalms or psalm imitation. The Homeric and Orphic hymns, however, and the hymns and odes of Callimachus and Pindar offered poetry with serious religious purpose (albeit directed to pagan gods) that made use of magnifi-

1. For a consideration of the tradition of the literary hymn from antiquity through the Renaissance and its application to Milton's Nativity Ode, see Philip Rollinson, "Milton's Nativity Poem and the Decorum of Genre," in "Eyes Fast Fixt": Milton Studies VII, ed. Albert C. Labriola and Michael Lieb (Pittsburgh: University of Pittsburgh Press, 1975), pp. 165–88. Carol Maddison also considers literary hymns as well as odes in Apollo and the Nine: A History of the Ode (London: Routledge and Kegan Paul, 1960).

cent and complex choral structures, employed striking figures and elaborate descriptions, and displayed a whole range of sophisticated poetic effects. Formal, ceremonial, and public, these choral odes were meant for public worship, not for private devotions. Hence, taking them for models, the poet could move away from a poetry that was purely personal to one that was more formal and ceremonial and might combine deep religious feeling with public praise. The poet was moving out, center-stage, so to speak, to lead the chorus. With Milton and Crashaw, the religious ode celebrates an important occasion—the birth of Christ—while at the same time keeping its character as a devotion of private faith, publicly expressed. With Cowley, however, the ode, though ostensibly written about a central religious mystery—the resurrection of the dead—is less a celebration of religious devotion and more the vehicle for poetic performance. Hence by the time Cowley endows Dryden with his poetical mantle, the ode, which earlier in the century had been borrowed from Pindar and Callimachus to sing praises to a Christian God, has become merely a form for occasional poetry and mostly secular songs of praise.

Puttenham in *The Arte of English Poesie* was one of the first commentators in English who recommended Homeric Hymn and the odes and hymns of Pindar and Callimachus as models for religious poetry, although Sidney some years earlier had recognized in *The Defence of Poetry* the seriousness of Greek divine poetry.[2] Puttenham remarked that classical hymns were among the earliest poetry, "the highest & the stateliest," and "were song by the Poets as priests, and by the people or whole congregation as we sing in our Churchs the Psalmes of *Dauid*."[3] Puttenham was not the only one to link psalm and hymn or David and Pindar; since the time of Jerome such comparisons were made. Nor were Renaissance Christians the first to contemplate adapting Greek hymn and ode for Christian subjects; a rich tradition of imitation goes back to Byzantine and Roman

---

2. George Puttenham, *The Arte of English Poesie* (London, 1589), pp. 33–35; Philip Sidney, "A Defence of Poetry," in *Miscellaneous Prose of Sir Philip Sidney*, ed. Katherine Duncan-Jones and Jan Van Dorsten (Oxford: Oxford University Press, 1973), pp. 97ff.

3. *Arte*, p. 23.

Christianity.[4] In some sense too the praise by ancient commentators and critics from Plato through Quintilian of the seriousness and piety of Homeric Hymn and Pindaric Ode also made this poetry acceptable to Renaissance Christians. Yet in the sixteenth century there were few truly Christian adaptations of Homeric Hymn and Pindaric Ode. The most famous imitations of both Pindar and Greek hymn were published by Ronsard in the 1550s, but Ronsard uses both Pindaric Ode and classical hymn alike to praise the king, members of the nobility, and friends in his own poetical circle.[5] If Spenser's *Hymne of Heavenly Love* and *Hymne of Heavenly Beautie* are imitative of Greek hymn, as some critics have urged, then they would appear to be the most notable use of the Greek model for divine subjects before the seventeenth century.[6]

4. For a discussion of the connection of the psalms of David to Pindar's Odes and Greek hymn, see Barbara Kiefer Lewalski, *Protestant Poetics and the Seventeenth-Century Religious Lyric* (Princeton: Princeton University Press, 1979), pp. 7–10. O. B. Hardison, in *The Enduring Monument: A Study of the Idea of Praise in Renaissance Literary Theory and Practice* (Chapel Hill: University of North Carolina Press, 1962), looks at the literary theory of imitation and its application in the Renaissance. For the use of the hymn in Latin Christian poetry, see F. J. E. Raby, *A History of Christian Latin Poetry* (Oxford: Oxford University Press, 1927). Byzantine hymns include those in the fourth century by Gregory Nazianzen ("Hymn to God," sometimes attributed to Proclus) and by Synesius ("Christ's Journey to Heaven"). There are hymns in the fifth century by Proclus (to Athene, to the Muses, and to all gods) that revive the traditions of the Homeric Hymns. Vestiges of this tradition may be found even in the sixth-century Byzantine Cantica, especially Romanos's Hymn on the Nativity. See Raffaele Cantarella, *Poeti Bizantini* (Milan: Società Editrice "Vita E Pênsiero," 1948); C. A. Trypanis, *Fourteen Early Byzantine Cantica* (Vienna: Boehlaus in Kommission, 1968); and *Sancti Romani Melodi Cantica*, ed. Paul Maas and C. A. Trypanis (Oxford: Clarendon Press, 1963). The edition of *Poetae Graeci Veteres* published by Roviere in 1614 prints not only Greek tragic, comic, and lyric poets (among them Pindar), but also the hymns of Synesius, Gregory Nazianzen, John of Damascus, and others.

5. See *Les Odes de P. de Ronsard* (Paris, 1617). The first edition of odes appeared in 1550, augmented in 1552–1553 by other odes printed with them in *Les Amours de P. de Ronsard* (Paris). The hymns appeared in 1555 and 1556. See *Les Hymnes de P. de Ronsard* (Paris, 1555) and *Le Second Livre des Hymnes de P. de Ronsard* (Paris, 1556).

6. During the sixteenth century several poets had imitated Greek hymn in Latin: Michael Marullo, *Hymni Naturales* (using pagan subject matter); Vida, *Hymns* (Christian subject matter with classical form); Scaliger (hymns to the Trinity and saints); and Pontano (Christian hymns). See Philip B. Rollinson, "A Generic View of Spenser's *Four Hymns*," *Studies in Philology* 68 (1971): 292–304.

Homeric Hymns were composed mostly in the seventh century B.C. and, though ascribed to Homer in antiquity, according to modern critics were not composed by him; they were judged authentic, however, in the Renaissance. Thirty-three in number and addressed to different gods of the Olympic pantheon, these choral hymns were thought by the Greeks to be among their oldest poetry. They were chanted by rhapsodes at the beginning of ceremonial occasions, such as the Pan-Athenaic celebrations. Most follow certain set formulae: they begin with the invocation of the Muse or an announcement of subject ("I shall begin by singing . . ."), proceed with a description of the honored deity and with accounts of his birth or childhood or with myths connected with him, and conclude with a farewell, a supplication of favor, and a promise to remember the deity in future songs of praise.[7] The Homeric Hymns become models for later choral poetry: for Pindaric Ode, for the hymns of Callimachus, and for the Orphic Hymns. The Orphic Hymns, though written much later than the Homeric Hymns and inferior in quality to them, were considered by the Renaissance the genuine poems of Orpheus and therefore of great antiquity.[8] Like the hymns of Callimachus in the third century B.C., they retain the dactyllic hexameter of the Homeric originals and the basic pattern of invocation, description, and supplication. Although Pindar and Callimachus also adhere to a basic tripartite structure, they are independent in developing each part, and Pindar in his odes uses different meters. Some modern critics attempt to make a sharp distinction between hymn and ode as different genres of poetry.[9] Such distinctions, however, ignore the fact that both are choral lyrics or songs. Indeed, the words *hymn* and *ode* both mean *song* and were used interchangeably: Pindar calls his odes both hymns and odes. Further, the choral ode in Greek, whether in the form of the choral ode in the tragedies or in the form of the

7. *Hesiod, The Homeric Hymns and Homerica*, ed. Hugh G. Evelyn-White (London: William Heinemann, 1914).

8. *Orphei Hymni*, ed. Guilelmus Quandt (Berlin: Weidmannus, 1955); Pindar, *Carmina*, ed. C. M. Bowra (Oxford: Oxford University Press, 1935); and Callimachus, *Hymns and Epigrams*, ed. G. R. Mair (London: William Heinemann, 1960).

9. See Rollinson, "Milton's Nativity Poem and the Decorum of Genre," pp. 166–80; Paul H. Fry, *The Poet's Calling in the English Ode* (New Haven: Yale University Press, 1980), pp. 4–7.

epinician or victory ode, developed historically from the older hymns and dithyrambs. Little attempt is made in antiquity to differentiate hymn and ode, and Renaissance critics, as we note with Puttenham, for the most part preserve this linking.[10]

Like the Homeric Hymns, the odes of Pindar are basically religious poetry. The games at Olympia, Delphi, the Peloponnese, and the Isthmus, for which the epinician or victory odes were composed, were festivals sacred to Zeus, Apollo, and Poseidon respectively. The odes include invocations and prayers to the deity whose festival they celebrate, and to other deities as well. While the odes were commissioned, it is true, to celebrate the achievements of the winning athletes and their sponsors, they also celebrate the gods who make such victory possible. The victory celebrations at which they were performed, moreover, were in the true sense festivals of thanksgiving to the gods. As Sidney's commentary in *The Defence of Poetry* illustrates, Renaissance critics did not always understand or appreciate the reverence that Greeks felt for such festivals.[11]

Many of Pindar's odes follow the model of the Homeric Hymn, opening with an invocation to the god, employing mythic stories digressively, and concluding with remembrance of the gods and thanksgiving for divine favor. Pindar is often even more reverent to the gods than are the earlier poets. He uses digressive myth pointedly to emphasize the importance of piety to the gods, and he rarely refrains from direct moral comment to impress his hearers with the rewards for virtuous acts and the penalties for vicious ones. Although neither connected with religious festival nor remarkably pious in attitude, the hymns of Callimachus, following two centuries after Pindar's odes and four after the Homeric Hymns, are plainly modeled on this earlier poetry. In his hymns to Zeus, Apollo, Artemis, and

10. See, for example, the opening of Pindar's "Olympia 2," where Pindar calls his songs "Lordly-lyred hymns" (Ἀναξιφόρμιγγες ὕμνοι). Renaissance editors of Pindar refer to his odes as both hymns and odes. See, for example, Benedictus (Saumur, 1620). Puttenham groups Pindar, Callimachus, and Anacreon as lyric poets, and he does not distinguish between Pindar's odes and Callimachus's hymns as separate genres (p. 20).

11. "And where a man may say that Pindar many times praiseth highly victories of small moment, matters rather of sport than virtue; as it may be answered, it was the fault of the poet, and not of the poetry, so indeed the chief fault was in the time and custom of the Greeks, who set those toys at so high a price . . ." (p. 97).

Pallas, Callimachus employs proper hymnlike invocations, narrative, and descriptive effects. But with artful commentary, witty puns, and playful reference, this master epigrammatist of the Alexandrine school creates something more like sacred parody than solemn hymn. Nevertheless, Renaissance critics such as Puttenham do not distinguish between the choral lyrics of Pindar and Callimachus; and some fifty years after Puttenham's *Arte*, Milton names these two poets together as supreme artists in the heroic lyric.

In *The Reason of Church Government*, Milton calls the odes and hymns of Pindar and Callimachus "in most things worthy" and compares them to the "frequent songs throughout the law and prophets," which surpass the Greek lyric, "not in their divine argument alone, but in the very critical art of composition."[12] Despite this later commendation of the Hebraic art of composition, Greek ode and hymn might have offered the younger Milton in 1629 certain rhetorical and structural features, certain descriptive effects and narrative modes more accessible to him then as a poet than the modes of psalm or Hebraic song. For example, in Greek hymns visual descriptions dominate, as well as interwoven brief (and sometimes extended) narrative—the kinds of effects Milton was used to imitating in his Latin elegies. The gods appear in the hymns and are characterized not only by descriptive adjective and epithet, but also by hair-color, dress, and personal possessions. For example, Demeter in the Homeric Hymn is "lovely-haired," the lady of the "golden sword" and "glorious harvest"; she is vividly and personally described at the very moment she loses her daughter Persephone. She rends the veil from her head, casts her dark cloak from her, and speeds, like a bird over land and sea, raging and carrying flaming torches in her hand. Similarly vivid is the scene of Persephone's rape: she is playing in a meadow with the daughters of Ocean and gathering flowers—roses, crocuses, violets, irises, hyacinths, narcissus. The flowers are individually named and the girl herself is compared to them. The Hymn to Demeter not only describes the goddess and her daughter Persephone, but also narrates in detail the story of Demeter's

---

12. *Complete Poems and Major Prose*, ed. Merritt Y. Hughes (New York: Odyssey Press, 1957), p. 669. Citations of Milton's poetry and prose are to this edition.

search for and recovery of Persephone (a story Milton alludes to compellingly in *Paradise Lost* 4.268–72). Other Homeric Hymns are similarly detailed in their narratives and descriptions—and so too are the odes of Pindar and the hymns of Callimachus.

Despite its wealth of description and its use of narrative, Greek lyric is neither basically descriptive nor narrative poetry; it is formal choral poetry of praise that is especially attentive to the occasion for which it is composed, designed to celebrate specifically that occasion and the persons and gods connected with it. Consciously choral in composition, it alludes not infrequently to the chorus that is performing. Callimachus describes at the beginning of the Hymn to Apollo the chorus of young men preparing for their song and dance. Pindar at the outset of Pythia 1 tells how the chorus responds with their dance steps to the melody of the lyre.

It is the Greek sense of occasion that Milton, Crashaw, and Cowley address as they organize their odes on the Nativity and the Resurrection. Milton's "On the Morning of Christ's Nativity" and Crashaw's "In the Holy Nativity of Our Lord God" are both choral odes or hymns, Milton's for solo voice with a chorus of celebrants, Crashaw's a chorus "Sung as by the Shepheards." Cowley's "The Resurrection" is included among his *Pindariques* and quite deliberately displays its debt to the Greek choral tradition by opening with a quotation from one of Pindar's odes.[13]

Although the Nativity Ode is firmly Christian in subject and concept, classical decorum guides Milton in his structuring of the poem. As in Greek hymn or ode, he opens the poem in the first four introductory strophes by setting the scene ("This is the Month, and this the happy morn" [l. 1]), by describing both Father and Son, and by invoking the Heavenly Muse. The Father is presented in relationship to the Son as "Heav'n's eternal King" (l. 2), just as Zeus in Homeric Hymn and Pindaric Ode appears in relation to his sons: the divine Apollo and the human

13. "On the Morning of Christ's Nativity," in *Complete Poems and Major Prose*, ed. Hughes; "In the Holy Nativity of Our Lord God" in Richard Crashaw, *The Poems: English, Latin, and Greek*, ed. L. C. Martin (Oxford: Clarendon Press, 1927); and "The Resurrection" in Abraham Cowley, *Poetry and Prose*, ed. L. C. Martin (Oxford: Clarendon Press, 1949).

Heracles. Throughout the Nativity Ode, moreover, Milton's descriptions of the Son make one recollect Apollo and Heracles. The first characterization of the Son as a God of light, sitting with "far-beaming blaze of Majesty . . . at Heav'n's high Council-Table . . . (in) the midst of Trinal Unity" (ll. 9–11) recalls the golden Apollo, son in the Greek trinity (Zeus, Apollo, and Athene), enthroned in Olympus at his Father's side, lyre in hand, honoring his heavenly Father. Just such a scene is evoked frequently by Pindar throughout his odes, as, for example, in Olympia 14, where Apollo, seated by the Graces, offers evermore honor in reverence to the Olympian Father (ll. 10–12). The sun/son comparisons throughout Milton's Nativity Ode recall the connection of Apollo with the sun in later Greek and Roman mythology.

Milton's ode is not merely an ode in honor of Christ, however; it is an ode that celebrates his birth and examines the implications in Heaven and on earth of that birth. Occasions of birth are important in Homeric Hymn and Pindaric ode, whether they are the births of the gods themselves—Zeus, Apollo, or Hermes—or the births of the sons of gods: Apollo's mortal sons or Zeus's. Zeus's birth on Crete and his nurture by the Great Mother is alluded to by Callimachus in his Hymn to Zeus, as the birth of Apollo is featured by Callimachus in the Hymn to Delos. The Homeric Hymn to the Delian Apollo renders a particularly poetical account of the god's birth, telling how the goddess Leto knelt in a soft meadow and, throwing her arms about a palm tree, gave birth to Apollo. Attendant goddesses gave a cry and the earth rejoiced when Apollo leapt to the light; then the goddesses bathed him and wrapped him in pure garments, and Themis gave him nectar and ambrosia. Milton takes his cue from the Greek hymn as he narrates the opening "hymn" section of his Nativity poem. Nature serves as an attendant goddess and, since it is winter, doffs her gaudy trim and presides at the birth in a saintly veil of maiden snow. Meek-eyed peace, the personification of order (as is the goddess Themis in the Homeric Hymn) is also in attendance; and the birds of calm, which sit brooding on the charmed wave, add a sense of pastoral quiet. Instead of goddesses, angels raise the paean to the newborn god and announce to a rustic and almost "Greek" band of shepherds that "mighty *Pan* / Was kindly come to live with them below" (ll. 89–90).

However prominent the birth account appears at the beginning of a Greek hymn, the aim of the hymn is not merely to celebrate the birth of the god, but to show in that birth anticipation of the god's future deeds and triumphs. Accordingly, in the Homeric Hymn to the Delian Apollo, the god is no sooner born than he displays his powers, pronouncing his mastery over the lyre and the curved bow, shooting afar, and beginning to walk over the wide-pathed earth. In the Homeric Hymn to the Pythian Apollo, his attributes as far-shooter, healer, and giver of prophetic oracles are specially featured, and he is named the slayer of the serpent Pytho. Milton's aim in the Nativity Ode is similar, for while he opens and closes the hymn proper in the manger, like his Greek models he alludes to the future powers and achievements of the newborn god, who, as he tells us in the first strophe of the ode, has come to release us from "deadly forfeit" and to "work us a perpetual peace" (ll. 6–7). Hence, Milton's ode looks back as far as the Creation and Fall and forward to the Redemption and the return of the Age of Gold. The powers that the Son is to exercise on earth as prophet, priest, and king, moreover, have a peculiar relevance to those very powers that Apollo, son of Zeus, acquired at his birth and which he must relinquish with the birth of a greater "son." Milton's Son has come to drive the pagan gods from their shrines, and Apollo is the first god named who is so dislodged. Like the greater sun come to earth to make the earthly sun hide his head in shame, Milton's Christ outshines the resplendent golden-haired Apollo. The musical jubilee he commands at his birth is more sweet and sublime than Apollo, the very god of music, could call forth. Welcomed by the shepherds as their true god and Pan, the Son dispossesses Apollo, the lord of flocks and shepherd-god, of an authority he once exercised. The Son takes on also Apollo's attributes of monster-slayer; for as Apollo was extolled in hymn and ode for his great feat of conquering the mighty serpent Pytho, the Son now limits and straightens "th'old Dragon under ground" (l. 168). Finally, to mark his complete assumption of the Apollonian role, the Son silences the god of prophecy at the oracle Apollo established with his birth, and Apollo in defeat departs with a "hollow shriek" (l. 178), bequeathing his authority to a new god of prophecy.

Important as Apollo is in the Nativity Ode as a classical model of the divine son with whom Christ is compared and contrasted, he gives place in the final section of the ode to Zeus's human son, Heracles, who like Jesus is the child of one divine and one human parent. The Heraclean reference occurs just at the end of Milton's catalogue of the fleeing pagan gods and in the antepenultimate stanza of the ode. Like Apollo, Heracles was one of the famous monster-slayers of antiquity; even in infancy he foreshadowed his future role by strangling in his cradle the two serpents Hera had sent to kill him. In describing Jesus as an infant who displays similar supernatural powers, Milton alludes directly to this story, well known in classical sources and prominently featured in Pindar's Nemea 1. Heracles, one of the most illustrious heroes of the ancient world, born in Pindar's own native Thebes, was a favorite of Pindar's and appears repeatedly throughout his odes. Pindar chooses to tell the story of Heracles's defeat of the serpents at the end of Nemea 1, perhaps to honor Chromius of Aetna, for whom he wrote the ode, since Chromius traced his descent from Heracles. Certainly, the principle of inherited birthright is important in this ode. Heracles, in strangling the serpents, proves his divine birthright even in infancy and gives a clear sign of the future heroic deeds he was to perform in a life also marked with long suffering and trial. This victory indicates—as the seer Teiresias prophesies in the ode—that despite adversity Heracles will triumph and achieve the destiny that his divine father ordained for him. In describing Heracles's struggle with the serpents, Pindar wishes to show that Heracles begins, so to speak, as he means to end.

> ὁ δ'ὀρ—
> θὸν μὲν ἄντεινεν Κάρα, πειρᾶτο δὲ πρῶτον μάχας,
> δισσαῖσι δοιοὺς αὐχένων
> μάρψαις ἀφύκτοις χερσὶν ἑαῖς ὄφιας.
> ἀγχομένοις δὲ βρόχος
> ψυχὰς ἀπέπνευσεν μελέων ἀφάτων.

> But he held his head upright,
> And for the first time tried his battle strength,
> With his two irresistible hands

Seizing the two serpents,
In short time caused them
To breathe forth their souls out of their monstrous bodies.

(Nemea 1.43–47; my translation)

Pindar's description stands, I believe, directly behind Milton's, for the likenesses of Pindar's Heracles and Milton's Son are far from incidental.[14] The Son is an infant god-hero in the Heraclean mold, who even from his cradle controls and routs the crew of monstrous gods, most dangerous among them Typhon, whom Pindar himself described in Pythia 1 and Pythia 4 as the preeminent foe of Zeus.

He feels from Judah's Land
The dreaded Infant's hand,
    The rays of *Bethlehem* blind his dusky eyn;
Nor all the gods beside,
Longer dare abide,
    Nor *Typhon* huge ending in snaky twine:
Our Babe, to show his Godhead true,
Can in his swaddling band control the damned crew.

(ll. 221–28)

Like Pindar, Milton suggests that this deed performed in infancy is the seal or proof of the infant-god's divine heritage; it is the sign of what is to come and of the hero's ultimate triumph at the end of his life. In the pattern of his ode and in the use of classical allusion, Milton reveals a deep indebtedness to the classical choral tradition that he seeks to Christianize, as the Son of God Christianizes the gods and heroes of antiquity that he supersedes.

The resemblances between Milton's "On the Morning of Christ's Nativity" and Crashaw's "In the Holy Nativity of Our Lord God" may in some measure be accounted for in that both poems follow closely the Greek choral model. Both are occasional poems that celebrate the birth of a god; both are consciously choral in reference and effect. Crashaw alludes to the shepherds as singing the hymn; he opens and closes the hymn

14. Milton again turns to a story connected with Hercules when he recounts the triumph of the Son of God over Satan in *Paradise Regained* 4.563–68, once more drawing his account, as Hughes points out, from Pindar's odes, Isthmia 3. See *Complete Poems and Major Prose*, p. 528n.

with full choruses, alternating in between with single and combined voices. Crashaw's hymn, like Milton's ode, is designed as an offering or gift to the infant god. Christ is both described and directly addressed. As in Milton's poem, he is in Crashaw's a "Noble Infant," a "Mighty Babe," and a "Great little one," the king. Nature is attendant upon his birth. The sun, as in Milton's ode, welcomes a greater light, and day dawns, "Not from the East, but from thine Eyes" (l. 22). Though Winter holds the earth, the North wind "forgott his feirce Intent; / And left perfumes in stead of scarres . . . Where he mean't frost, he scatter'd flowrs" (ll. 26–29). In this poem Mary becomes more than nurturing mother; she is almost a pagan nature deity, a Flora or "fruitful" Maja, who has given birth to a "soft King / Of simple Graces & sweet Loves" (ll. 103–4). The scene of the birth is like the scenes of transformed earth that are settings for the nativity of Apollo or Hermes in the Homeric Hymns. "All Wonders" are present "in one sight! / Aeternity shutt in a span. / Sommer in Winter. Day in Night. / Heauen in earth, & God in Man" (ll. 79–82).

Crashaw's attitude toward the infant god alternates between reverence and playfulness, for he does not know whether to address the baby as a deity or a child. The wordplay throughout the poem also suggests this paradox. Both in his playfulness and use of paradox he much resembles certain classical models. The Homeric Hymn to Hermes presents us with a baby who is both a prankish boy and a powerful god. Not content to be a baby in his mother's arms, Hermes is already setting out to perform boyish mischief. Encountering the tortoise, he transforms it into the first lyre; finding Apollo's cattle, he hides them from the older god and then returns to his cradle to act the part of the "wise" child. Apollo, seeking the thief of his cattle, finds only a mere infant, and he is in turn struck with wonder that this mere infant has outwitted him. Apollo is further bemused when Hermes takes up the newly invented lyre and plays on it music such as Apollo has never heard before. Then, instead of reproving the child, Apollo worships him as the most renowned of gods and accepts from him the gift of the lyre. The shepherds of Crashaw's hymn are a little like the Apollo of the Homeric Hymn. They can scarcely believe that the tender infant before them is their creator and king. He seems only a sweet-eyed babe in a "baulmy Nest," an infant with "new-bloom'd Cheek," who "Twixt's mother's brests is gone to bed" (ll. 67–68). Yet they recognize also in this baby the "Bright dawn of our aeternall Day" (l. 72), the one whose birth "Lifts earth to heauen, stoopes heau'n to earth" (ll. 83–84). Like Apollo, the shepherds do not know at first how to treat the "wise" child before them; but at last they humble themselves in worship, offering gifts, kissing his feet, and crowning his head.

Callimachus's Hymn to Apollo offers a different combination of playfulness and worship. It is structured, like Crashaw's hymn, as a kind of epiphany: a revelation of god to man. Callimachus begins with a description of the god knocking at the door of the temple. The Delian palm tree trembles, giving a sign to the young men who prepare a song that they are about to enter into the god's presence. Commencing their song, they sound the tortoise-shelled lyre, and Callimachus archly comments that the tortoise when alive was silent, but now when dead is tuneful. Kind Apollo is now present in their midst; welcoming him, the chorus describes his appearance and praises his attributes, punning at the same time on the supposed etymology of the name *Apollo* from the Greek word *poly* (πόλυ), meaning many or much. Apollo appears to them poly-golden (πολύχρυσος) and poly-possessed of riches (πολυκτέανος) (ll. 34–35). Even the cry, "Hie, hie, Paeon," which summons the god to the celebrants, and the sound of the god shooting his arrow are puns in Greek on Apollo's name:

> ἄλλον ἐπ᾽ ἄλλῳ
> βάλλων ὠκὺν ὀιστόν, ἐπηύτησε δὲ λαός,
> "ἰὴ ἰὴ παιῆον, ἵει βέλος."

> one after another,
> He hurls a sharp arrow, and the people cry,
> "Hie, hie, Paeon; let fly an arrow." (ll. 101–3)

Cleverly Callimachus has made this whole passage sound as though the chorus were calling upon Apollo, even as he describes the god and the people. In the conclusion of the hymn Callimachus effects one more witty touch, for he makes Apollo speak as though in comment on the hymn in his honor that he has just heard. Spurning the suggestion of Envy that all poets should aspire to epic performance in order to please their hearers, Apollo commends the well-made brief poem. Comparing the epic to the Euphrates River and the brief hymn to the pure stream, Apollo says that though the Assyrian river is great, it carries much garbage on its waters. Moreover, not from every water will the bees sip, but only from the undefiled spring. Callimachus has concluded his hymn by having the god of poetry compliment the very kind of verses he has written.

Crashaw's hymn, like Callimachus's, delights in paradox and clever wordplay. Here too is an unconventional performance that takes considerable liberty with its solemn subject. Coming into the presence of their god, Crashaw's chorus expresses its surprise in discovering "loue's Noon in Nature's night" (l. 2). The baby opens his eyes, and the chorus comments, "In spite of Darknes, it was Day" (l. 20). These conceits and many of those that follow are metaphysical, to be sure. Donne's divine poems might have prompted some of these Christian paradoxes. For example, Donne had expressed in "La Corona" the paradox of the creator having made the very world into which he was created. But Donne hardly prepares us for the saucy humor of Crashaw's phoenix who builds his own nest:

> The Phaenix builds the Phaenix' nest.
>   Love's architecture is his own.
> The Babe whose birth embraues this morn,
>   Made his own bed e're he was born. (ll. 46–49)

Nor is there anything quite comparable in other seventeenth-century poetry to the gentle wit of the next section, in which Crashaw archly inquires what place is both soft and warm enough for a divine infant to lay his head. Dismissing snow as too cold and fleece as impure, he arrives wittily at the compromise of the Virgin's breasts: "no way but so / Not to ly cold, yet sleep in snow" (ll. 69–70). As Callimachus made us visualize the chorus coming into the presence of the god, as he made us see the young men react to the god's person, so Crashaw makes us look with the shepherds' eyes, as they react to and discover their deity before them. In a warmly appropriate gesture, the shepherds promise to bring their first-born lambs to the dread Lamb of God before them, thus repaying his sacrifice in part by one of their own. As the poet offered his skill as poet to the god of poetry in the ancient hymn, so here Crashaw makes his shepherds offer gifts appropriate to Christ as Lamb. Yet it is not specific echoes or even examples that link Crashaw to Callimachus, but a matter of attitude. Crashaw was an expert classicist who took classical technique and models seriously, as is well demonstrated by his adaptation of forms such as the classical epigram to Christian subjects. Callimachus's hymns might well have demonstrated to Crashaw that the hymn form need not be treated solemnly, for Callimachus showed Crashaw how the deity could be approached with banter and wordplay. Crashaw, following his lead, creates a hymn on the coming of Christ that is not cold and distant, but warm and intimate.

While classical models teach Milton and Crashaw to express more fully and variously the Christian experience, they lead Cowley to secularize the Greek ode. Cowley's Pindarique "The Resurrection" is a poem that is religious in name only. Its ostensible subject is the final resurrection of the dead at the Last Judgment, one often treated in religious poetry and never perhaps so successfully as in Donne's sonnet "At the round earth's imagined corners." There Donne creates imagistically the aura of the final moments when souls will reassume their bodies, and then pleads, as a sinner about to be condemned, for time to repent while yet on earth. Cowley deals with the Last Judgment in only one of the poem's four strophes, the next to the last, where his treatment bears some verbal resemblances to Donne's:

> Then shall the scatter'ed *Atomes* crowding come
>   Back to their *Ancient Home*,
>
> . . . .
> And where th'*attending Soul* naked, and shivering stands,
>   Meet, salute, and joyn their hands. (ll. 37–38, 44–45)

Though presented in ode form, these lines more resemble their metaphysical model than that of Greek hymn or ode. Missing particularly is the sense that the ode is addressed, as Pindaric ode usually is, to the deity either in praise or supplication or that it explores in its narrative or descriptive passages the relationship between God and man. Cowley's description of the Last Judgment is almost impersonal and inspires neither awe nor mystery. Yet, at the same time, Cowley marks his poem as a formal imitation of Pindar, including it among his *Pindariques* and paraphrasing in his opening lines the beginning strophe of Olympia 11:

> Not *Winds* to *Voyages* at Sea,
> Nor *Showers* to *Earth* more necessary be,
> (*Heav'ens* vital *seed* cast on the *womb* of *Earth*
>   To give the *fruitful Year* a *Birth*)
>   Then *Verse* to *Virtue*, which does do
> The *Midwifes* Office, and the *Nurses* too: (ll. 1–6)

Olympia 11 is a brief poem of one triad only (strophe, antistrophe, and epode); containing no myth, it does little more than promise a future ode in honor of the boxing victory it here commemorates. But in so doing it makes an important and typically Pindaric statement about the relationship between virtuous deeds and the poetry that celebrates them. Both the ability to perform the virtuous deed and the skill needed to commemorate it come from God. God alone makes a man flourish in virtue and brings that virtue to fruition in an act nobly achieved. God also commands the poet to sing and makes him confer the poetic laurel to crown the heroic man with lasting honor. Hence, when a poet wishes to sing a worthy deed, he calls upon the Muses to inspire him and to join with him figuratively in singing the victory songs, those honey-voiced hymns (μελιγάρυες ὕμνοι) that are the true reward of the victor. Pindar's entire poem is in a way the elaboration of the striking opening figure, imitated by Cowley, with which it begins.

> Ἔστιν ἀνθρώποις ἀνέμων ὅτε πλείστα
> χρῆσις· ἔστιν δ᾽ οὐρανίων ὑδάτων,
> ὀμβρίων παίδων νεφέλας.
> εἰ δὲ σὺν πόνῳ τις εὖ πράσσοι, μελιγάρυες ὕμνοι
> ὑστέρων ἀρχὰ λόγων
> τέλλεται καὶ πιστὸν ὅρκιον μεγάλαις ἀρεταῖς.

> For men there is a time
> When winds are most needed,
> Time for heavenly waters,
> For the storm children of clouds;
> And if anyone performs well with toil, then honey-voiced
>   hymns
> Lay down the foundation of future tales,
> Even a trusty witness of noble virtue. (Olympia 11.1–6)

In this figure Pindar establishes a relationship between man and the heavenly forces sent by God—either rain or song—to insure that virtue will not wither and die but be preserved. Though brief, Pindar's poem is an important statement of his creed as the divinely inspired bard.

Cowley's ode, it is true, attempts in part to deal with this Pindaric theme, for it looks at the relationship between poetry and the earthly fame it confers. Verse, says Cowley, "*feeds,*" "*cloathes,*" "*embalms*" virtue and "erects a *Pyramide* / That never will decay" (ll. 7–10). Verse will last while the earth does or "till *Heaven* it self shall melt away, / And nought behind it stay" (ll. 11–12). Missing from Cowley's praise of the lasting quality of verse, however, is the sense of divine sanction that Pindar insists allows both virtue to triumph and verse to record it for posterity. God does not call forth Cowley's ode. Yet Cowley attempts in some measure to duplicate the occasion of the Greek ode without its calling. The ceremony is present in strophe 2; like an ancient Greek choragus, Cowley urges the chorus to "Begin the *Song,* and strike the *Living Lyre*" (l. 13). He compares the years to come to a "well-fitted *Quire,*" which advances "hand in hand" to accompany the song with the "smooth and equal measures" of a dance (ll. 14–16). This choral performance, Cowley pronounces, will last, moreover, until the "*Universal String*" is untuned and the thunder of the Last Judgment is heard. With this evocation of the Last Judgment, Cowley introduces the description of the resurrection that occupies the whole of the third strophe and justifies, so to speak, the title of the ode, if not its main subject.

If Cowley's Pindarique has a principal subject and is not merely a digressive exercise, it would appear to be the power of poetry. Certainly, that is what concerns him most in the first, second, and the final strophes of the poem. In this fourth strophe he calls upon his Muse to allay her "vig'orous heat"; the very force of poetic inspiration, which he names his "*Pindarique Pegasus,*" is carrying him away. It is "an unruly, and a *hard-Mouth'd Horse,* / Fierce, and unbroken yet," which "now *praunces* stately, and anon *flies* o're the place," threatening to throw both writer and reader (ll. 57–64). In fact, it is the Pindaric manner, rather than the Pindaric matter, that Cowley takes as the essential of this ancient Greek form. For Cowley, Pindar is a poetical and not a religious model. Instead of looking to the ancient ode for what it might teach about writing a modern Christian ode, Cowley sees in it the model for a new poetics of a loose occasional poem. "The Resurrection" thus is almost a kind of experimental fragment on how to write Pindaric verse. Cowley's first note on the poem provides the clue; he explains, "This Ode is truly *Pindarical*, falling from one thing into another, after his *Enthusiastical manner*."[15] Cowley is not truly celebrating a religious event in this poem; unconcerned with either gods or heroes or the ancient poet's view of the divine forces that inspire them, Cowley imitates Pindar's "enthusiastical" manner of moving from subject to subject. Focusing on the poet's figures, he secularizes his theme: verse becomes a medium merely for celebrating verse.

*   *   *

The publication of Cowley's *Pindariques* in 1656 marks the end of one era and the beginning of another of classical imitation. Cowley differs from Milton and Crashaw, who had turned to Greek hymn and ode in order to adapt its form, its choral format, its narratives and description of gods and heroes for Christian odes on religious occasions. Cowley is not looking for a new form for the Christian ode; indeed only two of his original set of *Pindariques*—"The Resurrection" and "The Plagues of Egypt"—touch on religious subjects. He is looking for a poetic model for the occasional poem. The form that Milton and Crashaw had used for hymns and odes to Christ, Cowley will use to praise the Muse, to celebrate Thomas Hobbes, or to commemorate the birth of the Royal Society. Hence, Cowley's Pindaric experiments are a kind of watershed. Turning to a medium once used for religious expression, Cowley adapts it for secular praise, preparing the way for the secular hymns and odes of Dryden and for the occasional odes of the eighteenth century. What

15. Cowley's use of the word *enthusiastical* to describe Pindar's style is significant. It is a word traditionally used in the Renaissance (as in E. K.'s headnote to Spenser's "October" of the *Shepheardes Calender*) to describe the bard's direct inspiration from the god—being filled by the god as the prophet or priest might be. In the seventeenth century it was being applied to the popular style of extempore preaching, sometimes in a not wholly approving way. Cowley seems to be saying here, following the ancient critique by Horace of Pindar's style (see *Carmina* 4.2), that Pindar's enthusiasm can carry him away. In this he is a dangerous master to imitate.

started as an impulse among Renaissance poets to Christianize the hymn to pagan gods ends with the creating of a kind of occasional poetry that is utterly purged of the heavenly muse's divine notes.

12

"IN COPIOUS LEGEND, OR SWEET LYRIC SONG": TYPOLOGY AND THE PERILS OF THE RELIGIOUS LYRIC

Joseph Wittreich

Joseph Summers has reminded us of a story about how C. S. Lewis taunted both students and friends: "Don't you rejoice with that chorus [in *Samson Agonistes*]":

> While their hearts were jocund and sublime,
> Drunk with idolatry, drunk with wine
> And fat regorged of bulls and goats,
> Chanting their idol, and preferring
> Before our living dread who dwells
> In Silo, his bright sanctuary,
> Among them he is a spirit of frenzy sent,
> Who hurt their minds
> And urged them on with mad desire
> To call in haste for their destroyer . . . ?

"The young friend would protest, 'No! No! I don't! It's unchristian,' and Lewis would reply, 'Oh, come now, Rejoice! You're supposed to, you know.'"[1]

This story provides Summers with an occasion for counseling that, even if "many modern readers reject Samson, along

---

1. "Response to Anthony Low's Address on *Samson Agonistes*," *Milton Quarterly* 13 (1979): 106. This present essay is another version, with a somewhat different emphasis, of chapter 5, "Samson among the Nightingales," in my *Interpreting "Samson Agonistes"* (Princeton, N.J.: Princeton University Press, 1986), pp. 239–95.

with other military and national figures in the Old Testament, as spiritually alien and ethically benighted, most Christians of Milton's time seem to have accepted him as an authentic hero of the Chosen People's divinely guided history before the Christian revelation, and to have perceived significant relations between pre-Christian and post-Christian histories." Such musings are meant to substantiate Summers's claim that Milton's contemporaries (and indeed all subsequent readers) should "recognize in Samson a heroic servant of God who seemed to have lost and then to have won everything, 'Triumphing over Death, and Chance, and thee O Time.'"[2] Summers is not alone among Miltonists in leaving untested his thesis concerning the Renaissance Samson; nor is he alone in positing a spiritually triumphant Samson at the end of Milton's poem. Yet against Summers's thesis we might place this alternative formulation: that Summers's (and what he supposes to be Milton's) Samson survives within the sweet lyric song of Milton's century, but that at the same time the Samson of the religious lyric is continually being diminished by the Samson of secular literature and, more, by the copious legend still accruing to this supposed hero and *sometimes* celebrated type of Christ.

Since the publication of F. Michael Krouse's *Milton's Samson and the Christian Tradition* in 1949 there has been an alarming, and misguided, tendency to elide the Renaissance Samsons with the Samson of the Middle Ages and, through this elision, to collapse the very different Samsons of the Renaissance into one Samson or, in the instance provided by Krouse, into two Samsons, the one belonging to the religious and the other to the secular lyric. The saint of religious literature, says Krouse, stands in marked contrast with the sinner of secular literature:

> In nearly all the secular literature of England during the sixteenth and seventeenth centuries, Samson was treated exactly as he had been treated during the medieval period . . . . The poets of the Renaissance, almost without exception, adopted the medieval literary conception of Samson as a great man brought low by woman's treachery.[3]

2. "Response," p. 106.
3. Princeton: Princeton University Press for the University of Cincinnati, 1949, p. 72.

It is true that the restraints especially of the religious lyric engendered reductionist tendencies, eliminating the opportunity for including certain kinds of representations of Samson; yet the forms of reductionism commanded by the celebratory character of the religious lyric seem to have been countermanded in a secular literature that arrayed around the saintly image of Samson his various fallen forms, and not just that of a lustful hero snared by female treachery.

Let us recognize, first of all, that Samson's history was popular enough to have been the subject of two different plays in England, both now lost, the one dating from 1567 and the other from 1602.[4] Moreover, the details of his history were sufficiently disseminated that they could be referred to casually, even flippantly, as in these lines spoken by Quick-silver in George Chapman's *Eastward Hoe:* "I *Sampson* now, haue burst the *Philistins* Bands, / And in thy lappe my louely *Dalila*, / Ile lie lie and snore out my enfranchisde state."[5] By both Thomas Dekker and Shakespeare, the Samson story is referred to without explicit citation. In Dekker we read: "Humble mee . . . that . . . my heart may not swell up with pride . . . . As thou hast placed mee, to be a Pillar to uphold others, so grant that I may not proove a weaker Pillar, to throw my selfe downe; and with my fall to bruise others that stand under me."[6] Or in Shakespeare: Lear has just embraced Cordelia and thereupon tells her, "He that parts us shall bring a brand from heaven, / And fire us hence like foxes. Wipe thine eyes; / The good-years shall devour them, flesh and fell" (5.3.22–24).[7] In the example provided by Dekker, the speaker is the antitype of Samson, the strong not the weak pillar; in the Shakespearean example, however, he is Samson's antithesis, regenerate not degenerate, wiping away tears not occasioning them, pouring a balm upon the world not

4. See *Annals of English Drama 975–1700,* comp. Alfred Harbage, rev. S. Schoenbaum (London: Methuen, 1964), pp. 41, 84.

5. See George Chapman et al., *Eastward Hoe* (London: Printed for William Aspley, 1605), sig. C.

6. *Four Birds of Noahs Arke* (1609), ed. F. P. Wilson (Oxford: Basil Blackwell, 1924), "The Eagle," p. 35. Samson is probably behind Dekker's lines concerning the pulling down of justice on our heads ("The Dove," p. 3) and the driving away of all foxes ("The Eagle," p. 20).

7. Quoted from *King Lear,* The Arden Shakespeare, ed. Kenneth Muir (London: Methuen, 1972).

devastating it. And Samson is here invoked both to emblem-
atize the agent of division and fragmentation and to illustrate
the proposition that evil is self-consuming.

In view of these observations and these figurings of the
Samson story, certain propositions should be set forth immedi-
ately. Retellings of the Samson story pale against the prolifera-
tion of allusions, often implicit or muted, to that story; the
allusions themselves are evidence of the popularity of the Sam-
son story, of its being fixed, in all its details, within the Renais-
sance mind, of its being a significant part of the mental furniture
of the age. Such allusions suggest that the Samson story, by the
beginning of the seventeenth century, has acquired an overlay of
political significance and further that it has become netted
within a typological scheme, both secular and sacred, that
exhibits a tarnished Samson—a Samson who, nurtured in
blood, delights in vengeance, and whose enterprise entails the
wretched interchange of wrong for wrong. The Samson
typology, once used to establish an identity between Samson
and Christ, is now being used, in the happy formulation of Ray-
mond Waddington, to mark "the modulations of difference."[8]
Typological systems, of course, are always founded upon sim-
ilarities and differences; yet the Samson typology during
Milton's own century changes in its inflections, with the accent
falling ever more insistently on differences, disparities between
Samson and Christ. Very simply, a disjunctive displaces a con-
junctive typology.

In the seventeenth century, biblical narratives, no less than
the Bible's inlays of wisdom, are sometimes translated into lyri-
cal effusions:

> O What a number more there are,
>   time will not serve to tell,
> Of Barac, Samson, Gideon,
>   Jephe, Dauid, Samuel.
> P Rophets also, which all through faith
>   kingdomes subdu'd and gain'd,
> Wrought righteousnesse, Rop't Lyons mouche,

8. "Milton among the Carolines," in *The Age of Milton: Backgrounds to
Seventeenth Century Literature*, ed. C. A. Patrides and Raymond B. Waddington
(Manchester: Manchester University Press; Totowa, N.J.: Barnes and Noble,
1980), p. 352.

and promises obtain'd
Q Vench'd violence of flaming fire
escap'd the sword in fight.
Of weake made strong and valiant,
great Armies turn'd to flight.[9]

The Old and New Testaments brought an extraordinary collective inspiration to the religious lyric of the Renaissance, a poetry often fueled by biblical paraphrases such as the one just cited.[10] Such poetical fancies, or spiritual epitomes, whatever their gains for art may be, exhibit the customary losses of translation: narrative probity and nuance, ambiguity and complexity are sacrificed to lyrical simplicity and intensity; ideological rifts opened in biblical narratives, more often than not, are concealed within the restraints, ideological and aesthetic, of the religious lyric; analytical power gives way to typological play; modulations of difference modulate into similitudes. The presence of the Samson story, its infiltration of the religious lyric, provides a striking example.

Typological parallels, *express similitudes*, are highlighted in the religious lyric. Witness the example provided by George Herbert in "Sunday": "As Sampson bore the doores away, / Christs hands, though nail'd, wrought our salvation, / And did unhinge that day" (ll. 47–49).[11] Or witness the complicated, and complicating, instance offered by Thomas Traherne in *The First Century* (1.90): "In Death it self, will I find Life, and in Conquest Victory. This Samson by Dying Kild all His Enemies: And then carried the Gates of Hell and Death away, when being Dead, Himself was born to his Grave."[12] Artful accommodation of theological commonplaces, through the device of typology, is a part of the story told by lyric and prose poem alike. But another, more interesting part of the same story involves the extent to which a typology that had proved binding to scriptural texts and that had

9. Simon Wastell, *Microbiblion or the Bibles Epitome* (London: Robert Mylbrune, 1629), pp. 467–68, but see also pp. 52–53.

10. For elaboration, see Ernest Rhys, *Lyrical Poetry* (1913; rpt. London and Toronto: J. M. Dent and Sons; New York: E. P. Dutton, 1933), p. 221; and Barbara Kiefer Lewalski, *Protestant Poetics and the Seventeenth-Century Religious Lyric* (Princeton: Princeton University Press, 1979), p. 144.

11. *The Works of George Herbert*, ed. F. E. Hutchinson (Oxford: Clarendon Press, 1941), p. 76.

12. *Poems, Centuries, and Three Thanksgivings*, ed. Ann Ridler (London: Oxford University Press, 1966), p. 208.

effectively sealed their fictions, largely through the coun-
terthrusts of the secular lyric and drama, often had the effect of
sabotaging the commonplaces of religion and, with them, the
conventional typologies. One of the blurring effects of the Sam-
son typology was achieved by identifying Samson and Christ in
the perception that both figures, in their respective deaths, slew
God's enemies and thereby opened the gates into paradise. Their
deaths, that is, were construed as births, with each of these heav-
enly champions being a resplendent image of "earth's bright
Glory"[13]—a bright shoot of everlastingness.

Herbert's formulation, and to a certain extent the one by
Traherne, may be correlated with Daniel Featley's "Sermon III:
A Christian Victory: or, Conquest over Death's Enmity" (1639),
where we read that when Christ "rose againe, then he spoyled
him of his power, and tooke his weapons away, and triumphed
over him intoken of conquest, as *Samson* took *the Gates of Gaza
on his shoulders*, and carried them to the top of the hill."[14]
Correspondingly, the formulations by Herbert and Traherne call
to mind Matthew Griffith's declaration that, like Samson, "we
shall be victorious, even in death it self; at which time we shall
see the heavens open."[15]

In triumphing over their enemies, Samson and Christ alike
bruise the head of the serpent, defeat Antichrist and all his
limbs. Samson's carrying off of the gates of the city, and
especially his hurling down of the temple, are the episodes sanc-
tioning and securing the typological connection between him
and Christ. In taking the gates of Gaza, Samson was recognized
as "A figure of Christs glorious resurrection"; and at the pillars
he was perceived as one who "humble[s] himself to the death,
that he might have his people out of the hands of all their spir-
itual enemies."[16] In his death, Christ is a second mighty Sam-

13. Quarles, *The Historie of Samson* (London: John Marriott, 1631), p. 140.
14. In *Threnoikos: The House of Mourning* (London: John Dawson, 1640),
p. 273.
15. *A Patheticall Perswasion to Pray for Public Peace* (London: Richard
Royston, 1642), p. 45.
16. See John Trapp, *Annotations upon the Old and New Testaments*, 5 vols.
(London: Robert White, 1662), 1:90; and John Downame et al., *Annotations upon
All the Books of the Old and New Testament*, 2 vols. (London: Evan Tyler, 1657),
annotation to Judges 16:30. But see also Thomas Taylor, *The Works of That
Faithful Servant* (London: John Bartlet, 1653), pp. 378–79, and Theodore Haak,
The Dutch Annotations upon the Whole Bible (London: Henry Hills, 1657),
annotation to Judges 26:31.

son overcoming his enemies—and at a time when he seems most overcome by them, says Thomas Taylor; and in rising from the dead, Christ is "another mighty *Sampson* [who] rose in his might, [and] carried away the gates and bars of death." In virtually the same breath, however, Taylor will use these episodes through which typological identification had often been achieved to underscore typological distance and difference. Only Christ is never "ouercome" by his enemies: "The Philistines desired to get *Samson* into their hands, and preuailed: but here is an inuincible *Sampson*, his enemy cannot hold him."[17] Implicit in such comparisons is the realization that, finally, the heavenly Samson is qualitatively different from the earthly Samson; and from that realization issues a host of comparative formulations intended to mark their difference: "our better Samson," "our better Nazarite" truly conquers in dying; Christ alone leads captivity captive, is "the true *Sampson*, who by his death brake the bands of death, and destroyed his and our enemies."[18]

In the illustration provided by Herbert, then, Samson and Christ are express similitudes; but in the one afforded by Traherne, that typology begins to crumble as a speaker becomes the third term in a comparison wherein he associates himself with not the type but its antitype and thus represents himself not as a recapitulation but as a fulfillment. As it happens, Herbert's easy associationalism is less characteristic of the seventeenth century than Traherne's dissociationalism, which in a

---

17. *Christs Combate and Conquest: or, the Lyon of the Tribe of Judah* (London: Cantrell Legge, 1618), pp. 58, 60, 37, 193; cf. *The Works of Thomas Goodwin*, ed. John C. Miller and Robert Halley, 12 vols. (Edinburgh: James Nichol; London: James Nisbet, 1861–1866), 3:96. Elsewhere Taylor writes: "although *Sampson* the type was at last ouercome by his enemies: our true *Sampson* is inuincible, and hath gloriously triumphed over them all" (*Christ Revealed: or the Old Testament Explained* [London: M. F., 1635], p. 56; see also p. 60). In the sixteenth century, Henoch Clapham was compelled to distinguish between Samson "A Nazarite" and "our Nazaret Annointed, who by his death on the Crosse, overcame Death, and destroyed all power infernall, to the Faithfull" (*A Briefe of the Bible* [London: Robert Walde, 1596], p. 69). The tag of invincibility placed on Samson by Martin Luther is gradually detached from him in the seventeenth century; see *Luther's Works*, ed. Jaroslav Pelikan et al., 55 vols. (St. Louis: Concordia Press; Philadelphia: Fortress Press, 1955–1976), 8:281.

18. See Joseph Hall, *Contemplations on the Historical Passages of the Old and New Testaments*, 3 vols. (Edinburgh: Willison and Darling, 1770), 1:351, 361; and Trapp, *Annotations upon the Old and New Testaments*, 1:89.

similarly mild form is evident in Robert Southwell's poem "At Home in Heaven," where "our heavenly *Samson*" (l. 13) is compared with his earthly counterpart, and which is also evident in a more extreme form, typical of secular literature, in the stress John Donne places in "The Calme" on Samson's essential fallenness and hence effeminate slackness: "like slack sinew'd Sampson, his haire off, / languish our ships" (ll. 34–35).[19] The pressure exerted by secular literature early in the seventeenth century becomes so considerable that later in the same century hermeneutic texts, no less than religious lyrics, can no longer formulate parallelisms between Samson and Christ without formalizing the disparities. What can be presented as tabloids of differences by the commentators are coded into the religious lyric, where, as in the examples afforded by Traherne and Southwell, there is a straining toward such formulations. In this way, unexpected meanings may be seen breaking through the surfaces of poems with which those meanings also seem incompatible, indecorous, or to which they seem simply irrelevant.

Like all lyrics, the religious poem is constrained by demands for abbreviation and abridgment; such poems are still lifes in comparison with the expansive canvases of narrative and drama where there is leisure for detailed exposition. Even so, the religious lyric does not destroy itself, as Ira Clark argues, by overlooking typological discrepancies or by blurring differences.[20] Rather, it accommodates them by introducing as a middle term in its typological comparisons a speaker/persona and, if only implicitly, a readership that will itself be measured by resemblance now to type and now to antitype, here to Samson and there to Christ. The religious lyric, as Sharon Cameron has so astutely remarked, had been acting as a vise on certain fictions, housing them "within the walls of its own limitations."[21] Through the introduction of a middle term to typological comparisons, the hold of that vise is effectively bro-

19. *The Poems of Robert Southwell*, ed. James H. McDonald and Nancy Pollard Brown (Oxford: Clarendon Press, 1967), p. 58; and *The Complete Poetry of John Donne*, ed. John T. Shawcross (Garden City, N.Y.: Anchor Books, 1967), p. 193.
20. *Christ Revealed: The History of the Neotypological Lyric in the English Renaissance* (Gainesville: University Press of Florida, 1982), p. 139.
21. *Lyric Time: Dickinson and the Limits of Genre* (Baltimore: Johns Hopkins University Press, 1979), p. 22.

ken. The hold of that vise is loosened, certainly, by a secular literature, which thrusts against similitudes in order to brandish not a regenerate but instead a fallen Samson into whose heart women "so finely steale themselves":

> That strongest Champion, who with naked hands
> A lyon tore, who all arm'd and bound
> Heap't mounts of armed foes on bloody sands;
> By woman's art, without or force or wound
> Subdu'de, now in a mill blind grinding stands.
> That Sunne of wisdome, which the Preacher crown'd
> > Great King of arts, bewitch't with womens smiles,
> > Fell deepe in seas of folly by their wiles
> Wit, strength, and grace it selfe yeeld to their
> flatt'ring guiles.[22]

Samson's is a lechery, suggests George Gascoigne, that dwells "Not outwardly, but inwardly," that "marreth and corrupteth every age, . . . every sect, . . . every order, and . . . overthroweth every degree. For it invadeth young and olde, men and women, wyse and foolish, higher and lower, unto the laste generacion . . . [it] cursed *Ruben*, seduced *Sampson*, and perverted *Salomon*."[23] The secular parries with the religious lyric in such a way as to capitalize on the drama, not the dogma, inherent in the Samson story and does so, at least initially, by problematizing, as will Donne and later Bunyan, the supposedly triumphant close of Samson's life.

Donne allows that Samson dies with the same zeal as Christ and that, if Hercules is a type of Samson, in his death Samson is a type of Christ, but in the context of *Biathanatos*, where the murdering of Christ is contrasted with Samson's "selfe-killing" and where contending traditions of exegesis are brought into play: "it is argued by some that Samson's principal desire is for the death of Philistine's, not his own death; by others, that the responsibility is God's for he inspires Samson's acts."[24] This scrutiny of Samson's final days eventually has its

22. *The Apollyonists* by Phineas Fletcher, 4.22–23, in *Giles and Phineas Fletcher: Poetical Works*, ed. Frederick S. Boas, 2 vols. (Cambridge: Cambridge University Press, 1908–1909), 1:169.

23. *The Complete Works of George Gascoigne*, ed. John W. Cunliffe, 2 vols. (Cambridge: Cambridge University Press, 1907–1910), 2:248.

24. *Biathanatos*, ed. J. William Hebel (New York: Facsimile Text Society, 1930), pp. 199–201.

consequences for the religious lyric, where, in an example provided by Bunyan, his scriptural paraphrase cancels the events of the entire sixteenth chapter of Judges, thus emphasizing not the supposedly heroic feats of Samson's life but the problem-ridden times of a now domesticated figure whose sanctuary is his parent's home: "unto his father's house returned."[25] That special form of "Vertue transcendent and heroycall," which the scriptural commentators had sometimes ascribed to Samson, was already under challenge by Donne and would come under challenge often, not just by calumnists, but by those who recognized that the spirit of revenge often borrows the vizard of fortitude and that its only sanction, in the instance of Samson, seems to be his claim of divine instinct.[26]

Whether or not he approves of the situation, Joseph Wybarne describes it accurately: "The deeds of *Sampson* are scoft at by many," especially by poets, who misunderstand what Wybarne believes to be the scriptural intent, "which was to describe a man indued . . . with eminent vertues, yet not exempt from humaine passions." When described by the poets, Samson's peculiar brand of heroism is seldom "free from all tincture of folly," as Wybarne well knows, because such "bloody covenants are commonly drawn from Sathan."[27] Especially in their dealings with the Samson story, poets review and, from Wybarne's perspective, revile the commonplaces of theology valorized by scripture. Even epic poets assault the cult of heroism in the belief that heroes, none of them faultless, should be represented in their various and contradictory aspects, and this is true not only of feigning poets like Homer and Virgil but of modern ones like Spenser who, less prone to err, says Wybarne, "have set downe men of heroycall vertues, yet darkened like the Moone with some blot; therefore as well the sinnes as the vertues of *Moses, Sampson, David* are registered with the point of a Diamond in the glasse of true history"[28]—and registered in such a way as to exalt present over past history and modern heroes

25. *The Whole Works*, ed. George Offer, 3 vols. (London: Blackie and Son, 1862), 3:393.

26. See Joseph Wybarne, *The New Age of Old Names* (London: William Barrett and Henry Fetherstone, 1609), p. 72.

27. Ibid., pp. 27, 67, 72.

28. Ibid., p. 73.

over their antecedents. Typology, in the seventeenth century, has become a kind of subterfuge for including, especially in religious poetry, what might otherwise have to be excluded: it is now being used not to deny but to diminish earlier heroism and, at the same time, to promote the idea that true heroism is being fully realized in the modern age by a new breed of protagonists. There are twists and turns in such poetry to which we are only now beginning to pay proper attention. Another way of presenting Wybarne's objections to the poets would be to say that they resist the prejudicially black and white judgments of then-current Christian mythology and the special pleading of certain tradition-bound commentators who would ignore cruxes in the Samson story and thus halt further inquiry into the Samson legend.

Donne resists just this sort of special pleading, as both Shakespeare and Spenser had done before him. In *Love's Labor's Lost*, where wenches "prove plagues to men" (4.3.385) and great men become gnats, and within a context in which great spirits grow melancholy and lose the light of life by going blind, Samson is numbered among love's fools.[29] Samson is here a revenger revenged for submitting to the mockery of women who, having proved false to him, cause Samson to prove false to himself. Armado asks, "What great men have been in love?" (1.2.67–68), and is informed by his page Moth of two: "Hercules, master . . . Samson master. He was a man of good carriage, great carriage, for he carried the town gates on his back like a porter—and he was in love" (1.2.69, 74–76). Armado thereupon remarks: "O well-knit Samson! Strong-jointed Samson! I do excel thee in my rapier as much as thou didst me in carrying gates. I am in love too. Who was Samson's love, my dear moth?" (1.2.77–80). "A woman, master," Moth tells him, whose complexion is "sea-water green" and who has "a green wit" (1.2.81, 86, 95). Through this exchange, Shakespeare conjures up several different faces of Samson: that of the lustful lover, that of the strong man scant on wit who had "small reason" for loving Delilah (1.2.92), a man deformed by love and because of that refashioning his obligations, thus betraying them just as he himself has been betrayed. Contrary to Shake-

29. Quotations from this play, given parenthetically within the text, are from *Shakespeare: The Complete Works*, ed. G. B. Harrison (New York and Burlingame: Harcourt, Brace and Company, 1952).

speare, and perhaps accounting for the anti-Shakespearean senti-
ments in the preface to *Samson Agonistes*, Milton seems to have
thought that the Samson story is no matter for a "Christmas com-
edy" (5.2.462) but instead the stuff of tragedy. And it is with
Milton that Spenser seems to have concurred.

In book 5 of *The Faerie Queene*, Artegall is linked
typologically to earlier mythic and historical figures, among
them Samson. Echoes from the Book of Judges reverberate
throughout Spenser's Book of Justice, where Samson's effemi-
nate slackness illustrates the "wondrous powre [of] . . . wom-
ens faire aspect, / To captiue men, and make them all the world
reiect" (5.8.2). "That mighty Iewish swaine," with hardened
heart "enur'd to blood and cruelty," says Spenser, did "lay his
spoiles before his leman's traine" (5.8.1–2).[30] Artegall is num-
bered with those men—not just Samson but also Hercules and
Antony—who have been beguiled by women; yet once Artegall
is dissociated from his types in terms of his outer strength, the
Hercules and not the Samson analogy is developed by way of
revealing Artegall's inner strength and newly acquired wisdom.

The aura of prophecy and millennial expectation once asso-
ciated with Samson now comes to surround Artegall, as if to
suggest that whereas Samson represents an extreme of
injustice, Artegall embodies the mean of justice. Samson, not
Artegall, emblematizes those times, described by Eudoxus in *A
View of the Present State of Ireland*, when "swordes are in the
handes of the vulgare," and never really out of their hands, for
even when they seem wearied by war and are "broughte downe
to extreame wretchednes . . . they Creepe a little . . . sue for
grace" and, recovering their strength, go forth to slaughter still
others.[31] Spenser may affirm the proposition that arms occa-

30. Quoted from *The Works of Edmund Spenser*, ed. Edwin Greenlaw et al.,
11 vols. (Baltimore: Johns Hopkins Press, 1932–1945), 5:89. The following critics
offer particularly incisive commentary on this passage: Jane Apetaker, *Icons of
Justice: Iconography and Thematic Imagery in Book V of "The Faerie Queene"*
(New York and London: Oxford University Press, 1969), p. 180; Angus Fletcher,
The Prophetic Moment: An Essay on Spenser (Chicago: University of Chicago
Press, 1971), pp. 147–50; and James Nohrnberg, *The Analogy of "The Faerie
Queene"* (Princeton: Princeton University Press, 1976), p. 374. It was noted long
ago that *Samson Agonistes* may owe something to a parallel description of
Artegall in *The Faerie Queene*; see *The Poetical Works of John Milton*, ed. Henry
John Todd, 7 vols. (London: Printed for J. Johnson, 1801), 4:372.
31. *The Works of Edmund Spenser*, ed. Greenlaw et al., 10:55.

sionally further the divine purpose, but only in those instances when they are employed to maintain the public right over private ends. Those who judge others, Spenser seems to be saying, must themselves be just; and their justice stands in marked contrast to such injustices as cruelty, barbarity, and savagery. In book 5 of *The Faerie Queene* identity is forged between Samson and Artegall by way of forcing a distinction.

Not just Samson's fall but the consequences thereof—the hardening of his heart, his becoming enured to violence—are gathered into focus here, and in such a way as to give priority to Artegall, Spenser representing Artegall, by no means a perfect hero, as superior to his type, the bringer of justice to a world (as Samson never quite managed to do) where laws do not exist or perhaps have failed to work. In its largest extension, this typology reaches beyond the poem to envelop the poet and his queen as well, and in the process the sacred is secularized: typology invades history in order to explicate it, envelops its protagonists to elucidate their objectives and accomplishments. If history had been in times past crossbred with mythology, with Spenser typology comes to be crossbred with current history and in the process becomes an agent by which present is exalted over past history, the neotype over the type.

Wybarne may believe that poets, even if unwittingly, are dismantlers of myth and deconstructionists of the Samson legend; yet it is equally true that in the seventeenth century poets participate in the rehabilitation of this story, but still a typology of difference prevails. In "On Iesus and Sampson," included in *Divine Fancies*, Francis Quarles sets forth the typological associations between these scriptural figures and their respective stories, starting with the annunciation scenes that forecast their births: both are Nazarites and deliverers, both marry Gentiles, speak riddles, exhibit ire, slay lions, befriend harlots, and eventually burst their bonds. Yet Jesus also purchases a higher fame than Samson did:

> *Iesus*, the first, and second day, could be
> The *Graves* close pris'ner; but, the third, was free:
> In this they [Jesus and Samson] differ'd: *Iesus* dying Breath
> Cry'd out for Life; but *Sampson* cald for *Death*:
> *Father forgive them*, did our *Iesus* crye;
> But *Sampson, Let me be reveng'd and dye*:

> Since then, sweet *Savior* tis thy *Death* must ease us,
> We flye from *Sampson*, and appeale to *Iesus*.[32]

This typology of difference emerges from Quarles's more sustained meditation, *The Historie of Samson*, published the year before. That poem ends, as Milton's tragedy will also end, with a celebration of Samson's name and fame, both lasting and flourishing until the end of time:

> [Samson's] name shall flourish, and be still in prime,
> In spight of ruine, or the teeth of *time*:
> Whose fame shall last, till heav'n shall please to free
> This *Earth* from Sinne, and *time* shall cease to be.[33]

The celebration of Samson one year becomes more measured the next, one supposes because of the sorts of reflections and reasonings that Quarles had already pored over in his studied review of Samson's checkered history.

Within this broad context of charting the gradual erosion of parallels between Samson and Christ and the demise of an old typology, Samuel Pordage's post-Restoration representation of Samson as Christ's type, bursting the bonds of death and throwing open the bar standing between this world and paradise, may seem but a throwback to an earlier and by now outmoded typologizing of the Samson story. But it is more than that and, in this, an unexpected prefiguration of Milton's last poems. Pordage's "Sacred Poem" reaches from the loss of paradise by Adam to its apocalyptic restoration by Christ but is also eminently concerned with the redemptive process in history resulting from human effort rather than divine intervention, with the way in which man himself repairs the ruins of the Fall and wrests comedy from tragedy. Thus Samson and Jesus are typologically coupled by way of reinforcing the point that heaven is reached not by divine but by human effort:

> O Noble Work! O mighty strength of the
> Blest Son of God's glorious Humanity!
> 'Twas his Humanity this work did do,

---

32. See *The Divine Fancies: Digested into Epigrammes, Meditations, and Observations* (London: J. Marriott, 1632), pp. 55–56; see also p. 54.
33. See *The Historie of Samson*, p. 141.

Or else no passage here had been for you,
Not for an' humane Soul.[34]

Samson appears here, with all his typological trappings, but
now as a foil less for the heroism than for the humanity of Jesus.
Still, the most important reflection upon Milton's Samson, as
we shall presently see, comes in a Marvellian parenthesis, the
implications of which depend upon Marvell's own perception of
what by now is, at least as a literary tradition, nearly a century-
old practice of typological differentiation.

Typological differences are registered increasingly as the
Samson story comes to be treated less and less reverently. Sam-
uel Butler's Sir Hudibras is promptly identified with "that stub-
born Crew / Of Errant Saints, whom all men grant to be the
Church *Militant*":

Such as do build their Faith upon
The holy Text of *Pike* and *Gun*;
Decide all Controversies by
Infallible *Artillery*;
And prove their Doctrine Orthodox
By Apostolick *Blows* and *Knocks*;
Call Fire and Sword and Desolation,
A godly-thorough Reformation,
Which always must be carry'd on,
And still be doing, never done . . . . (1.1.190–202)

Thereupon, this errant Knight's tawny beard is likened to
"*Sampson's* Heart-breakers":

. . . it grew
In time to make a nation rue:
Though it contributed its own fall,
To wait upon the publick downfall. (1.1.251–54)[35]

Scornful allusions of this sort, stressing (as John Dryden will do
in *The Medall*[36]) that Samson is the betrayer and destroyer of a
nation, provide an ambience for Andrew Marvell's unflattering

34. *Mundorum Explication . . . A Sacred Poem* (London: Lodowick Lloyd,
1661), pp. 233–34.
35. *Hudibras*, ed. John Wilders (Oxford: Clarendon Press, 1967), pp. 7, 9.
36. See *The Medall* (73 ff.), in *The Works of John Dryden*, ed. Edward Niles
Hooker and H. T. Swedenborg, Jr., 19 vols. (Berkeley and Los Angeles: University
of California Press, 1961), 2:45.

reference to Samson by way of flattering Milton in "On Mr. Milton's *Paradise Lost.*" The "Argument" to *Paradise Lost* causes Marvell, for awhile, to doubt Milton's intentions and to fear that Milton might

> ruine (for I saw him strong)
> The sacred Truths to Fable and Old Song,
> (So *Sampson* groap'd the Temples Posts in spight)
> The World o'rewhelming to revenge his Sight. (ll. 7–10)[37]

Better perhaps than any poet of the seventeenth century, Marvell reveals the extent to which Samson, once a figure around whom to spin witty conceits, gradually became one inducing sober reflection. Behind the "iron gates of life" (l. 44) in "To His Coy Mistress" may lie a playful allusion to the gates burst by Samson in anticipation of Christ's later opening of the gates into Paradise; and more probably, the Mower's "Revenge" in "The Mower's Song," reducing the world to a "Common Ruin" (l. 30), harbors an allusion to Samson's revenge in hurling down the pillars, itself an anticipation of the great ruin at the end of time. The Samson who could once be, as here, a figure in "a comic Apocalypse"[38] becomes after the failure of the Revolution an image of that horror; previously a figure in sweet lyric song, he now emerges as a principal protagonist in the tragedy of history. Allusions that once were evidence of a poet's typological skill and mode of thought are now replaced by ones in which the poet not only withholds but resists such typological play as he fixes attention to the temple holocaust.

It has been said that when Samson hurls down the temple/theater, he destroys not only himself and others but drama as well, and that in this demolition of drama (and more notably of tragedy), Milton, through the final speech of Manoa, insinuates a poetic anticipatory of "another [poetic] mode, 'legend' and 'lyric song.' The claim that *Samson Agonistes* never was intended for the stage," argues Nicholas Jose, "is a tactical move in the interests of higher truth," with the modes of narrative and

---

37. *The Poems and Letters of Andrew Marvell*, 2d ed., ed. H. M. Margoliouth, 2 vols. (Oxford: Clarendon Press, 1952), 1:131–32. All other citations of this poem, given parenthetically within the text, derive from this edition, and other of Marvell's poems cited in this essay are likewise from this edition.

38. Bruce King, *Marvell's Allegorical Poetry* (New York and Cambridge: Oleander Press, 1977), p. 143.

drama now giving way, by virtue of their inferior truth claims, to the reign of lyric.[39] The question lurking behind Jose's observation may be stated thus: what do poets hear when they listen to the song of a nightingale, its song or a myth? Or thus: what do readers of *Samson Agonistes* hear in Milton's poem, a song of joy or a tragic lament? what do they see therein, the phenomenology of faith which is the province of the religious lyric,[40] or some other phenomenology that ordinarily comes within the purview of tragedy? What is implicit in Jose's argument was rendered explicitly early in our own century: that whatever Milton accomplished in *Paradise Lost* and *Paradise Regained*, it is less than he had already achieved on the plane of lyric song; that lyric effusions intervene insistently in the narrative mode of these epics, especially *Paradise Lost*; that *Samson Agonistes* is a progressive regression—"a very deliberate attempt at lyric drama" by way of recovering "the irrepressible song of the man's own soul."[41] Such an argument presses the questions upon us: what did Milton intend for us to hear? do narrative and drama reign over lyric or not?

As others have done, Jose presumes that *or* means *and* in *Samson Agonistes*, especially when Manoa promises that Samson's "Acts [will be] enroll'd / In Copious Legend, *or* sweet Lyric Song" (ll. 1736–37; my italics),[42] when, in fact, those lines seem to participate in the gathering cloud of prophetic irony that settles over the concluding verses of Milton's tragedy. Manoa's remark, more probably, anticipates the double-form of the Samson story, his contrarious fame, the negative aspects of which will find conveyance in legend, the positive aspects in lyric song. Manoa's lines are genuinely prophetic of Samson's "double-fact . . . double-mouth'd" fame (l. 971), but ironic, too, inasmuch as Milton, contrary to most of his contemporaries,

39. *Ideas of the Restoration in English Literature 1660–71* (Cambridge, Mass.: Harvard University Press, 1984), p. 158; cf. Earl Miner, "The Reign of Narrative in *Paradise Lost*," in *Composite Orders: The Genres of Milton's Last Poems*, ed. Richard S. Ide and Joseph Wittreich (Pittsburgh: University of Pittsburgh Press, 1983), pp. 3–25.

40. See William Elford Rogers, *The Three Genres and the Interpretation of Lyric* (Princeton: Princeton University Press, 1983).

41. Rhys, *Lyrical Poetry*, pp. 223–27.

42. Quotations from *Samson Agonistes*, given parenthetically within the text of this essay, are from *The Complete Poetry of John Milton*, rev. ed., ed. John T. Shawcross (Garden City, N. Y.: Anchor Books, 1971).

will house his version of the Samson legend not in sweet lyric song but in stately tragedy and, contrary to his chief Renaissance rival in dramatic form, will judge Samson's story to be the stuff of Christian tragedy, not Christmas comedy. Insofar as *Samson Agonistes* is a dramatic poem with lyric embedments, walled within its choral odes are the commonplaces and platitudes of the Samson tradition that Milton interrogates and, for the most part, discredits.

Harbored in Manoa's lines is a profound critique of lyric poetry, of its propensity for simplifying and thereby mutilating myth and legend, and thus a recognition of the poet's need to move beyond lyric if he is going to restore dramatic ambiguity and narrative probity to the Samson story, the very qualities of which it had been divested by the religious lyric, where poets are inclined to strong-arm temporal sequence and where, so often, they mediate the space between this world and the next, themselves and God, by distorting, even annihilating, that space altogether. As Barbara Hardy explains, "the advantage of lyric . . . is its concentrated and patterned expression of feeling"; and she continues, "This advantage is negatively definable: the lyric does not provide an explanation, judgment, or narrative; what it does provide is feeling, alone and without histories and characters." That is, lyric poetry is, by definition, a poetry of sentiment but a poetry also of exclusions, "more than usually opaque because it leaves out so much of the accustomed context." The very fact that lyric poems are an embedment in larger schemes, or more encompassing genres, that often they encroach on other genres, is one indication, says Hardy, that the poets themselves "are sometimes aware of the limitation of the lyric declaration" and hence of the need for an enlarged perspective.[43] Far from reverting to lyric in *Samson Agonistes*, Milton, who had earlier strained at its boundaries, now strains to get beyond lyric, not through an act of annihilation but through a gesture involving the accommodation and absorption of lyric. The Samson legend, Milton seems to be saying, captures disparate orders, different facets of human experience. Politics and history, religion and psychology, must all come into play in any

43. *The Advantage of Lyric: Essays on Feeling in Poetry* (Bloomington: Indiana University Press, 1977), pp. 1, 2, 6. Cf. Cameron, *Lyric Time*, pp. 244–45, 248, 257.

faithful rendering of that legend. Yet it is just this multifaceted-
ness against which the lyric of the seventeenth century, with its
religious fervor and facile typologizing, militates. Or put
another way: lyric poems, for all their shifting forms and
images, would perfect and clarify both and, in the process,
deform both by unperplexing, uncomplicating them. Lyric may
stand for a moment in, and hence be an aspect of, all poetry—"a
swerving aside . . . from the usual axis of narrative" or, in the
case of *Samson Agonistes*, of drama.[44] But the tendency is also
for lyric to collapse again into other kinds of discourse, other
modes of poetry, where the figure or image of Samson, let us say,
can be presented less starkly and more provisionally.

The typological lyric could acknowledge but not anatomize
ambiguity; it could expose discrepancies and differences
through a linguistic code but not explore them as dramatic and
narrative forms might do. Its limitations may be imposed by the
restraints of genre but, in the seventeenth century, are surely
intensified by a larger cultural phenomenon. In the realm of her-
meneutics, typological readings displace allegorical readings,
and figural are displacing literalistic interpretations. In these
displacements, there is loss, obliteration, especially when the
narrative books of the Bible are made a concern: scriptural nar-
ratives, if not altogether ruined, become disfigured; cumulative
patterns, doubling perspectives, chronological sequence, nar-
rative shape (the foci of literal reading) fall by the wayside. The
ascendancy of typological reading throws biblical narrative,
even drama, into eclipse.[45] When typological reading ceases to
work in concert with literal interpretation, it begins to subvert
biblical narratives as narrative. Such concepts as "typological
evolution" and "typological continuity"[46] reveal more about
the cultural spirit of the Renaissance than they do about the
texts they are devised to explain. Insofar as such concepts imply
a concern with unity, it is the extrinsic unity of dogma, not the

44. See the intriguing, sophisticated discussion by Daniel Albright, *Lyri-
cality in English Literature* (Lincoln: University of Nebraska Press, 1985), p. 3.
45. See Hans Frei, *The Eclipse of Biblical Narrative: A Study in Eighteenth
and Nineteenth Century Hermeneutics* (New Haven: Yale University Press,
1974), p. 134.
46. See, e.g., Lynn Veach Sadler, *Consolation in "Samson Agonistes":
Regeneration and Typology*, Salzburg Studies in English Literature (Salzburg:
University of Salzburg, 1979), p. 39.

intrinsic unity of art; and insofar as they host an ideology, it is that of a rationalistic age which, as Hans Frei remarks, saw fit "to alter the ending of *King Lear* in order to bring it into harmony with more advanced moral ideas";[47] it is one that would obliterate the original Hebrew tale, because of its supposedly false consciousness, and replace it with the reigning Christian consciousness of the Samson story. In the process, past history is obliterated in the interests of present history, and meaning is wrung from the mind of the interpreter, *his* historical consciousness, and not the Samson story itself. Or as Kenneth Gross would probably state the case, typological readings of the Samson story, especially in the seventeenth century, are a form of reader-nostalgia for "earlier, more secure centers of meaning," and have the effect of turning readers into stone and of making their gaze a "reflection back from a text's unbroken surface of stoniness . . . the reader himself . . . imposed upon it."[48] Secure centers of meaning may finally have very little to do with the Samson story's real center of concern, and typology itself may have the unfortunate effect of veiling the tortured energy in much religious poetry of Milton's century.

Typology may be a peril of the seventeenth-century religious lyric and a manifestation of its limitations; but it is likewise a bond between different kinds of religious poets, between very different kinds of poetry, between literatures both sacred and secular. It is a functioning device in *King Lear* no less than in *Samson Agonistes*, in *The Faerie Queene* no less than in *Paradise Lost*, in Donne's *Anniversarie* poems no less than in "Lycidas," and in "Lycidas" no less than in Marvell's Cromwell poems, although in each instance typology seems to function differently. Now it is a device for exalting the present over the past, and now for collapsing the past into the present. Here it measures a middle term in relation to a type and there in relationship to the antitype; sometimes the middle term is advantaged and other times disadvantaged by the comparison. Now the middle term is the poet's persona or the poet himself, and now the poet's audience.

Typology is both a peril of and a procedure in the seven-

47. *The Eclipse of Biblical Narrative*, p. 313.
48. *Spenserian Poetics: Idolatry, Iconoclasm, and Magic* (Ithaca, N.Y.: Cornell University Press, 1986), p. 66.

teenth-century lyric; and we need not transfer to a later time, as Barbara Lewalski has done, what are its conspicuous character traits at this time. According to Lewalski, "Typology is not unimportant in later poetry . . . , but given the changes in consciousness and religious attitudes, good poets necessarily used it obliquely and ambiguously."[49] Good poets of the seventeenth century often use typology obliquely, ambiguously; and the shifts in religious attitudes, the alterations in human consciousness of which Lewalski speaks, are part of the tale of seventeenth-century culture and hence a manifestation in that century's poetry. Even the religious lyric, however indirectly, has the capacity for registering, if not for explicating, advances in consciousness, alterations in attitude. Poets simply cannot revert to the commonplaces of their ancestors without falsifying their newly acquired cultural awareness; poets are the purveyors of such awareness, moreover, not protectors against it.[50] Initially a revelation of Christian "truths," typology would eventually be used against itself to reveal the *truths* of the Bible. An agent in the deconstruction of Old Testament narratives, typology would eventually be used, as in *Samson Agonistes*, to effect their restoration.

As for the Samson typologies (and they are my example here), they became, in the course of the seventeenth century, a mirror upon individual failure and national disaster, upon the tragedy of the Puritan Revolution through which one could glimpse the full tragedy of human history. "This is heroic tragedy," says J. R. Hexter:

> It is tragedy because circumstance and event provide the setting in which Puritanism, through its own inner flaws and failings, thrusts itself down the path to disaster. It is heroic because Puritanism itself in the days of its triumph and its catastrophe was no trifling, hole-in-the-corner affair—because Puritanism was indeed heroic, magnificent in its virtues and force, magnificent in its failings: Samson Agonistes, but Samson still.[51]

49. *Protestant Poetics and the Seventeenth-Century Religious Lyric*, p. 144.
50. See C. Day Lewis, *The Lyric Impulse* (Cambridge, Mass.: Harvard University Press, 1965), p. 23.
51. *Reappraisals in History: New Views on History and Society in Early Modern Europe*, 2d ed. (1961; rpt. Chicago: University of Chicago Press, 1979), pp. 247–48.

The celebratory character of the religious lyric necessarily veils the tragedy of Samson, its typological progressions always attesting to God's bringing good out of evil and to history's metamorphosing from tragedy into comedy. That part of the Samson legend pushed into the basement of sweet lyric song is the same part glimpsed by Milton, and thereupon anatomized, in his tragedy of "Blood, death, deathful deeds . . . / Ruin, destruction at the utmost point" (ll. 1514–15). In *Samson Agonistes*, lyric, tragedy, and narrative may coexist; but the poem's lyric and narrative elements are overruled by a tragedy which registers all that current history taught Milton to see in the Samson story.[52] As a genre, lyric poetry rings changes on a single, limited perspective, the limitations of which are burst by narrative and drama—and in such a way as to remind us that the eye altering alters all.

*   *   *

The eye cast by *Samson Agonistes* on the Judges story was instrumental, it seems, in effecting reinterpretation, both by telegraphing a bold reminder that this scriptural book is a "Mirrour of Magistrates *and Tyrants*"[53] as well as a looking-glass on contemporary history, and by unsettling received interpretation of the Samson story, thereby raising problematical questions about its meaning. It is more than coincidence that the first commentator on *Samson Agonistes*, John Dunton, should be adamant in asserting Milton's orthodoxy in the representation of Samson's death as a triumph and in the registration, through his portrayal of Dalila and in accordance with the Judges narrative, of a "terrible *Satyr* on *Women*." When Dunton turns his own eye to the Book of Judges, more telling than his answers are the questions he raises: for example, "*What are we to think of the Salvation of* Cain, Eli, . . . Sampson . . . ?"[54] By the end of

52. Joseph Mazzaro observes that lyric and tragedy seldom exist contemporaneously and, further, that "The predicaments that sowed the seeds for the shift of the lyric into the narrative and epic genres also sowed the seeds for its possible shift into the dramatic form" (*Transformations in the Renaissance English Lyric* [Ithaca, N.Y.: Cornell University Press, 1970], p. 149).

53. See Samuel Torshell, *A Designe about Disposing the Bible into a Harmony* (London: A Miller, 1647), p. 27 (my italics).

54. *The Athenian Gazette: or Casuistical Mercury*, 2 vols. (London: John Dunton, 1691), pt. 1, no. 14.

Milton's century, such questions were being debated, in part because of the bold interpretation Milton seemed to be advancing in *Samson*, where, on the one hand, it is made evident that "Women have a very powerful Influence upon all sorts of Transactions in the World,"[55] and, on the other hand, it is rendered suspect that the same book which seemingly condemns Delilah should cry up Deborah and Jael, especially in view of Milton's eliding the supposedly good and bad in the Dalila-Jael equation. There is a Dalila typology that Milton deploys as subversively as he does the Samson typology.

Dalila expects to be "Not less renoun'd then in Mount *Ephraim*, / *Jael*, who with inhospitable guile / Smote *Sisera* sleeping through the Temples nail'd" (ll. 888–90). As Dalila does with Samson, so Jael practices her deceptions upon Sisera with "faire and alluring words," her story raising the question, says Richard Rogers, of "whether *Iael* did well or no, in thus deceiuing him" and leading some, like Milton's Dalila, to think her murderous act not "blessed," but a "barbarous cruelty & trechery."[56] Milton thus allows Dalila herself to call into question the received reading of this story wherein Jael is represented as God's instrument, doing in His if not her own enemy, and the people's deliverer; and in the implied contrast between Jael and Dalila, Milton also hides the suggestion that Dalila may finally be less treacherous than the celebrated Jael, usually exonerated of her crimes, even on one occasion by Milton himself.

Indeed, we might now conjecture that it was a poem like *Samson Agonistes*, using dramatic probity to expose the typological clichés of Christian orthodoxy often embedded within the religious lyric, that enabled William Walsh, writing under the pseudonym of "Eugenia," to carry such questioning still further: "we might defend some of those women [in Judges] . . . , and excuse the rest. For *Dalilah* I shall say nothing, out of respect to the Scripture, that represents her as an Ill Woman." But Walsh, in fact, *does* say something:

> . . . 'tis possible were she [Delilah] alive, she might tell you in her own defence, that what account you have of her, is from her pro-

---

55. Robert Allestree, *The Ladies Calling* (Oxford: n.p., 1673), unpaginated preface.

56. *A Commentary upon the Whole Book of Judges* (London: Felix Kyngston, 1615), pp. 221–22.

fest Enemies: That however taking the thing as they tell it; if she
did commit a piece of treachery, it was against an Enemy of her
Country; and that it is very hard she should be so much run down
for the same thing they have so much admired in *Jael* and *Judeth*
. . . ; she would perhaps push her defence further, and tell you,
that tho she deliver'd *Samson* to the *Philistines* to be kept pris-
oner, yet she neither drove a Nail through his head, nor cut it off.[57]

To view the Samson story from this—modern readers will
say, Empsonian—perspective may cause us to despair, as Milton
seems to have done, over Samson's final victory—over his being
numbered among the brave men and great soldiers of history.
And it is in just this way that, through a belated understanding,
Samson Agonistes came to be viewed at the turn into the nine-
teenth century, by John Aikin for example: "It has been invid-
iously suggested, that Milton chose the Samson story for the
opportunity it gave him to satirize bad wives. I should rather
imagine, that the assertion of pure religion, and the resistance of
tyrannical power, were the chief circumstances which gave him
a predilection for this fable . . . ." But then Milton's mind—the
range of its consciousness—"knows no limits," according to
Aikin, except "those impassable by the human intellect."[58]

---

57. *A Dialogue Concerning Woman. Being a Defence of the Sex* (London:
Richard Bentley, 1691), pp. 80–81; see also pp. 50, 79.
58. These statements are quoted by Lucy Aikin, in *Memoir of John Aikin*
(Philadelphia: Abraham Small, 1824), pp. 194, 195.

Notes on the Contributors

James Andrew Clark is Assistant Professor of English at Auburn University. He has previously published articles on Sir Thomas More and John Milton. He is currently studying the typology of "Temple-work" during the Puritan Revolution.

M. Thomas Hester is Professor of English at North Carolina State University. He is author of *Kinde Pitty and Brave Scorn: John Donne's Satyres*, founder and coeditor of *John Donne Journal*, and coeditor of the satires volume of *The Variorum Edition of the Poetry of John Donne* (forthcoming). He has just completed a book-length study of Donne's poetry entitled *Reading Donne: An Anatomy of Wit* and an edition/translation of Justus Lipsius's *Epistolica institutio*.

Ted-Larry Pebworth is Professor of English at the University of Michigan–Dearborn and a principal organizer of the Dearborn conference series. He is author of *Owen Felltham*; coauthor of *Ben Jonson*; editor of *The Poems of Sir Henry Wotton* (forthcoming); coeditor of *The Poems of Owen Felltham* and of collections of essays on Herbert, on Jonson and the Sons of Ben, and on Donne. He is author or coauthor of numerous critical and bibliographical studies of seventeenth-century literature and serves as a member of the Advisory Board and textual coeditor for *The Variorum Edition of the Poetry of John Donne*.

Patricia Garland Pinka is Professor of English at Agnes Scott College. She is author of *This Dialogue of One: The Songs and Sonnets of John Donne* and of several articles on Donne.

Mary Ann Radzinowicz is Professor of English at Cornell University. She is author of *Toward "Samson Agonistes": The Growth of Milton's Mind* and editor of *American Colonial Prose: John Smith to Thomas Jefferson*. She is also author of numerous articles on John Milton, and is completing a book-length study of Milton's epics and the Book of Psalms.

Stella P. Revard is Professor of English at Southern Illinois University, Edwardsville, where she teaches courses in both English literature and Greek. Her book, *The War in Heaven: "Paradise Lost" and the Tradition of Satan's Rebellion*, received the James Holly Hanford Award of the Milton Society of America. She has published numerous essays on Milton and other seventeenth-century figures. She is currently completing a book on the influence of Pindar on sixteenth- and seventeenth-century English poetry.

Lorraine Roberts received the Ph.D. from the University of Missouri–Columbia in 1982 and teaches in the Department of English at the University of Kansas. She has delivered papers on Milton as well as Crashaw, and is working on essays on Crashaw's voice, on the development of Counter-Reformation themes from Southwell to Crashaw, and on Southwell's "A vale of teares."

Michael C. Schoenfeldt is Assistant Professor of English at the University of

217

Michigan–Ann Arbor. He has published on Herbert and is currently working on a book-length study of Herbert and Renaissance courtesy literature.

William A. Sessions is Professor of English at Georgia State University. He is a founder and editor of *Studies in the Literary Imagination*, having edited the volumes on Bacon, seventeenth-century prose, and Sidney. He is author of *Henry Howard, the Poet-Earl of Surrey*, essays on Bacon, Herbert, Milton, and Spenser, and a monograph, *Spenser's Georgics*, in *English Literary Renaissance*. He is now writing a biography of the Earl of Surrey and a second critical work on his poems.

William Shullenberger teaches literature at Sarah Lawrence College. His previously published work includes essays on Milton's poetry and poetics, Beaumont and Fletcher's *The Maid's Tragedy*, Keats, and Wordsworth.

Claude J. Summers is Professor of English at the University of Michigan–Dearborn. He is author of books on Christopher Marlowe, Christopher Isherwood, and E. M. Forster; coauthor of *Ben Jonson*; and coeditor of *The Poems of Owen Felltham* and of collections of essays on Herbert, on Jonson and the Sons of Ben, and on Donne. His book on Forster was designated an Outstanding Academic Book by *Choice*, the journal of the American Library Association. His essays include studies of Marlowe, Shakespeare, Donne, Herbert, Herrick, Vaughan, Forster, Auden, Isherwood, and others.

Joseph A. Wittreich is Professor of English at the University of Maryland, College Park. He is editor or coeditor of several books, including *The Romantics on Milton, Calm of Mind: Tercentenary Essays on "Paradise Regained" and "Samson Agonistes," Blake's Sublime Allegory, Composite Orders: The Genres of Milton's Last Poems*, and *The Apocalypse in English Renaissance Thought and Literature*. In addition to numerous articles, principally on Milton and Blake, in various journals and collections of essays, he is author of *"Image of that Horror": History, Prophecy, and Apocalypse in "King Lear"* and *Interpreting "Samson Agonistes."*

R. V. Young is Associate Professor of English at North Carolina State University and an editor of *John Donne Journal*. He is author of *Richard Crashaw and the Spanish Golden Age* as well as articles on the poetry of Jonson, Crashaw, Marvell, Góngora, and Bembo. He is currently at work on a book on seventeenth-century devotional poetry.

INDEX TO WORKS CITED

This index includes only primary works. Anonymous works are alphabetized by title.